P9-DML-885

HIGH PRAISE FOR
STREET SOLDIER

"THIS BLACK MAN'S STRUGGLE IS A HUMAN STRUGGLE. A *MUST* READ FOR MEN AND WOMEN AROUND THE GLOBE!"
—John Singleton, director, *Boyz N the Hood*

"*STREET SOLDIER* IS THE RIVETING STORY of the enormous difference that caring adults actually are making in the lives of inner-city youngsters. It provides clues for rescuing them from poverty, prison or worse. It's high time policy makers and the public catch on by reading Joe Marshall's engrossing story."
—Hugh B. Price, president, the National Urban League

"A PASSIONATE, PERTURBING ACCOUNT . . . Interspersed with riveting first-hand accounts by the youth portrayed in this book . . . *Street Soldier* poses a challenge to all Americans."
—*Kirkus Reviews*

"INSPIRING." —*Chicago Sun-Times*

"AN UPLIFTING STORY . . . [a] stirring account of saving African-American youth . . . a practical and clear approach to what can be done." —*The Buffalo News*

Please turn the page for more extraordinary acclaim. . . .

"INSPIRING . . . EVERY BLACK MAN IN AMERICA SHOULD READ THIS BOOK, AND THEN *DO* SOMETHING."
—Spike Lee

"COMPELLING . . . The emotion and detail in his writing convincingly portray the way he connects with young people. . . . His motivation is a genuine concern for future generations."
—*Toledo Blade*

"THIS BOOK IS A CALL TO EACH OF US TO HELP OUR CHILDREN GROW STRONG."
—*Marion Star & Enterprise*

"Marshall stresses in this compelling call to arms that simply because you can't save everybody doesn't mean you can't save somebody."
—*Publishers Weekly*

"He eloquently tells the compelling tale of his path to activism . . . and shares the success stories of some of the 'graduates' of his organization."
—*Booklist* (starred review)

"Joe Marshall's *Street Soldier* is a revelation!"
—Denzel Washington

STREET SOLDIER

One Man's Struggle to Save a Generation— One Life at a Time

Joseph Marshall, Jr.,
and Lonnie Wheeler

Delta
Trade Paperbacks

A Delta Book
Published by
Dell Publishing
a division of
Bantam Doubleday Dell Publishing Group, Inc.
1540 Broadway
New York, New York 10036

Copyright © 1996 by Joseph E. Marshall, Jr., and Lonnie Wheeler

Omega Boys Club, Street Soldiers, 1-800-SOLDIER, The Knowledge
Conference, and The Omega Institute are trademarks of the Omega
Boys Club.

All rights reserved. No part of this book may be reproduced or
transmitted in any form or by any means, electronic or mechanical,
including photocopying, recording, or by any information storage and
retrieval system, without the written permission of the Publisher,
except where permitted by law. For information address:
Delacorte Press, New York, New York.

The trademark Delta® is registered in the U.S. Patent and Trademark
Office and in other countries.

ISBN: 0-385-31706-9

Reprinted by arrangement with Delacorte Press

Manufactured in the United States of America
Published simultaneously in Canada

Book design by Susan Maksuta

August 1997

10 9 8 7 6 5 4 3 2

BVG

To Malcolm X: They may have killed you, but they didn't kill your spirit. Thank you for your love of the people. I heard you loud and clear.

And to my grandmother, Louise Pierce, who said to me when I was six years old, "The more you know, the more you owe."

Contents

Acknowledgments   ix

Credits   x

Foreword   xi

Introduction   xxi

Chapter 1: Black Man 101   1

Chapter 2: "If I'm So Damn Good, Why Is
        This Boy Strung Out on Dope?"   33

Chapter 3: Homies Anonymous   51

Chapter 4: Turf   69

Chapter 5: Throwaway Kids   97

Chapter 6: Norris U.   117

Chapter 7: A Warm Thursday Night   139

Chapter 8: *Street Soldiers*   157

Chapter 9: Risk Factors   189

Chapter 10: Uncut Diamonds   213

Chapter 11: Letters   237

Chapter 12: L.A.   263

Chapter 13: The More You Know, the More You Owe   287

Acknowledgments

The authors would like to express their thanks to those whose efforts helped make this book possible, including:

Steve Davis, Philmore Graham, Avon Kirkland, Harold Logwood, Enola Maxwell, Ave Montague, Keith Naftaly, Kevin Nash, Katherine Preston, Dennis Sweeney, Martie Wheeler, Preston Worthy;

KMEL and KKBT radio stations;

Saundra, Malcolm, Sydney Nicole and Cassie Marshall, Ella Lyons, Gue Gue (Louise Pierce), Joseph and Odessa Marshall and the entire Marshall clan;

Steve Ross, who was the first to imagine the book; David Black, who makes things happen;

Andre Aikins, Philip Bounds, Macio Dickerson, Zachary Donald, Michael Gibson, Marcel Evans, Terrence Hanserd, Enoch Hawkins, Lamerle Johnson, Jermaine King, Norflis McCullough, Otis Mims, Corey Monroe, Nate Pique, Johnny Releford, Sam Robinson, Ali Satchel, Kershaun Scott, Joe Thomas, Raymond Willis, and the rest of the Omega family;

the wise Wilbur Jiggetts, the gracious Margaret "Doc" Norris, and the one and only Jack Jacqua.

Credits

Sources for statistical and general information included: the Black Community Crusade for Children; the Casey Journalism Center for Children and Families; the Children's Defense Fund; the National Center for Health Statistics; and the United States Census Bureau.

Foreword

I often drift off around 11:24 P.M., unable to outlast the interminable commercials that follow the weather and postpone the sports. On numerous occasions in the past year or so, however, this ritual has been aborted by an outburst from the telephone at my bedside, a ring I recognize as Joe Marshall's.

It is three hours earlier in San Francisco, and through the haze of my semiconsciousness I can visualize Joe alone at his post in the old frame schoolhouse a couple of eclectic miles south of downtown. I see him wearing nylon sweatpants and a Georgetown sweatshirt, leaning back nearly too far in his chair and rubbing his eyes with one hand, his tall-man's tennis shoes propped up on the desk, positioned between the Harriet Tubman poster and the archive nook of the ample former classroom that Frederick Douglass's picture on the door unofficially identifies as the office of the Omega Boys Club.

By any ordinary standard, he doesn't have to be working late. Nobody is paying Marshall to be at the office, and there is no personal advantage in it. He is there basically for two reasons— one, because the phone slows down a little bit at that hour, which enables him to turn to his agenda for the day, at last; and two, because there are still kids to be saved.

Saving kids is Joe Marshall's business, and there are many who believe he's the best there is at it. That judgment is based on the success of the boys club that he and Jack Jacqua co-founded late in 1987, although much of the credit for this success is owed to the peerless trench work of Jacqua, who, with a hardcore reticence that characterizes him as distinctively as his sixties-length gray hair, is loath to accept or even discuss it. Marshall, meanwhile, is no less modest on the first-person level but much readier to hoist the banner of the boys club and carry it from forum to forum, which makes him Omega's emcee and public champion.

It is a job for which he maintains around-the-clock enthusiasm, a quality that comes across whether he is speaking on the radio, in Congress, at a juvenile detention center, or over the telephone lines at 11:24 P.M. Eastern time. When Marshall shares this enthusiasm, his voice tends to take off soaring from its customary station, leaving tenor and alto behind on its fanciful flight north. He is one of those blessed individuals who gets genuinely excited about his work, to which he, like his co-founder, is consummately devoted.

It is more than enthusiasm, though, that keeps him at his duties often until the A.M., when he drives groggily home to his wife and two daughters (his son is already grown) in the Oakland suburb of Pittsburg, occasionally pulling off at a convenience store or some stopping place in Contra Costa County to catch some sleep in the car. It is more than devotion that makes him do that. It is a sense of urgency. Marshall fervently believes—and his case is powerful, especially when *he* makes it—that there is no work more vital than saving the kids.

When delivering their animated appeals to teenage boys and girls at the Potrero Hill Neighborhood House (where Omega holds its meetings), or at the San Francisco Youth Guidance Center, or at the San Bruno County Jail, Marshall and Jacqua place this urgency in the context of black genocide. What the kids call "the life"—the gangbanging, drive-by shooting, selling crack, dropping out of school, making babies—the Omega patriarchs refer to broadly as "the death." The life is the death not only to the young people themselves and to their friends and brothers and sisters; not only to legitimate hope for a family and a future; but to a virtual generation of black men.

Marshall knows this from being in touch with the streets

and the kids and the schools where he used to teach, and from the feeling in his stomach every time he hears that another of his former students or the grandchild of a grieving friend is in jail or working a corner or lying dead. He knows by names and faces what anyone can and ought to know by numbers, at least.

For example, these numbers:

- Every four hours, an American black child is killed by a gun.
- More young black men are murdered each year in this country—most of them by guns and each other—than were killed by lynching in all the inglorious years of its history.
- Youth violence takes more than twice as many American lives every year as cancer, heart disease, and car accidents combined.
- In 1990, there were 22 handgun deaths in Great Britain, 68 in Canada, 87 in Japan, and 10,567 in the United States.
- Over the last twenty-five years, the total of Americans who have been killed by themselves or another—nearly a million and a half—represents approximately three times the number of American battle deaths in all the foreign wars of the twentieth century. Between 1988 and 1991, more Americans were murdered with firearms than were killed throughout the nearly nine years of the Vietnam War.
- Nationwide, juvenile arrests for murder nearly doubled between 1987 and 1991.
- During the 1980s, arrests for drug abuse among black juveniles rose by more than 150 percent. Arrests for heroin and cocaine abuse increased ten times faster among black juveniles than among white juveniles.
- Well over half of America's black children live without fathers in the household, twice the rate of 1970, twice the rate of Hispanic children, and more than three times the rate of white children.
- Nearly half of the black children in this country (46 percent) live in poverty.

- Every eleven minutes, a black juvenile is arrested for a violent crime and a baby is born to a black teenage mother who already has a child.
- Every 69 seconds, a black baby is born to an unmarried mother.
- Of the black men between ages twenty-five and thirty-four who have dropped out of high school, 75 percent are in prison or on parole or probation.
- Although blacks make up only 12.4 percent of the general population of the United States, they constitute more than fifty percent of the inmate population. ("That's the number that gets me," Marshall says. "Blacks make up a majority in the NBA, the NFL, and the prison system.") In the city jails of San Francisco, blacks outnumber whites by a ratio of fourteen to one.

Most of us, incredibly, are unmoved by these numbers, resigned to them as unsightly aberrations on our statistical landscape. But where we see numbers, Marshall sees kids. He sees intelligence, talent, sensitivity, ambition. Where we see wantonness, he sees potential. Where we see hopelessness, he sees college.

It isn't necessarily the best and brightest only—the most earnest, tractable, studious black boys and girls—that the Omega Boys Club sends on to better things, including higher education. Largely, it's the mean-muggers, the gangbangers, the delinquents, felons, addicts, runaways, and dropouts. Omega dutifully takes on the worst of the worst. What it does with them more famously than perhaps any other youth organization is change their outlooks from top to bottom. The club stands apart by revealing lifestyle alternatives to kids who never knew they had any.

To accomplish this, Omega works inside out, reconfiguring a street kid's way of thinking about himself and the world he occupies. Operating on the premise that choices are the residue of mentality, it reforms his values, his patterns, his habits, and his goals. For those Omegas who go, in a year or two or more, from jail to college, college is not the predetermined solution but the natural outcome; it's where their new lifestyle and knowledge have inevitably taken them.

The knowledge is the thing, specifically, that consumes Joe Marshall. According to the Marshall plan, knowledge is the lifeline with which young people can be rescued from the murderous throes of crack and guns and overwhelming peer pressure. His unremitting efforts are committed not just to sharing knowledge but also to acquiring it through watching, listening, reading, and reasoning. For him, saving kids is more than a business and more even than a passion; it's a science.

I haven't forgotten what Marshall said to me toward the end of our first telephone conversation. He had been given my name as a possible collaborator on this book, and one of the purposes of his call was to find out whether I might be one with whom he could franchise some of his enthusiasm, which he presented persuasively. At the outset, I was sold on him, curious about the club, and skeptical about my suitability for such a project. In addition to being a couple thousand miles away, I knew little about the Bay Area and less about the complicated goings-on of young black men in the inner city. I didn't know a Crip from a crepe. It was a testament to Marshall's confidence as a communicator that he didn't care about any of that. "Your discovery," he said, managing to sound honestly excited about my very ignorance, "will be the greatest part of it."

At that, he had no idea about the extent of my naïveté concerning his world. On my initial visit to the Potrero Hill Neighborhood House, for instance, I finished interviewing a couple of veteran Omegas named Corey Monroe and Pooh McCullough, then placed my briefcase on a table in the main room while I slipped into the office to make a phone call. When I came out two minutes later, I was startled to find my tape recorder missing from the briefcase. "Oh, man," Pooh said, pushing back his stocking cap and, out of politeness, refraining from shaking his head, "you can't leave stuff like that lying around in here."

After listening to the remarkably candid and graphic street histories of more than a dozen Omegas, I gradually picked up a working familiarity with their turf. As the tales unfolded, I began to see ahead when a payback was coming and sometimes what form it would take. I began to hear what was left unsaid and to understand the kids' colloquial language. But I never got past the feeling of being conspicuously out of context in their company. I'd been the only white person in a black church during an emotional school desegregation protest in small-town Mississippi; in obscure crannies of Detroit and Cincinnati; in remote regions of North and South Carolina; but I'd never felt quite as I did the first time I sat in a crowded room of juvenile inmates at the San Francisco Youth Guidance Center. One wary, restless boy—he couldn't have been more than twelve—sampled several locations around the room that night in search of a place to sit down, scarcely looking at me but somehow making it clear that I was the source of his uneasiness. Bigger kids glanced at me and then whispered to each other. And at the YGC, I wasn't the only white person; there was, of course, the long-bearded Jack Jacqua, who commanded the floor in his famous evangelistic manner, pacing it and occasionally giving it up to a testifier in baby blue. When the session was over, a bright, outgoing eighteen-year-old approached laughing and said, "I was tellin' my potna that if we had seen you on the street all by yourself like that, we'd have jacked you in a heartbeat."

The fact is that white people appear so infrequently in the lives of inner-city black kids that, when they do, they are swiftly categorized—cop, mark, social worker; whatever. The categorizations, in turn, provide telling commentaries. At the Neighborhood House one Tuesday evening, I was walking down a flight of stairs with an Omega kid when a teenager sitting on the bottom step looked up and asked matter-of-factly, "You a probation officer?"

In light of their inherent suspicions about someone like me, however, the kids were amazingly forthcoming about their private lives, even to the point that we've had to change some names and tinker with some details to protect them. I attribute this candor to their trust in Marshall, who assured them that talking to me was like talking to him.

It was in these conversations that I experienced the discovery Marshall had alluded to. Kid by charming kid, I was escorted into a horrifically complicated universe dominated by guns, drug money, and the ruthless pursuit of respect. To the former gangbangers who personify the Omega Boys Club, violence was a currency with which adolescence was brutally negotiated, a means of acquiring the reputation and respect for which they were starved to the point of depravity. Violence was so endemic, so essential, so common to their lives that they faced its prospects with quiet anxiety but without any salient terror—roughly the way most teenagers confront pop quizzes in history class. Their fear of dying was perhaps mitigated, and their instinct to stay straight was no doubt confused, by an absence of ambition that some might ascribe to nihilism. There were no idyllic futures—no sweet mental pictures of themselves at twenty or thirty—that they were afraid of screwing up. It wasn't as if, by carrying and moving amongst guns, they were jeopardizing career plans in medicine or law, or throwing away the dreams of watching their children play Little League.

To the kid of the city street, for whom there is nothing particularly compelling about the tomorrows of adulthood, ambition is an item of immediacy. It's about accumulating respect and its various accoutrements—about getting the rep, about having things; about making people envious or intimidated if not both. The pressure on the homie is not to get into Stanford but to be a man; to be a man *here* and *now* because it's time to do something and people are watching. The black city kid is no different from his white suburban counterpart in the desperate desire to fit in—to be cool and popular—but there is a yawning disparity in the terms. The latter functions from a context defined, to an extent, by college, prosperity, and parents at home. For the young people of that world, there is a vividly imagined future to be inherited, and the pressure—peer, parental, professional, or self-imposed—amounts basically to so much teenage stuff. Meanwhile, the urban dropout, left to his own devices, seeks his validation, along with his livelihood, from the streets.

The unabridged scenario is not quite that simple, of course. It is a delicate, controversial, overanalyzed social dilemma that can't be reduced here to a phrase or two. But it doesn't take a government study to determine that the crisis known as the black urban male has a lot to do with role models. For the boys in the 'hoods, it comes down largely to men—the lack of, and the consequent need to be.

Joe Marshall and Jack Jacqua recognized that condition when they worked for the San Francisco public schools, and they took on as much of the attending burden as they could shoulder, which, over the past eight years, has been a considerable amount. Through the Omega Boys Club, they have been the fathers that the kids lack and the role models that they require, providing extended families and essential knowledge to those who have come asking. (To *come* to the Omega Boys Club is to come tacitly asking.) There is nothing vague about what they do. Their work is idealistic to the maximum and falls clearly under the category of do-good, but if it weren't compellingly real, it wouldn't reach kid one. In the form of academic help, college scholarships, rules for living, time, wisdom, and dozens upon dozens of peer counselors—Omegas who have turned their lives around and are pleased to share the experience— Marshall and Jacqua have furnished tangible, functioning alternatives to the death game that so many of the young brothers have tragically mistaken for a rite of passage. Omega's co-founders have shown the homies not only how to become a man but how to become a black man.

The former was a lesson Marshall learned from his father, the latter from the writings of Malcolm X. For the kids who have neither in their lives, Marshall has tried to be both the dad and the Malcolm. He has shown them that responsibility and blackness can go together; that love and pride can change a person; that support and knowledge are the great equalizers. He has unfolded manhood on terms they can accept as their own. Rather than requiring its young people to buy into a program that already has them at a disadvantage, Omega has offered them family and culture in the best African-American tradition.

The issues the club has taken on, however, are by no means exclusively black in nature. Youth violence in this country has not been restricted by matters of race or color. The recent rise of hate crimes among zealous white groups ought to be evidence enough of that, but white violence certainly doesn't stop there. In Cincinnati, for example, it took a provocative twist in 1994 when a fatal shooting was attributed to a band of teenagers who called themselves the Wiggers—for "white niggers"—and were known for their hip-hop clothes and music. Meanwhile, Mexican-American sets remain among the most feared in California, as Hispanic gangs have historically been on the East Coast. Nationwide, city to city and now even in between, the market for antiviolence work is virtually unlimited. Fortunately, so are the requisite raw materials, reason and commitment, both of which can be carried freely and effectively across ethnic lines. That was demonstrated on *Street Soldiers,* the radio show that Marshall co-hosts, when Omega-style counseling defused an explosive situation between the Samoan and Filipino communities of the Bay Area.

Nor does the boys club's message apply only to boys. On any Omega meeting night, as many as a third of the young people at the Potrero Hill Neighborhood House will be girls, while on any *Street Soldiers* program, more than half the callers might be female. All of that notwithstanding, however, the conditions to which Omega has attached itself are symbolically male in nature. The individual whom America most fears these days, and not without reason, is the young black inner-city male—the homie. He is why the Omega Boys Club exists. He is the one the club is openly dedicated to saving.

Of course, it can't save all the homies. It can't save all of them in California or San Francisco or even Potrero Hill, but it has saved a lot of them in its first eight years, and it has done so in a fashion that is stirring. Omega has taken street kids from jail to college. It has ripped off their masks and turned their mean-mugs into slow smiles. It has kept teenage fathers home with their babies. It has made big-time players lay down their assault weapons and crack dealers flush their inventory. It has been responsible for personal insults going unchallenged and retribution unpaid.

"We're talking here about a couple of underpaid schoolteachers with nothing more than a desire to make a difference," says Wilbur Jiggetts, the Omega volunteer and grandfather figure whom all the kids know respectfully as Coach. "And in a short time, they have done more than all the poverty programs of the sixties. That's what can happen when someone makes it a high enough priority."

Imagine what could happen if other people, lots of them— say, for instance, the readers of this book—made a high enough priority out of saving the kids. Marshall's voice would be breaking crystal.

L.W.

Introduction

My most vivid memory of childhood is that of my father getting up at five-thirty every morning to dig ditches for the Southern California Gas Company. I would groan and roll over in my bed, not the least bit aware of how lucky I was to have such a role model in the house.

A short while after Pops returned home every afternoon, soiled and sweaty, my mother would leave for her job as a night nurse. One of my parents was nearly always home, and one of them was nearly always working. Through such an arrangement, they miraculously managed to send all nine of the Marshall children to college. It was an incredible feat that took me a long time to fully appreciate.

The upshot of all the parenting and sacrificing and nurturing that went on in our house was that it created enough of a buffer against the madness of the inner-city streets to keep me not only alive and free but healthy, straight, and relatively safe. That might not sound like much, but for a black city boy growing up in our society, it's about the best you can hope for.

Because of my home life, I was luckier than many of my friends and acquaintances in South Central Los Angeles, and from the start it made me a little different. It made me relatively tranquil —at least by comparison with the scowling, bullyish brothers who hung together in clusters in the parks and on the street corners— and it also made me ambitious in a way that might have been more socially responsible, or perhaps legitimate, than was the local custom. But even so, there was a thread of union and communion that ran through all of us. We were all young and black, each trying in his own way to survive on the cold hard streets of urban America.

In general, and now in retrospect, the overwhelmingly positive nature of my own upbringing—and that core of union and communion between all of us—has left me with the unshakable conviction that people can be made immune to their surroundings, however vile or pernicious. I hold tightly to the belief that inner-city teenagers can be taught and raised in such a way that they don't have to become part of the wantonness swirling around them. They can be persuaded to steer clear of guns when everyone else is packing M.A.C.-10s; to stay sober when everyone else is drinking forties; to stay clean when everyone else is either selling crack or smoking it, if not both. They can—and given the opportunity, frequently do—become part of the solution.

What makes this possible is the peculiar fact that the players of the urban game actually hate the game they play. Although few show it and fewer admit it, many of them inwardly despise the violence and the degradation that rule the neighborhoods and bring so much anger and pain to them, their families, and their friends. They join the game only because they can't beat it; or more to the point, because they *think* they can't beat it. Because it's all they see, they think it's all there is. And because they recognize no alternative, they become the very thing they despise: players in the game. To some, playing the game means getting crazy-rich off crack. To most, it means taking care of business. To all of them, without exception, it means earning a rep. Tragically, it means being a predator so as not to be prey.

The homie does these things because, unlike me thirty-something years ago, he has no fortification against an environment that has escalated its attack upon him. He inhabits a different world than I did. He faces serious unemployment issues that discourage the legal work ethic it takes to compete in mainstream American society. He has to deal with weapons of war that have been literally dumped on the streets of America—AK-47s, Uzis, nine millimeters, glocks, M.A.C.-10s. But most of all, he has to deal with crack cocaine, the worst thing to hit black America since slavery. Hell, crack is *worse* than slavery. Crack cocaine pulls young men into the *illegal* work ethic—some as young as age nine or ten —and most of them never manage to get out of it, ending up dead or in jail. But there is something even more pernicious, even more insidious, about crack. Crack has been able to do something even slavery couldn't do: It has stopped the African-American woman from mothering her child. Imagine that—a force stronger than motherhood! The effects of crack are nothing short of unbelievable.

So here sits the homie with a daddy he never sees, hardly knows, and deeply resents. Hell, Daddy's probably in prison anyway. Mom's home being both Mom and Dad, but too often now she's strung out herself, buried too deep in her own problems to worry about fixing snacks or checking the bookbag when her son gets home from school. And dude's angry about that because he knows he's getting screwed. Other adults, meanwhile—the extended community—well, they're scared to death of him because he's been terrorizing them from the age of thirteen.

So the homie goes where people are there for him, at least ostensibly. He goes to the streets to hang out with the other brothers who have nobody at home, either, and who share the same problems. As a group—a gang, a set, a clique, a posse, whatever you want to call it—the lot of them try to be for each other what they desperately need in their lives: men. Of course, they don't know how to do that because nobody's shown them. Nobody has shown them about getting up at five in the morning to dig ditches; about responsibility; about values; about what's really important; about what works and what doesn't work. They think taking care of each other means protecting each other's backs from homies in the next 'hood who are also trying to protect each other's backs.

The information process has obviously miserably failed these young men. Instead of fathers and mothers at home giving them information to live by, they have homeboys and homegirls in the streets giving them information to die by. The communication crisis is like a virus that has been sweeping over the inner cities ever since I grew up in South Central. But it's not incurable. It can be arrested. I believe—hell, I *know,* I've seen it *proven*—that with the right information and guidance, the homies' immune systems can be built up to a level at which the kids have some protection against themselves. We can put a stop to black genocide by inoculating the young brothers with knowledge and tender loving care. It must be done, and if their own parents aren't up to the task, it has to be done by one of us, the lucky ones. Actually, it has to be done by *a lot* of us. It is our duty and special privilege to open up our lives to the children whom fate has dumped on the street and society has left there. By making our resources their resources—by giving them some of the time and support that every kid needs—we can make them just a little luckier. Very often, that's all it takes.

For a long time, I thought I could do this as a schoolteacher, or better yet, a principal. The problem was: at school, the bell always rings. There's no bell on the street, however, and as a result I was out of tune. I found it hard to teach math to kids who had sold drugs all night and had some for breakfast. It was even harder to teach the ones with fresh bullet holes in their chests.

After watching a lot of our middle schoolers die, I concluded that the rest of them needed information more than algebra. They needed to know the kind of things my mother and father and grandmother taught me. They needed to know that there was another way to live. Hell, they needed to *live.* Rather than living, the homies were acting out a *death*style, and for them, the kind of turnaround I had in mind would be tantamount to a cultural revolution. If I truly intended to change their lifestyles—to *give* them lifestyles—I would have to train the boys in the 'hood as revolutionaries. Historically, that was something they had demonstrated a readiness to become. A quarter of a century before, in South Central, I'd seen the Black Panthers introduce a revolutionary culture to the Slausons and the Gladiators, which were the Crips and Bloods of my day.

There weren't many Crips and Bloods in San Francisco, where I worked for the public school district, but there were plenty of turf warriors in neighborhoods like Hunters Point and Fillmore and Sunnydale and in nearby cities like Oakland and Richmond and Vallejo and East Palo Alto. There were plenty of funerals. There was plenty of work to do.

When I teamed up with Jack Jacqua, an unlikely partner but kindred spirit who was on the staff with me at Potrero Hill Middle School, that work took the form of the Omega Boys Club, which in the ensuing eight years has developed a profile that neither of us could have imagined. What's surprising is not that we've given new life to so many of the homies—we knew that they were good kids ripe for saving—but that our grassroots efforts have expanded to the degree that they have and attracted such fanfare on not only the regional but also the national level. That growth and attention has become our advantage, and it is my intention, through this book, to play that advantage to its fullest effect. Lord knows, we need all the advantages we can get in the grim struggle to save the kids.

One of the incalculable benefits the boys club has realized from so much publicity was the opportunity I had in 1993 to speak before a joint congressional committee consisting of Christopher Dodd's Senate Subcommittee on Families, Drugs and Alcoholism and the House Committee on Children, Youth, and Families. It was a humbling occasion that I used to inform the legislators of what can be accomplished if they—or anybody—will simply make the commitment that is necessary to salvage a generation of black males. "It's funny," I said on the Senate floor, much as I'm saying here and now, "but this is not unlike going into a prison or going onto a street corner, where I have to convince the [homeboys] to stop doing what they're doing—to stop dealing drugs, stop gangbanging, stop shooting people. And the key to the whole thing is to get them to believe that it's possible. I feel the same way here. You need to know that it's possible. And it is. I gotta say that in the beginning. It is.

"I wrote this purposefully," I continued that day, and the same can be said for the book you are holding, "to tell you what can happen if you intervene. You can achieve success, all right? Hopefully, you'll be able to understand that if you really want to solve the problem, you *can* solve the problem. All I know is that it's a lack of effort, a lack of will.

"I'll get right to the point. In just six years, the Omega Boys Club of San Francisco has been able to place 108 young people in college, many of them former gang members and drug dealers. We have been able to elicit community support to help pay for their education. Six years ago we began with fifteen members. Today we have over three hundred [and as I write this, the number has nearly doubled]. We have since added a weekly radio call-in program which enables us to reach an additional two hundred thousand. We do peer counseling on a weekly basis in the juvenile detention centers of San Francisco and Oakland. It is not uncommon for us to meet a young offender through our peer counseling program, stay with him through the duration of the adjudication process, and send him to college. It is not uncommon for us, via the airwaves, to deter a youth from engaging in the sale of crack cocaine or packing a gun to school or retaliating against a member of another gang. Later this year we will have our second Youth Conference, at which some three thousand youth will gather to devise strategies to cope with and change the destruction in their communities. We have been profiled on CNN, the NBC Brokaw Report, in *Essence* magazine, and the *Los Angeles Times* and have been honored at the White House.

"Now, what does all of this mean? The success of the Omega Boys Club proves one thing loudly and clearly: Violence can be curbed, children's lives can be spared, and communities can be made safer, but only if—and this is a big if—only if we are willing to devote the time, the energy, and the personal and economic resources to making it happen. Don't be shocked. I am a volunteer. I teach high school by day and do the boys club at night. I started the boys club because I simply got sick of losing too many young people to drugs and violence. Along the way, I've been able to find others who felt the same way I do and who have joined with me in the fight to save our youth.

"Many people," I told the committee, as I've told many audiences many times, "seem to believe that it's easier for young people today. Well, it's not. The lack of employment, the availability of weapons of all types, and the presence of crack cocaine have all combined to make things interminably worse for them, especially in the inner cities of our nation. But—and this sentence is very key, people—armed with the belief that young people *want* a way out but just *don't know how to get out,* we have been able to save individual lives, and better yet, to empower others to reach out and do the same.

"This is a terrible thing to say, but I am almost convinced that as a society we would rather let those young men die than do something to save them. But we can't say anymore that we don't know *how* to save them, or that we don't have a successful model we can emulate. The success of the Omega Boys Club demonstrates that it is not necessarily *they* who have given up on *us,* but *we* who have given up on *them.* The ball is in our court."

When I was about six years old, my grandmother told me, "The more you know, the more you owe." I didn't know what it meant then, but I sure know what it means now. I've learned a hell of a lot; therefore I owe a hell of a lot. After you read these pages and find out what's possible for the youth of America, you will, too.

The ball is now in *your* court. As I said to the subcommittee, "Service, anyone?"

J.M.

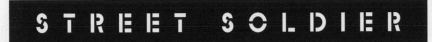

STREET SOLDIER

1

Black Man 101

Spike Lee, the filmmaker, was two rows in front of me on the other side of the aisle—all the honorees had aisle seats —and when my turn arrived on the program, he swiveled to face me, framed his eyes with his hands, thumbs touching, and locked in, squinting a little and cocking his head this way and that for the best angle. The next thing that happened was even stranger. While Morgan Freeman finished his introduction and called me to the stage to receive my Essence award, Spike and Jesse Jackson and Denzel Washington and Eddie Murphy and Quincy Jones and all the other illustrious people at the Paramount Theater rose to their feet applauding. At that frozen moment, I realized that the Omega Boys Club would never again be exclusively mine and my partner's or even San Francisco's. By the time I shook Morgan Freeman's hand and turned to address the crowd of tuxedos and gowns, I was in awe not only of the scene but of the apparent magnitude of what Jack Jacqua and I had unwittingly created out of common concerns and spare moments at Potrero Hill Middle School.

Needless to say, when we started the club in 1987 I never

considered the possibility of winning something like an Essence award, or a Children's Defense Fund Leadership Award, or a Mac-Arthur fellowship, or being on the Oprah Winfrey show and every major television network, or even signing a book contract, all of which happened within the course of one whirlwind year. I didn't think those were things that came from working with city kids.

All of that stuff still blows me away, but what I understand now is that public recognition *has* to come to those who work with city kids. If America is going to acknowledge and address its most devastating social dilemma—the moral and biological demise of the urban youth—it has to glorify those who are saving the kids, perhaps above all others. It has to recognize that those who are saving the kids are inherently saving the cities. I say this not to be self-serving; on the basis not of what I do but what I *see.*

What Jack and I saw eight years ago was a generation in jeopardy and a culture in ruin. We saw kids—good kids—dying, dealing, packing, and going to jail before they finished middle school, and it disturbed us beyond distraction. The cheapening of young life was a crisis that undermined not only what we were trying to accomplish at the school where we worked but the future of every boy and girl in that building. We both felt that we couldn't go on without doing something about it.

Once we made up our minds to embrace some of the kids through a boys club, the rhythms of the city and country took over. Because the time was right for us—because we were the right answer to an urgent problem; the right product for a desperate market—one thing inevitably led to another, which led to our radio show, which led to a crazy amount of media coverage, which led to Spike Lee's imaginary camera and the heady words that were coming from Morgan Freeman on the stage of the Paramount: "Joe Marshall," I dimly heard him say as the strains of "The Greatest Love of All" played in the background, "for rescuing our children and restoring their belief in themselves and in their future, we are honored to present you with the 1994 Essence award."

The groundswell had obviously been gathering for some time, but that made it no less mind-boggling when the crowd that had applauded politely for Spike Lee and Eddie Murphy turned it up a notch for the co-founder of a boys club in San Francisco. The whole night, as I sat next to my son, Malcolm, and gawked at the people filing in—Maya Angelou, Aretha Franklin, Betty Shabazz, Sugar Ray Leonard, Michael Jackson and his escorts—it had been difficult for me to come to terms with what I was doing there, in that lofty company. Prior to 1994, *Essence* magazine had given its annual awards only to women, and so it was from a wide-open field that I was selected along with Jesse Jackson, Denzel Washington, Robert Moses, Quincy Jones, Eddie Murphy, Spike Lee, and Dr. Ben Carson. *Essence* picked me when it could have picked Michael Jordan or Bill Cosby or Colin Powell. I was still trying anxiously to justify all of that when, after a few winning minutes of film clips about the club, I stood up to walk toward the stage and everybody else stood up with me.

Under the circumstances, the speech would have been difficult had I not spoken to so many tougher crowds at the club, on the radio, and in the schools and prisons. "Oh, wow," I said, groping to find my legs. "I'm overwhelmed. I'm stunned. . . .

"You know, a man is only the sum total of all that has been put into him, and certainly I have had much put into me. I'm the oldest of nine children, and have a great mother and father. I have to thank my grandmother, who's eighty-seven years old, who told me, 'The more you know, the more you owe.' I want to thank my own family that allows me to run around the country being a surrogate father to so many other young people. Lastly, I gotta thank the group that put me up here—that's all the homies. All the boys in the 'hood; all the ones that people say would not listen, wouldn't give me five minutes. They gave me five minutes, they gave me ten minutes; that ten turned into twenty, that twenty turned into a lifetime.

"If you wanna find me, I'll see you in the 'hood."

There was more standing and clapping as I returned to my seat, and by the time I got there, Spike Lee had handed me a business card with his home, work, and fax numbers on it. Then Luther Vandross sang me a song. Denzel Washington was next to receive his award, and in my daze I heard him say something about God blessing me. When he was back in the audience, he stopped in front of me, knelt down, and said, "Thank you for what you're doing, Mr. Marshall. If I can ever be of any help, let me know." Later, Sinbad talked to me about making a television movie out of the boys club, and Spike Lee insisted that we get together for breakfast in San Francisco, which we ultimately did.

The last honoree on the program that night was Jesse Jackson, and the theme of Jackson's speech, as it has often been lately, was the incarceration rate and neighborhood violence among young black males, the combined effect of the two being virtual genocide. In many ways, it was the same talk Jack and I had given to our club members two or three times a week for seven years. Now, however, through Jackson and other activists and various books and our radio show and a snowballing awareness in the national media, the entire country is starting to pay attention. For its *own* best interests—not just the kids'—it has to.

Frankly, that's about the only way we can expect anybody to pay much attention to any problem—by making them see that it's *their* problem, which this one emphatically is. Even a man like Jack Jacqua, who is white and has no children of his own, recognizes, through reason and open eyes, that the urban youth problem is very much his problem because it's his city's problem and America's problem and humanity's problem.

For my part, I determined long ago that anything pertaining to the black condition pertains intimately to me. I had arrived at that conclusion during my college years.

In 1964, I enrolled at the University of San Francisco because I wanted to go to a school that had a substantial black population. I had closely followed the USF basketball team on television, having become a fan when Bill Russell and K. C. Jones led the Dons to consecutive national championships in the midfifties and remained one through the lesser likes of Joe Ellis, Ollie Johnson, and Huey Thomas, all of whom were black. Since the team was heavily integrated, I assumed that the same applied to the USF student body. When I arrived on campus and looked around, however, I realized, with a certain amount of discomfort, that the basketball players and I were seriously outnumbered.

My little miscalculation notwithstanding, the ambitions I carried to USF were similar to those of most college students. I was in pursuit of the American Dream—my specific goal was a couple of cars—and as many good parties as I could work into my schedule without flunking out. With the latter in mind, I joined a black fraternity. Since there weren't enough blacks at USF to form one, this entailed commuting fifty miles to the Omega Psi Phi fraternity house at San Jose State University. San Jose offered the Bay Area's only Omega chapter, which included students from nearly every school around, including Stanford, Cal-Berkeley, Cal-Hayward, San Francisco State, and Santa Clara.

Not having a car of my own, I caught a ride with another pledge a few days after arriving on campus and pulled up at the big Omega house on fraternity row for my first smoker. There was nothing in my experience that gave me a clue as to what I would find inside, and the other pledges and I were waiting nervously in the living room when, from around the corner, the evening began suddenly with the words of the famous Omega song, "Zoom":

> . . . *So hard to make Omega,*
> *So hard to make Omega,*
> *Sweat blood.*
> *Sweat blood and tears.*
> *Sweat blood.*
> *Sweat blood and tears.*

As they sang, the Omega brothers stomped into the room with an arresting syncopation reminiscent of the Grambling or Southern University marching bands. They were all wearing their purple and gold fraternity sweaters, looking extremely collegiate and practically mesmerizing us with that damn chant. If they had asked me at that moment to remove my clothes and walk the

Omega flag all the way to USF, I would have carried it out the door stomping.

When the singing stopped, Gerald Hughes, an upperclassman who was on his way to becoming a doctor, gave us the rundown on the history and purpose of Omega Psi Phi. His words were mostly academic, though, because what really mattered was Gerald himself . . . and Leon Roundtree, who was on his way to becoming a lawyer, and John Maupin, who was on his way to becoming a dentist and president of Meharry Medical College in Nashville, and all the rest of the brothers who were clearly on their way to something high and mighty. Those guys—and the frat house seemed to be full of them—represented a world I had never glimpsed before. I said to myself, "Damn, this is bad! These guys are real *students.*" I was awed by the air of achievement that charged the room. Then, after the traditional segment of the smoker was over, about two dozen of the best-looking girls I had ever seen suddenly appeared out of the woodwork.

Although the social aspect of the fraternity was probably sixty percent of it, which suited me fine, the thing that most impressed me was the fact that the brothers all seemed to be working together for legitimately high ideals. You have to understand how *different* all of that was to me. Where I grew up, on 62nd and Denker in South Central Los Angeles, every stranger was a threat —at best unfriendly and at worst a hell-bent enemy. If you didn't know somebody, you just hoped he wouldn't be openly hostile toward you. Having gone to an all-white Catholic high school (the fraternity brothers called me Guiseppe because of that), my experience had taught me that white guys were serious students and black guys were serious only about fighting each other for control of the neighborhoods. Until I saw the fraternity in action, I really didn't believe that young black men had the means or the wherewithal to come together for positive purposes. From the beginning, it was obvious to everybody in the fraternity that I was ultrasincere about its ideals. The other guys would say things like, "Hey, he really *believes* this stuff," and they were right. I took it to heart. If I hadn't, I don't think I would have chosen to endure the brutal pledge process that was then the fashion— the "sweat, blood, and tears" immortalized in "Zoom."

What it amounted to was that the big brothers beat the shit out of us. They would tell us to bend over and grab our ankles, then proceed to flail our backsides with paddles or whatever was available. This sort of treatment would go on for months and months until they thought the pledge was ready to be an Omega. After a while, the ordeal became psychological, a matter of how badly one wanted to join the fraternity. In my case, I wanted it so desperately that I would have suffered through anything I could bear to be initiated.

The brothers considered it their sacred duty to make certain I was granted this privilege. When I was back in Los Angeles over the summer, for instance, an Omega from South Central named Wilson Simmons took a special interest in me, advising me that while he realized I was off limits when school was out of session, he had big plans for me in the fall. When he had been a pledge, Butch, as we knew him, had nearly been killed by the older Omegas for knocking out a big brother who was trying to brutalize him. But his objection to hazing apparently had nothing to do with the principle of it. Given the license to pick on pledges, Butch had established a reputation as a fellow to be feared. I wasn't particularly worried, however: come September, he would be nearly four hundred miles away.

After school started up again, I was hanging around the fraternity house one evening, waiting to leave for a party, when the door opened and big Butch Simmons walked through. I saw him coming and said, "Oh, shit!" He saw me, too. Sure enough, when the time came for everybody to go to the party, Butch instructed me to stay behind. "See, little brother?" he said. "I told you I was gonna get you." As soon as everybody else was gone, he led me into one of the bedrooms—I had no choice but to follow—and pulled out Silent Sam, a legendary fraternity weapon made out of a twisted coat hanger. That was the only time in my life I ever had to pull my pants down to have my rear end beaten. The whipping probably only took a few minutes, but it seemed like an hour. The whole time, Butch was saying, "Now, you gonna remember this, little brother. I want you to make Omega the *right* way." Afterward, he actually tried to console me with the same words fathers use after punishing their kids: "You know, I did that for your own good. It hurt me more than it hurt you." The hell it did.

When my interminable pledge period was finally over and I was initiated into Omega Psi Phi, it was apparent that I was not a bit different from Butch Simmons or any of my tormenters. I was so gung-ho for the fraternity that I subscribed wholeheartedly to all that it did and stood for, including the brutalization of pledges, concerning which I was somewhat insane. Before long, the brothers were calling me "Bloody Joe" Marshall. "Big Brother Marshall wants to see some blood," they would say to the poor bent-over pledges. I wanted initiation in Omega Psi Phi to really *mean* something, and its price, consequently, had to be painful.

In retrospect, I suspect that my zeal to attach significance to Omega membership might have been an attempt to override my questions about it. As much as I admired the scholarship and personal ambition of the Ques (pronounced "cues"), as Omegas were called, I recognized that the fraternity stood principally for brotherhood, as attested by its motto: "Friendship is essential to the soul." I was all for the friendship—in fact, I reveled in it, permitting fraternity life to dominate my college experience for a while— but deep down, I had to wonder about its price.

In the years since, I've given a lot of thought to the pledge experience. Why did I allow myself to be beaten like that—sometimes so severely that I couldn't sit down—and why did I then turn around and inflict the same punishment on those who came after me? I've never really made complete sense of it—I'm not sure anybody has—but it seems to me that, somehow, the Omega pledge process was a manifestation of our history; that in many ways, pledging represented the best and worst of being a black American, the African part and the European part—what we've retained from the motherland and what we've inherited from our slave ancestry here in America. I regarded pledging, including its hazing aspect, as a rite of passage and in that respect very African, very tribal, not unlike the elders taking out the adolescents for manhood training. There was an intrinsic fraternal unity in the whole process—the big brothers passing along their history and traditions to the pledges, the underlying interest in each other, the way the whole pledge line worked and played together—a spiritual magnetism so powerful that it enabled eager pledges like me to silently suffer, and in some ways even appreciate, the physical and psychological pain that was brought down on us. The paddling, meanwhile, was horrifically reminiscent of slavery times, scarcely different from the horsewhippings our ancestors endured at the hands of the overseers. In tragic irony, African Americans have evolved over the past two centuries as a self-punishing people. This tradition has been cruelly carried on by the unconscionably savage "jumping-in" requirements that modern-day street gangs commonly demand, including the maiming and murdering of strangers and even family members. There's historic poignancy in all of that black brutality, and somehow, as a naïve teenage pledge, I *felt* it. I'm certain it affected me. At the time, though, I couldn't have identified or articulated any of it. There was very little I understood about being black in America.

Until then, racial sensitivity was something I had been conditioned to put aside. As the oldest child in a happy home of nine kids, with a mother and father and grandparents who loved us and did all the right things, I harbored no discernible anger inside me. On the few occasions that racism had intruded upon my experience—such as the times when my white schoolmates would mimic my high-pitched South Central style of speaking with an exaggerated minstrel kind of voice—I had been puzzled and certainly offended by it, but my response was always softened by the coolheaded style that my family had brought from St. Louis or by the crystal-clear expectations of the white authorities.

The vice-principal of Loyola High School, for instance, conveyed to me the establishment point of view. I appealed to him concerning an incident during a lunch-hour intramural basketball game in which I had been shooting unusually well and as a result my team had been on the verge of upsetting a squad of cocky jocks.

One of them, the star tight end on Loyola's conference-champion football team, was unable to stand it, and his answer was to start flinging around every sentence he could think of with *nigger* in it: "You're not going to beat us, nigger!" "We'll run you out of here, nigger!" "You don't belong here, nigger!" I was more appalled than angry, stunned by the unexpected explosion of latent racism and profoundly hurt. What hurt the most was not the football fool exposing his true colors but the fact that neither my teammates nor the lunch-hour supervisor, a Jesuit who was standing right there, offered a word in my defense.

Determined to see justice served, I stormed into the vice-principal's office and delivered my side of the story. The vice-principal was in charge of discipline at a very disciplined school, and I had no doubt that he would swiftly collar the tight end and punish him on the spot. The more we talked, though, the more obvious it became that he had no such intention. I was getting hotter by the minute. "If you don't do something about it," I finally blurted out in frustration, "I'm gonna bring my boys in here and we'll take care of it ourselves." That went over big. "If there's any trouble," he replied, "you won't graduate." If anyone from the school administration ever spoke to the football player, I didn't hear about it. The entire episode left me completely bewildered.

A comparable thing happened at USF near the end of my sophomore year, the spring of 1966. A group of students had gathered in the dormitory television room to watch the NCAA basketball championship game between Kentucky and Texas Western, most of them not surprisingly rooting for Kentucky. Texas Western was the first prominent college team to start five black players, and that fact was foremost in the minds of everybody in the room, including me. As the prospect of Texas Western winning—which it ultimately did—became more formidable, two or three of the guys right in front of me started shouting at the TV, saying things like, "Don't let those niggers win!" I might as well have been invisible and for the moment elected to remain that way.

I couldn't wipe the incident out of my mind, however, and as the days and months went on, things started to tumble and swirl in my consciousness. While the civil rights movement had been confined largely to the South throughout the early sixties, California had weighed in violently with the Watts riots of August 1965, and I found it was impossible to remain unaffected. By then, my family had moved from Denker to 108th Street, and the National Guard tanks rolled right past our door on their way to Watts. I remember thinking, "Damn, this is like Vietnam." A curfew was imposed for the entire area, and one night, when I was returning home late from a party, National Guardsmen shot at my car as I passed their position. During the daytime I worked at a service station on Manchester and Central, which the authorities shut down for a while because customers were using our gasoline to make Molotov cocktails. Later in the week, during the state of emergency, I attended a Rams game at Los Angeles Coliseum, and as my friend and I were driving away from the stadium, a couple of policemen stopped us and put shotguns to our heads. They tore apart our car and made me open my trunk, which had a couple of baseball bats in it. The cops didn't want to believe that I carried the baseball bats for playing baseball. They let us go, but not before making certain they had ruined our evening.

By 1966, the atmosphere of rebellion had me surrounded even in the insulation of my conservative Jesuit campus. Just across the Bay Bridge in Oakland, Huey Newton and Bobby Seale were organizing a group of aggressive, heavily armed young men who that fall became known as the Black Panthers. In Berkeley, meanwhile, just a few miles farther north, social unrest seemed to have taken over the Cal curriculum. Everybody seemed to be searching, including me.

Under these influences, I was impelled to do the most radical thing I'd ever done. I picked up a book about Malcolm X. Malcolm had been murdered early in 1965, and although the event had little effect on me, I was still curious about the man. All I knew of him was what I'd read in the newspapers, which depicted him as a raging conflicted militant. I suppose it was all the commotion over Malcolm that intrigued me, and I figured that if I understood *him* a little bit, I might understand the times a little bit.

What I hadn't counted on was that by understanding Malcolm a little, I would come to understand myself a lot.

I started out with *Malcolm X Speaks*. For me, that was Black Man 101. Through *Malcolm X Speaks*, I began to see that the public portrayal of Malcolm, by the press and policymakers, was completely simplistic, mainly erroneous, and grossly self-serving. I was exposed to points of view regarding Malcolm that I hadn't glimpsed through the mainstream channels, and it made me angry that the media had so distorted and shortchanged this great brilliant man. My response was to read *The Autobiography of Malcolm X*. With that, my life changed.

Traditionally, if you're a young black person in this country, you know that something's wrong but you don't know exactly what it is. Malcolm showed me what it is. He explained the rage through the triumph and tragedy, the achievement and oppression, the dignity and degradation of black history. He explained it with bold, chilling logic. As I turned the pages of that incredible book, Malcolm showed me why it was that a group of black kids who didn't even know me had beaten me up over a baseball game when I was eleven years old. He showed me why the vice-principal at Loyola High had virtually endorsed the football player's verbal attack on me. He showed me why South Central Los Angeles was so menacing, even then; why kids who lived just a few blocks from me, who by all appearances were just like me—the same nappy hair and everything—scared the hell out of me. He showed me why none of my neighborhood friends joined me in college. *The Autobiography of Malcolm X* unlocked the door for me and flung it wide open.

After reading Malcolm, I realized that my Catholic education—which, in this respect, was no different from a public education—had included absolutely nothing about me as a black man. I had never even heard of Booker T. Washington or Frederick Douglass or W.E.B. Du Bois or Paul Robeson. The only black person mentioned in my history classes was George Washington Carver, the peanut doctor, and he was recognized, no doubt, because of his contributions to the mainstream (that is, white) economy. It was as if black history were of no real significance whatsoever, which implied, in turn, that black people were of no real significance. Malcolm not only enlightened me about black history, but he turned me on to the fundamental fact that there *was* black history. More than that, he showed me how that great and scandalous history was still playing itself out in our homes and in our schools and in our communities and in our minds. From the tribal abductions to the planter's libido to the Klansman's hood to the brother's habit, he put it all in perspective—oh God, did he ever. Many of the things he wrote have since become so ingrained in my consciousness that they seem elementary to me now, but in 1966 I'd never read or heard anything like, for example, Malcolm's explanation of the black American's cultural emasculation, as described in part through his conversations in prison:

"I began first telling my black brother inmates about the glorious history of the black man—things they never had dreamed," he wrote. "I told them the horrible slavery-trade truths that they never knew. I would watch their faces when I told them that, because the white man had completely erased the slaves' past, a Negro in America can never know his true family name, or even what tribe he was descended from: the Mandingos, the Wolof, the Serer, the Fula, the Fanti, the Ashanti, or others. I told them that some slaves brought from Africa spoke Arabic, and were Islamic in their religion. A lot of these black convicts still wouldn't believe it unless they could see that a white man had said it. So, often, I would read to these brothers selected passages from white men's books. I'd explain to them that the real truth was known to some white men, the scholars; but there had been a conspiracy down through the generations to keep the truth from black men. . . .

"It's a crime, the lie that has been told to generations of black men and white men both. Little innocent black children, born of parents who believed that their race had no history. Little black children seeing, before they could talk, that their parents considered themselves inferior. Innocent black children growing up, living out their lives, dying of old age—and all of their lives ashamed of being black."

With my stomach growling for more black history, my next

book was *Before the Mayflower*. I devoured it. There was my heritage right in my lap, like a lost chapter of the Bible. I was enthralled, and the deeper I plunged into my discovery, the more piqued I became over the white man's reconfiguration of history, over his systematic attempt to dupe me and my race, depriving us of knowledge that would make us proud of our culture. When I found out that George Washington had owned slaves, I thought, "You've got to be kidding." I had the same reaction upon reading that Abraham Lincoln had favored deporting blacks to Central America. So overtaken was I by this vast new knowledge that it was all I could talk about. At my urging and on their own, my fraternity brothers and black friends were beginning to read the same books, and discussing them became the focus of our extracurricular lives. We read from the works of Douglass and Du Bois and then moved on to more current popular volumes: *Manchild in the Promised Land; Crisis of the Negro Intellectual; Native Son; Invisible Man.*

In Richard Wright's *Native Son,* I found the rage of the black man searingly conveyed, but even so, it was Malcolm who explained to me, first and always, why the rage was there. The more I read, the more I realized that Malcolm's writings, Malcolm's lessons and logic, hit me harder than anyone else's and made the most sense. They set my course. My father had taught me how to be a man, but Malcolm taught me how to be a black man. For that, I felt a deep-seated, almost congenital, connection to Malcolm. Even now, hardly a day goes by that I don't picture him in a pool of blood on the floor of the Audubon ballroom; the only difference time has made is that the picture doesn't bring me as often to tears.

It was more than knowledge that Malcolm gave me. When he received the knowledge in prison, Malcolm knew that he had to *do something* with it, and when I received it in college, I knew that I, too, had to put it to use. No longer could I be content to collude in my own oppression. I had no grandiose illusions about being another Malcolm, but I knew that the knowledge itself was not enough. It had to change me. And I, in turn, had to change the conditions for black people.

I wasn't doing anything particularly wrong at the time, except that I wasn't doing anything particularly right. I was just being a normal carefree college student—going to parties, enjoying my fraternity, and when things were quiet, losing myself in jazz and particularly Nancy Wilson. (When I was seventeen, I'd been seduced by a Ramsey Lewis album, *Barefoot Sunday Blues,* and another, *Take Five,* by Dave Brubeck. After that, I was on a mission to acquaint myself with virtually every jazz musician who ever cut a record. I credit Nancy Wilson with getting me through college.)

Although I didn't perceive it that way at the time, jazz, and to a lesser extent soul, no doubt helped put me in touch with black culture. It was sort of a warm-up act for Malcolm. But my basic perspective was unaltered until I fell under Malcolm's influence, and when I did, I started thinking about something my grandmother had said many years before on the front porch of her house on Paris Avenue in St. Louis.

When I was six or seven years old, I had asked Gue Gue (pronounced "Goo-goo") what she wanted me to be when I grew up, and in her soft-spoken, firmly elegant manner, she replied without hesitation that she hoped I would be a teacher. Gue Gue always enjoyed teaching me things—before we moved from St. Louis to Los Angeles, she would often dress me up in little suits and take me on the bus to Forest Park, where she would point out all the different birds and flowers—and she was impressed with the knowledge I was always eager and able to absorb. (My parents were amazed that I could somehow pick out record albums when I was three or four years old. They would say something like, "Billie Holiday," and I would go fetch the recording they wanted.)

My apparent appetite for information was a big part of the reason why Gue Gue wanted me to be a teacher: so that I could share my knowledge with other people in the same manner that she consciously shared hers. Gue Gue was uncommonly dedicated to the sharing of knowledge. As a young woman in Mississippi, her dream had been to start a private school for black boys. That had not been possible in light of her resources and geographical situation, but through the power of her own ideals she had kept alive the premise on which it would have been founded. "The more you know," she told me on her porch that day and many times thereafter, "the more you owe."

While Gue Gue imagined me as a teacher, it seemed that just about everybody else in my extended family—including two great-aunts, my grandparents, and even my brothers and sisters—had their own plans for me when I was growing up. My mother had the priesthood in mind, and my dad wanted me to be a lawyer or a baseball player, like Jackie Robinson.

I was born the year Jackie Robinson broke the color line (1947), which made me feel sort of star-crossed because Jackie Robinson was sacred around our house. Although we didn't go to many ball games in St. Louis, my grandfather made a point of taking me to Sportsman's Park to watch the Dodgers play the Cardinals in 1954. I don't remember who won the game, but I'll never forget my grandfather pointing to the on-deck circle and saying, "See that number forty-two? That's him."

I was as big a Jackie Robinson fan as anybody, but—probably because I was realistic about my own ability or lack of it—I never gave much thought to following in his footsteps. My own dream was to play the piano. When my grandmother heard that, she went to the Aolean Piano Company in St. Louis and bought me one.

Gue Gue (her real name is Louise Pierce) always seemed to be in tune with what I was thinking and dreaming. She had an omniscient quality about her, which I ascribe to her deep sense of religion. Every time she knocked on our door, Gue Gue recited John 3:16 (*For God so loved the world, that he gave his only begotten Son, that whosoever believeth in him should not perish, but have everlasting life.*); we wouldn't open up unless we heard it. To this day, when someone calls her on the phone, the first words out of her mouth are, "Jesus loves you."

Gue Gue lived a few blocks away from us in Los Angeles, and she knocked virtually every day, which I welcomed. I felt blessed in her company, warmed by her assurances that the Lord had something special in mind for me. I also missed having her around all the time. We had lived on the second floor of Gue Gue's house in St. Louis, where she was an unofficial grandmother to all of the neighborhood kids and for a while also ran a restaurant that specialized in tomato rice soup and fried apple pie. I often went to the restaurant with Gue Gue, and at home, where she was the esteemed elder of the house, I clung as close to her as I could. (As the oldest of the nine Marshall children, I was the one whose baby talk produced her nickname.) She was, almost literally, my security blanket. In the middle of the night, I would wake up and traipse downstairs to crawl in bed with Gue Gue. Like clockwork, the younger kids would follow—first Deborah, then James, and on down the line.

Without assistance from my father's father, Gue Gue had raised her only child, Joseph Earl Marshall (she called me Junior) in the Baptist churches of Vicksburg, Mississippi, and St. Louis. My mother, who was also raised Baptist, converted the family to Catholicism shortly after I was born—in part, perhaps, so that we could attend Catholic schools. By the time I was old enough for kindergarten, Gue Gue took me down to Rock Church in St. Louis to sign up, only to find out that she had taught me too much for kindergarten; I had to go straight to the first grade.

Having acquired a taste for learning from Gue Gue, I was content with the structure and scholarship of a Catholic education, although the same could not be said for my brothers. After we settled in South Central, where a black kid in a parochial school was painfully conspicuous and consequently had to prove his mettle every day, a couple of them smarted off to the nuns and got kicked out. James, in particular, was uninterested in anything that smacked of capitulation. He ended up fighting a lot of my fights as I tried to reason my way out of conflict. I could never understand fighting, and he could never understand not fighting.

Los Angeles, in fact, was a place I had a hard time understanding in general after the Gue Gue world of my early years. Shortly after arriving there, I wandered over to the Harvard Playground, which was just across the street from our house, and a neighborhood kid asked me where I was from. I said, "St. Louis." He narrowed his eyes and replied, "Are you trying to be funny or something? I ought to kick your ass." It was only later that I realized he had wanted to know what gang I was with. It didn't occur to him that the geographical implications of his question might extend beyond South Central.

Our Denker Street address was located in what is now near Rolling Sixties territory. The Crips were still many years away, but South Central was already divided into gangs with names like the Businessmen, the Del Vikings, the Rabble Rousers, the Slausons, and the Gladiators. My friends were Gladiators, which made me one by association. I never joined in spirit or battle, however, mainly because of my father. I had more to fear from him than from any gang. The Gladiators put me through the little ritual by which they jumped guys into the gang—that is, they beat me up in the park—but as soon as they jumped me in, my father jumped me out.

In addition to instilling me with a stern sense of right and wrong, my father imparted the work ethic by example. When I was eleven years old, I started working as a box boy at the corner grocery for eighty-five cents an hour, and after that I was never without a summer job. Where other kids in the neighborhood hustled to put nickels together, I always trusted the fact—and a lot of people in our neighborhood didn't consider it to *be* a fact—that money could be made legally.

We had come to Los Angeles in the first place so that Pops, who had a junior college education, could dig ditches for the gas company, which he did the rest of his working life. He was also in charge of the kids while Mom worked the swing shifts at Kaiser and County hospitals, and it was a role he took very seriously. Having been raised without a father, Pops was determined that his children would have the benefit of manly discipline. Whereas my grandmother directed us with the Bible, my father preached the gospel of the rod, when necessary. He and his rod persuaded me, for instance, that I didn't *really* want to process my hair like my friends were doing. Pops was my stopper. He convinced me that I didn't want to do *a lot* of things that the other kids in South Central were doing.

In that regard, though, he didn't have too much to worry about. Because of my parallel life in the Catholic school, I never felt fully connected to South Central. I played Little League and sandlot baseball with guys from the neighborhood and considered them my friends, but they apparently recognized nothing bonding about baseball. I found that out one day at Harvard Playground, when we became involved in a pickup game with four unfamiliar kids from a set called the Baby Businessmen. I was waiting for my turn to bat when the guy ahead of me slid into second base and was called out by the other team. Instinctively, I yelled, "Man, are you nuts? He was in there easy." The next thing I knew, I had eight fists coming at me.

Because they were in a gang, and because I had spoken up to them, and because they had to assert their presence in a neighborhood where apparently nobody knew enough to let them have their way, the Baby Businessmen found it necessary to beat the hell out of me. It was their way of saying, "Who do you think you are, talkin' to us like that, nigger? Look, we're the gang. We're in charge here, and you don't know nothin' about nothin'." After they had all gotten in their licks and my mouth was bleeding pretty good, they backed off and left one of them—the smallest—to fight me himself. When I started kicking the little guy's ass, the rest of them jumped back in and pounded me some more. Meanwhile, my buddies watched, which is something I can't explain to this day. Maybe my so-called friends thought I *needed* to get beaten up. Maybe they thought I needed to get with the program, to get with the neighborhood and fight like a Gladiator. Whatever the reason, it didn't make any sense to me.

My problem was that I never felt that fighting proved anything, and beyond that, I never felt I had anything to prove; Moms and Pops and Gue Gue had done too good a job making me feel worthwhile as a son, a student, a child of God, and a human being. Even Gue Gue marveled that I so infrequently hit back when I was hit—maybe she thought I *should* hit back now and then—because

I was tall and wiry and capable of inflicting some damage. But rather than fight, I preferred to lecture my antagonists about the fruitlessness of fighting. Even then, as their peer and sometimes their victim, my response to brawling, preying, self-destructing street kids was to try to talk some sense into them. Instinctively, that seemed to be my role, even my calling. I can see that now, and Gue Gue could see it then. She had seen it from the beginning. That was why she had told me what she told me on the porch that day: The more you know, the more you owe.

Once I came to know the real story of black history and combined that with Gue Gue's porch wisdom, I felt I owed big-time. As a college student, I was in an unusual position—for a kid from South Central—to make good on that obligation, and I began to seriously consider my grandmother's advice about being a teacher. But I was also interested in law school—or more appropriately, in a lawyer's salary—and intended to pursue that possibility, if it existed. Either way, it was imperative that I cut down on the partying and get busy with my obligations, academic and social.

Although the black population at USF was still negligible, I grew increasingly sensitive to the fact that there was not a Black Student Union on campus. Most of the colleges in the area had one, and in fact four or five of my Omega fraternity brothers were BSU presidents at their schools. In the spring of 1968, I was actively kicking around the notion of a BSU on my snow-colored campus while working part time at a pharmacy in San Francisco's financial district. My job was delivering prescriptions—a good way to learn every section of the city—and on the afternoon of April 4 I was returning from a delivery when I flipped on the truck radio and was jolted by the news out of Memphis: Martin Luther King had been assassinated by a sniper.

I was extremely shaken—the thought kept coming back, "Why in the world would anybody want to kill someone as peaceful and good as Dr. King?"—and sort of stumbled into the rear of the drugstore when I arrived there. Inside, the first person I saw was the pharmacist, a Japanese-American, and I said to him blankly, "They shot Martin Luther King." My boss looked past me and replied, "Well, he shouldn't have been going around trying to change things." I was so angry and disoriented that I just said, "I gotta go," and took off.

It was soon evident that the majority of white students and faculty members at USF felt the same way about Dr. King—and by extension, about civil rights—as the pharmacist, which quickened my resolve about starting our own BSU. By the next fall, I had succeeded in organizing one in spite of resistance from the USF administration, which said that it could not authorize a campus club conceived on the basis of race. Consequently, we operated unofficially and underground at first, trying to stir things up without defeating our purpose by alienating the entire university community.

From the perspective I occupy thirty years later, it's easy to see that establishing the BSU was my first assignment in what would become a life's work. It's also easy to see that destiny had a hand in that work from the beginning. I wouldn't have even been at USF in the fall of 1969 if I hadn't blown my law school exam. I had already been recruited for the minority program at the University of Michigan law school and was mentally preparing myself for torts and snow. But on the morning I was designated to take the LSAT, I somehow managed to show up five minutes late. They wouldn't allow me to take the test, and there wasn't another one scheduled before the fall. When he heard that, the dean of USF's education department suggested that I enter the credential program for a teaching certificate. Since I had nothing else planned and Gue Gue's voice was in my head, I surrendered to the inevitable and became a teacher.

The credential program took a year, and I capitalized on that year to implement my start-up agenda for the BSU. While some of the BSU members were revolutionary in their ambitions and ideology—studying Maoism or observing the Black Panthers with particular interest—I angled for small practical breakthroughs. For the campus cafeteria, I wanted some food that I was accustomed to eating instead of all the Ozzie and Harriet junk we were fed exclusively. I wanted some jazz and soul on the student union jukebox to go along with the Beatles and Burt Bacharach. I wanted more black faculty members and black-awareness classes. I wanted some black *history,* for God's sake. My objective was a little more color—no, a *lot* more color—on campus. I wanted the black students to be represented.

The pragmatic low-key approach helped us gain accreditation after a bespectacled white English teacher named John Canney put his neck on the line by stepping up to be our faculty adviser. We were given operating space at Phelan Hall, next to the office of the student newspaper (*The Foghorn,* for which I had covered sports a couple of years before), and I spent large portions of my days and nights there. I loved the idea of having a home base for black culture. Often, after everybody else had left and gone to bed, I would settle in for a long cozy night of BSU scheming or communing with Malcolm X. I reread everything Malcolm wrote and, stimulated by the possibilities of the BSU, listened over and over to tapes of his speeches.

Although comparatively small in number, the BSU soon became the most conspicuous group on campus. Actually, our color alone would have accomplished that even without our sunglasses, leather jackets, dashikis, and natural hair styles. (My natural left much to be desired, as it grew only on the top of my head.) Judging mostly by our appearance, the students at large thought we were a little frightening and more than a little nuts.

That was all right with us, though, because our high profile was essentially a form of free advertising. As our visibility picked up, it was not uncommon for me to be walking out of a class or down a campus sidewalk and find myself engaged in a spontaneous and often agitated political discussion with a ring of white students, the subject always being the racial topic of the moment. Other times, the BSU scheduled town halls and campus forums in which we would present and kick around the issues that concerned us. Gradually, the faculty and student body became sensitized to our point of view, if not entirely won over by it. We got their attention, for instance, when we assembled in the student union and parodied the university's homecoming ceremony, even crowning our own queen. The idea of a black homecoming queen was fairly preposterous at the time—the school didn't even have *coeds* until my first year there, 1964—but we drove home our point, which was to make the campus self-conscious about its lily-whiteness.

Although, in the context of the period, we were not militant, I'm certain that outsiders perceived us to be. And I could understand why. We *were* determined, which was no doubt evident in our attitude, and unquestionably we put a sharp edge on the political dialogue that took place on campus. On one memorable occasion, we arranged for Angela Davis and Muhammad Ali to speak on the same dais. It was a wild combination—Angela the communist, shrill and intellectual, and Ali the Muslim, who of course believed ardently in capitalism and was also funny as hell. Several of us spent the afternoon with Ali, and he kept us entertained the entire time, at one point calling Joe Frazier on the phone—or at least pretending to—and going through his famous routine about Frazier being a gorilla.

We also invited Eldridge Cleaver shortly after he became involved with the Black Panthers. Cleaver cussed out Governor Reagan, President Nixon, Pope Paul, and any other influential white person who came to mind. At one point, he had practically the whole auditorium—blacks and whites alike—chanting with him: "Fuck Ronald Reagan! Fuck Ronald Reagan!"

Beyond Cleaver's visit, however, we had very little contact with the Panthers. I didn't agree with their policy of carrying guns, and their rhetoric was too volatile for my purposes, but I admired the school they had opened in Oakland and their free breakfast program, both of which were operated by Panther women. In many subtle ways, we took our cues from the Panthers. We patterned our hierarchy after theirs, calling our officers chairmen and ministers. We gave away turkeys at Thanksgiving, endeavoring, as they did with the free breakfasts, to become a benevolent presence in the community.

We considered community involvement to be important not only to us as a BSU but to the University of San Francisco. USF's reputation was that of the cloistered Jesuit school on the hill, far removed from the realities of the city—especially the inner city. We viewed it as part of our role to close the gap between the school and the community. To that end, we provided tutoring for San Francisco city kids and staged special campus activities for their benefit, such as riding them from the Fillmore district to USF in cable cars for a day at the BSU penny carnival. We also conducted recruiting forays into the city schools, in effect making black and minority students newly aware of the educational opportunities at the forbidding Jesuit university on the hill. Later, we expanded our recruiting efforts when BSU members Harold Logwood and Bill Riley joined me on trips to high schools throughout Northern California and also Los Angeles.

All of those activities were specifically directed at making the university more relevant, which was an issue that concerned many of the Jesuit colleges around the country. Even the Vatican had taken it up in the form of a directive authored by Father Arrupe, a black Spaniard who had campaigned for Jesuit institutions of higher learning to become more active in community outreach and the recruitment of minority students, teachers, and faculty members. When it seemed that our attempts to make USF relevant were not receiving the unqualified support of the university, Harold Logwood, who was a Vietnam veteran and a USF football player, telephoned the Vatican and spoke to Father Arrupe.

Most of us in the BSU were proud of our record for maintaining calm on the campus while significantly expanding its cultural and ideological horizon. In fact, despite all the disturbances by white activists on campuses like Berkeley and Kent State during those years, and the riots by black activists in cities like Angeles and Detroit and Newark, most of the BSUs in northern California were, like ours, nonviolent in their campaigns for social change. We partied together and took strength from the symbiotic relationship we cultivated. A particular friend and associate of mine at the time was Danny Glover, who was active in racial affairs at San

Francisco State, which was considered to be much more accessible
to blacks than USF. (There was a party at my house just before
Danny graduated, and I asked him, "What are you going to do
now?" He said, "I think I want to be an actor," to which I replied,
"Danny, you're too damn old to be an actor.") When Danny and the
black students at San Francisco State saw fit to go on strike, our
BSU was over there walking the picket line with them. They would
have done the same for us.

At USF, meanwhile, progress was slow and steady at best.
The university president, a reputedly liberal priest named Father
Albert Jonsen, seemed to be aware that the campus had some
catching up to do in the area of minorities. In retrospect, we were
making strides, but by my last year at USF—which was 1969–70,
by which time I had completed six years and a double major (political science and sociology) while closing in on my teaching degree
—the inevitable sluggishness of the process had become very frustrating.

Had my attention been undivided, I probably would have
been in a hell-raising frame of mind from the outset that year. As it
was, however, I was preoccupied with the practical matter of a full-
time student-teaching job (history and civics) at culturally eclectic
Woodrow Wilson High School in San Francisco, where I reported
every day in my dashiki and my lame Afro, carrying a briefcase full
of fire, brimstone, and Malcom X. I became the faculty adviser for
Woodrow Wilson's BSU and eventually led the black students in a
brief walkout over discriminatory school policies. I was young, and
I was pumped.

The teaching job gave me an outlet for my revolutionary
energy while, that winter, I turned over leadership of the USF
Black Student Union to Harold Logwood. I was looking forward to
riding in the backseat while Harold orchestrated another series of
black culture events, one of them being the appearance of the
renowned coeducational McClymonds High School drill team during halftime of a USF basketball game on a Saturday night in early
March. McClymonds was a predominantly black school known,
among other things, for its athletes and its drill team. It was Mc-

Clymonds that had given the incomparable Bill Russell to USF and the Boston Celtics. The USF crowd that night, however, was appreciative of neither McClymonds's gift nor its drill team. Long before the squad was finished with its routine, the audience began making sarcastic remarks, punctuated by a male cheerleader who picked up his megaphone and shouted, "Enough is enough!" Surly fans, emboldened by the cheerleader, yelled out, "Get your asses off the floor!" Spitballs came flying out of the bleachers and landed on the legs and uniforms of the McClymonds girls. The BSU had been extremely proud of bringing McClymonds to our campus, and the crowd's rudeness was a slap in our face as well as those of the humiliated high school students. We had no doubt that it was intended that way as well. Harold, who was a McClymonds graduate himself, got in several good licks on drill team abusers, and I had to talk him and several other BSU members out of starting a riot right there in Memorial Gym.

We were still in a nasty frame of mind the following Monday, when the BSU basketball team was pitted against a white fraternity team for the campus intramural championship. It was a fiercely contested game that was still tied at the end of two overtimes, at which point the official decided that there would be a center jump and the winner would be the first team to score. It had not escaped our attention—nor the white student referee's, apparently—that the other side's center was considerably taller than ours. We complained loudly, pointing out that basketball games are never decided by sudden death and that, other than the fraternity team's obvious advantage, there was no reason to make an exception in this case. While we argued, the ball was tossed up, and the Greeks won the tip, sprinted down the floor, and dropped in a layup to end the game.

For the first time in my six years at USF, I completely lost my head. For me, that stupid basketball game was the culmination of all the frustrations that had been building up ever since I'd arrived on campus. We had been screwed, and in that respect the basketball game seemed painfully symbolic of the screwing that my teammates and I and all the black people we knew had been getting too damn often for too damn long.

My anger spread quickly to the other guys and the BSU members who were there, all of whom were as ready as I was to take a stand. Some of them, in fact, had been waiting years for me to lose it. Acting instinctively at first, we grabbed up all the basketballs in the gym and took them to the south end, where we proceeded to demolish a couple of bulletin boards, the fire extinguisher cabinet, and the glass in the door leading outside. Then we ordered everybody else out of the gym—nobody was eager to stay in there with us, anyway—and huddled to figure out what to do next.

Between the shouting and cursing, about forty of us chose to form a beachhead at a student union meeting area known as the Green and Gold Room. Arriving there in force, with students shooting out of our path like leaves in a whirlwind, we declared it closed for a BSU meeting, chained the doors, then picked up where we left off at the gym, breaking windows, turning over vending machines, and essentially making a shambles of all the progress and good faith we had built up over the preceding years.

Before long one of the Jesuit administrators came by to try to calm us down, but we demanded to speak to Father Jonsen. The president was in San Rafael at the time, and while we waited restlessly for him to arrive, we demonstrated our impatience on the Green and Gold furniture, making special use of the pool sticks and balls in an adjoining recreation room. We had reason to believe that Father Jonsen was sensitive to our accumulated complaints, but when he finally walked in, his objectivity was severely impaired by the wreckage all around him. He persuaded us to disperse and meet again under more stable conditions, at which time disciplinary action would be among the topics.

We repaired as a group to one of our members' apartments, most of us still angry and some of us beginning to feel a little conscience-stricken. My delayed reaction leaned toward the latter, but it stiffened again when we learned that a San Francisco SWAT team had assembled at the edge of the campus, awaiting the signal to rush in. With that ugly bit of news, Harold Logwood picked up the telephone and started dialing the Vatican, intent this time upon talking to the pope. "Harold," I said to no avail, "you can't call the damn pope!" He settled for Father Arrupe, whom he informed that the University of San Francisco was in flagrant violation of the recent directive put forth for Jesuit institutions.

When we finally separated Harold from the telephone, we put together a formal list of demands—actually, we called them "concerns"—for Father Jonsen and the university. They included the creation of an ethnic studies program, the recruitment of black faculty and staff, a room honoring Bill Russell next to Memorial Gym, and the removal of Brigham Young University (which we perceived to be racist) from USF's baseball schedule.

On Saturday, Harold and I and other BSU members advertised our demands on pickets in front of the Commons. This elicited another visit from Father Jonsen, who advised us that if the picket line were not removed, we would all face possible suspension. We complied, and on Sunday it was Father Jonsen himself who sought a forum at the Commons, addressing an assembled crowd with his response to our demands and grievances. "I consider that these problems are serious and the complaints, in many cases, legitimate," he said in a statement later reported by *The Foghorn*. "I have pledged that the University Administration will act to remedy them quickly and fairly." While sympathetic to our causes, however, Father Jonsen made it clear in his speech that our little rampage would not go unpunished. "Any individual specifically identified as a perpetrator of vandalism," he said, "will be held responsible before University regulations and, if necessary, civil law."

The latter remark effectively promised that there would be at least a campus trial. As the first step in that procedure, the university initiated an investigation to be headed up by Father Robert Sunderland, the dean of men and a hard-nosed Jesuit conservative. According to Father Jonsen, the BSU membership as a whole would not be held accountable for the events of March 6, but Father Sunderland's investigation would attempt to identify and charge the individuals most responsible for the physical damage to university property. I expected that I would be seeing a lot of Father Sunderland.

In the meantime, the student body took up the cause and rallied to our defense. *The Foghorn* jumped in first with a supportive editorial. "That the blacks partly tore up the gym and the G&G hardly touches us; we take it as a valid response to the real disorder of USF itself," the paper wrote. ". . . We support the black grievances and demands." Then the Associated Students of the University of San Francisco (ASUSF) came out with its own list of demands, which essentially mirrored ours except that the ASUSF declaration started off by expressing its firm opposition to the investigation process that had been initiated against us: "We demand an end to any administrative hearings, investigations, and actions against those who were involved in the March 6th incident," the student group stated. "A special committee of the student senate shall conduct a full investigation into the underlying conditions leading up to such incidents as that of March 6 in the hope that the racial attitudes and conditions present on this campus be exposed."

Following up on the ASUSF action, the student senate in early May called for a multipurpose campus strike intended to support the BSU while simultaneously protesting the Kent State killings and the U.S. involvement in Cambodia. By that time, however, Father Sunderland—the Red Guard—had brought his charges, and several of us were scheduled to appear at a trial in the moot court of the university law building.

If we were found guilty of destroying campus property—Harold Logwood and I were also charged with inciting a riot—the university had the authority to expel us, to prohibit us from graduating, or in my case, to withhold my teaching credential, which would have been professionally crippling. It didn't look good for the defense. A few days before the trial, however, hope rapped faintly on the door when a law school professor, Robert Taggart, approached and said he'd like to represent our side.

On the day the court convened, the chamber was packed

not only with interested students but with representatives of the San Francisco media whom Harold had wisely contacted. Several of us were to be tried separately, and because of my leading role in the riot, I was the first defendant called. Father Sunderland's questioning revealed that I had indeed participated enthusiastically in the events of March 6 while encouraging my cohorts to do the same. That much was a given. The case would be made or broken on the cross-examination of our defense attorney.

'When his turn came, Taggart proceeded to lay out my entire life as a black student at USF, beginning with my first day on campus and my naïve expectation that the student body would have a much deeper complexion. He skillfully showed how my naïveté gradually, inevitably, gave way to rage. When he asked if I had ever been subjected to racial remarks at USF, I told about watching the Texas Western basketball game in the dormitory. When he asked if the USF community had been receptive toward the BSU's efforts to bring black culture to campus, I told about the McClymonds drill team. Taggart also permitted me to describe our work with city kids and our persistent attempts to make the university relevant in an awakening society. I was portrayed as a good guy who had become not bad, just mad as hell.

That characterization would have been much tougher to sell if I had arrived at USF as a street-trained revolutionary rather than the Jesuit altar boy that I literally was. In retrospect, my evolution as a student closely resembled that of the character Mookie, played by Spike Lee in his classic movie *Do the Right Thing*. I had tried with all my might to do the right thing for six years. My brand of activism was never truculent; it was never menacing. On the contrary, I had held the lid down on the hotheads of those who would have boiled over much earlier. But just as Mookie was the one who ended up throwing the can through Sal's window, I was the one whose rage was played out on the Green and Gold. When the cross-examination was over, I think everybody in the room understood what had happened on March 6.

What they might not have understood, however, was that mine was not the stereotypical black rage. Because I had a different background from a lot of other brothers—a family that taught and supported me—I was not as explosive as many of them, but the fundamental rage was still there. I may not have had much shit to sit on, as others did, but I had plenty of reasons to be angry—four hundred years' worth. For me, the essential thing about the anger was getting in touch with it, understanding it, and using it constructively, not destructively. Until March 6, I had been able to do that because my rage wasn't one that had been welling up since early childhood. I wasn't angry about my own background and home life. I wasn't angry about being poor or unloved. I wasn't angry about who I was. I was angry only at the injustice that made up my playing field. There's a profound difference.

The law professor, of course, was not concerned with the clinical dynamics of my anger—only that it could be demonstrated as justifiable. He succeeded notably on that score, convincing the courtroom that I had to be pushed awfully damn hard to reach the stage I reached at that intramural basketball game. Harold was the next to testify, and his military credentials enabled Taggart to effectively stay the course. By this time, public and media sentiment was squarely on our side—a factor that was probably not lost on the university when, the next fall, it implemented an ethnic studies program, hired black teachers and staff, and opened the Bill Russell Room at the basketball facility.

In the meantime, caught off guard by our back-door defense and the empathy it had engendered, the court recessed for a day after two days of testimony. When it reconvened—on May 12, 1970, my twenty-third birthday—Father Sunderland announced that the charges against me and the other students had been dropped. The place erupted.

That night, my friends at the BSU threw me a hell of a birthday party.

2

''If I'm So Damn Good, Why Is This Boy Strung Out on Dope?''

When my dashiki and I showed up at Woodrow Wilson in the fall of 1969, my mission—my purpose in life at that moment—was to impart the knowledge I had gained to the high school seniors of my civics, U.S. history, and black history classes, many of whom looked older than their skinny hustling teacher.

I not only looked young and was young (twenty-two); I *taught* young. In civics, for instance, the assigned topic was communism, but I disregarded that and focused on issues that I thought imminent high school graduates needed to be informed about—marriage, raising a family, employment, current events, and the like. At night, I opened a book on the Watts riot and read aloud into a tape recorder, which I played for the class the next day as I made my rounds of the room. I also spent a good portion of my negligible paycheck to buy books that I thought the kids ought to know about, such as *Before the Mayflower* and *Rivers of Blood, Years of Darkness*. I thought we had a hell of a class.

I practically lived at that school, devoting most of my extra-curricular time to the BSU. We had fundraisers, dances, barbecues, plays, and assorted "days of consciousness," such as one dedicated to all the black girls at Woodrow Wilson (we gave each of them a black balloon filled with helium; I can still picture the black cloud we created that afternoon when the girls released their balloons at three o'clock) and an African festival, for which the students built tribal huts in the schoolyard.

In my role as BSU adviser, I felt it was incumbent upon me to familiarize the black students not only with their heritage but also with their rights as young Americans and the methods available to secure them. That was the reason for the walkout I led them on. The issues were basic things such as staff representation —although the school was heavily integrated, most of the teachers were white—and black studies. The walkout was orderly, and after our list of demands was handed over to the principal, we returned peaceably to the classrooms. I was reprimanded by the principal, but my job security was not threatened—at least, not officially.

The status under which I had been placed at Woodrow Wilson was technically not that of a traditional student teacher but rather a student intern with the San Francisco Unified School District. As an intern, I was considered a long-term employee of the district and was thereby under contractual protection. I couldn't be terminated unless the district was willing to go through a protracted legal process. Nonetheless, it was evident as the year wore on that Woodrow Wilson didn't want me back. There were other student interns in the same position, and over the summer district officials tried to cut loose the lot of us. We made so much noise, however, that they were forced to reexamine their position. When the school board's own legal counsel advised that our contracts were valid, San Francisco Unified was stuck with us.

Even so, I would not be returning to Woodrow Wilson. The official reason given was that I had been a temporary fill-in for a teacher who was on sabbatical, but my reassignment was more revealing. For the apparent lack of a single history or civics opening in all of San Francisco, I was farmed out to the district's Guidance Service Center—that is, its clearinghouse for kids who had been kicked out of junior or senior high school.

Had the district been sincere about rehabilitating the Guidance Center kids and returning them to the mainstream, which was the mandate it professed, I would have regarded the new job as a special opportunity and tackled it with the rookie enthusiasm that got me sent away from Woodrow Wilson. But it was obvious from day one that the center was merely a dumping ground. For the first time—but certainly not the last—I saw adolescent kids being thrown away by the system. The program was contained in a classroom that was part of the old worn-out Buchanan YMCA building, situated in the Fillmore district of San Francisco, and there was never enough money to run it. We had a math teacher and an English teacher—both were exceptional—but everybody taught everything. We depended extraordinarily upon the dedication of the teachers, because we were given virtually no funding for books or any kind of teaching aids.

The special challenge of the Guidance Center was to maintain an academic curriculum while simultaneously addressing the issues that were germane to our uncommon student body. These were kids who had to learn to be citizens before they could be students. We had some real knuckleheads in that place—arsonists, burglars, pimps, purse-snatchers, drug dealers, the whole gamut of wayward teenagers. My job, consequently, was that of administrator, teacher, counselor, policeman, corrections officer, and disciplinarian. The mother of one of our purse-snatchers visited me at the center one time—that was a rarity—and said, "Mr. Marshall, do Arthur like a *man* would do him!" I knew what that meant, and I was not above it. There were several guys whom I would sometimes take into the gym and rough up a little. At the Guidance Center, we didn't concern ourselves too much with political correctness. We did our job the way they did surgery on *M.A.S.H.*

The most disheartening thing about the Guidance Center was that even the kids could see they were a low priority. Everybody there knew that it was only a matter of time until the program became a budget cut. I ran it for five years before the plug was pulled and, despite the obvious problems, consider the time to have been extremely well spent. The Guidance Service Center was my entree into the universe of the troubled black teenager.

It was a world with which I quickly and permanently became preoccupied. I was fascinated by the social dynamics—the differences and especially the similarities—of the kids who had been sent to us. Common to many of them was a fatherless and sometimes motherless home life and the resulting association with other kids in the same situation, creating virtual street communities of unloved, unnurtured, unsatisfied, unsupervised, and untamed teenagers. As I worked with them, sometimes effectively and sometimes not, the question that captivated me was whether the kids were merely going through developmental changes related to adolescence and temporary circumstances or if their social problems were of a deeper-seated, enduring nature. To pursue the issue further, I undertook a doctorate program in psychology at the Wright Institute, culminating in a dissertation entitled "The Effect of SONPAS (Significant Other Non-Parental Adults) on Black Male Adolescents." My theory was that nonparental adults could make a significant positive impact on black males, in effect filling the void created by absent or ineffectual parents. Without realizing it at the time, I was actually researching the concept and potential of a boys club. I ran out of money before I could complete my degree, but in my consciousness the subject was never closed.

After the Guidance Service Center was shut down, I was transferred to Aptos Middle School, where once again I took charge of student activities and became thoroughly involved with the kids. But the more deeply involved I became, the more clearly I could see that the school system was failing the young people of the city. The teachers simply couldn't do enough for them. That reality hit me in the face one day when I was leaving a conference in the Tenderloin district of San Francisco and a former student of mine named Darnell Oliver, gruesomely messed up on crack at the time, approached me on the street and said, "Mr. Marshall, you're the best teacher I ever had." I thought, hell, if I'm so damn good, why is this boy strung out on dope?

Darnell had been one of the brightest kids in my class, but

intelligence is no safeguard against the streets and virtually no factor in one's outcome. That fact made itself apparent to me in student after student. More than once, I heard a tap on my classroom door and opened it to find one or another of my former female students, matured to the matronly age of sixteen or so, stopping by to say hello and show me her children.

One of the finest boys I taught had trouble staying awake during class because he didn't have a home. He held a job in order to feed himself, and the only place he could sleep at night, when he got off work, was his aunt's basement. Years later, I ran into him during a visit to the San Bruno County Jail, where he was doing time for selling drugs.

I can't count the times I've been fooled by kids whom I presumed to be free from the snares of street life. One of my favorite students at Aptos was a quiet, sweet twelve-year-old girl named Shirley Brown, who had an equally cute and well-mannered older sister, Vanessa, who was fourteen. At lunchtime one day, I was talking to another teacher about the Brown girls and happened to mention how nice they both were. He looked at me curiously for a moment and said, "You know they're prostitutes, don't you?" I didn't believe it until he offered to take me to MacArthur Avenue in Oakland, where they worked. I declined the invitation. When I later started asking around about the girls, fishing for information on how I might get them off the streets, I was advised that if I interfered, I would have to contend with their pimp. Afterward, when I looked at Shirley or Vanessa sitting so attentively in my math classes, I often wondered if they knew what I knew. I could only assume that they did.

When I first encountered such horror stories at Woodrow Wilson, I took them to heart but remained relatively naïve about the incredible density of the teenage problem. While one could see at first blush that Wilson was a zoo, with kids smoking dope and dropping reds—the fashionable drug at the time—in the halls and bathrooms, I'd assumed that the school district had a handle on the problem and that solutions were in the works. Over the next five or six years, I came to realize that the district didn't have a clue and apparently wasn't looking for one.

Eventually, I began to reel from the weight of the accumulated Shirley Browns and Darnell Olivers. As a teacher who had set out to make a difference—and I had plenty of company in that respect—it was not only tragic but also disillusioning to witness all that promise being laid to waste at such a tender age. The most frustrating part was that I was *trying* to help. I had dedicated my career to that purpose, but in the greater scheme of things it seemed almost fruitless. There were teenagers all around me drowning in an ocean of neglect, and I was frantically rowing out to save them in a crepe-paper lifeboat. There had to be another vehicle.

As I grimly watched the kids of San Francisco slipping away one by one, it was furthermore obvious that the situation was not restricted to my city and school district. The same things were happening at an even more alarming pace back in South Central— a fact that hit home when I helped Gue Gue pack up and move to Inglewood after her husband died. For the first twenty years of her long stay at 109th and Figueroa, where she had eventually settled after coming to Los Angeles in 1955, Gue Gue had never felt threatened. There had been plenty of street fighting and gang violence during that time, but it wasn't random, it wasn't reckless; it didn't endanger even old ladies. Besides, the neighbors had always looked after each other's homes and families. When she walked to the grocery store, Gue Gue had sometimes left her door wide open without giving a second thought to what could happen while she was away. But lawlessness and dissolution began to take their toll. In the 1970s and 1980s the neighborhood disintegrated before her eyes, and the family right next door to Gue Gue represented a microcosm of the whole depressing process. Drugs and gangs literally made a shambles of that family, transforming their quiet home into a house of horrors. It was the same up and down the street. By 1980, armed teenagers had taken over the neighborhood. Gangs had shot into Gue Gue's house three times and pulled the bars off her windows. A little boy was killed on the corner. A dead man was tossed into the alley by her back gate. The son of one of her best friends was murdered at fifteen. She was frightened.

Grudgingly, Gue Gue made her escape to the seemingly safer community of Inglewood, but for me that couldn't be the end of it. The kids and the circumstances that ran my grandmother out of her home were the same kids and circumstances that turned Darnell Oliver to drugs and Shirley Brown to prostitution. One way or another, in San Francisco or Los Angeles or preferably both, I had to do something.

The place to which I was reassigned as a math teacher in 1980, Potrero Hill Middle School (PHMS), had something no other school could offer—a prematurely gray, hippie-haired, wild-bearded, three-day-jeans-wearing white man named Jack Jacqua, who was part coach, part counselor, part aide, and primarily a free agent able somehow to circumnavigate his official role, which nobody could precisely define anyway.

With or without the sanction of the school district—most likely without, knowing Jack and the school district—Jack had created a niche in which he served more or less as the students' faculty advocate. He was like their family representative on campus, the father figure or big brother or uncle—whatever the situation called for—who understood their special situations and took it upon himself to steer them through the daunting, sometimes treacherous corridors of middle school.

I had almost nothing in common with Jack except the thing that mattered most to both of us—the kids. From the day we met, Jack and I talked constantly about the kids. Through his largely self-created position, he knew them much better than I did. After school hours, Jack worked as a volunteer at the Potrero Hill Neighborhood House, where he would tutor kids or just talk to them or whatever. He paid particular attention to the boys who were in and out of Juvenile Hall, observing that more often than not, they were the brightest of the lot. He also made it a point to get to know the parents or the grandparents of the neighborhood kids, exchanging information that was mutually helpful. Jack's empathy for the kids was tangible because, as an ardent critic of San Francisco Unified and most other established public institutions, he knew all too well that they were getting a bum rap at school; he knew that the school was basically deaf to their extenuating circumstances.

He, by contrast, was there to lend an ear. But at the same time, Jack was much more than a well-meaning sympathizer. He helped the kids with their homework, he hooked them up with basketball and track teams, he gave them lunch money out of his pocket, and if they broke their promises or the law, he gave them hell. Jack was never soft, never easy on the kids. He expected from them as much as he gave them, and that was an arrangement they could understand. These were kids who understood street economics, who took it for granted that everybody was out for something, that everybody had his own hustle. The difference with Jack was that the thing he wanted in return was not material. That got their attention.

The kids sensed, also, that Jack was *real,* which meant everything in their estimation. It was also a major accomplishment for a middle-aged white guy. Jack's whiteness made the black kids naturally suspicious of why he was so interested in helping them. It was a suspicion that I shared at first. Because of my inherent skepticism as a black man, it took me some time to figure out where Jack was coming from. I wondered, for instance, why he railed so untiringly against the shortcomings and evils of the school system. "They don't give a damn about the kids," he would say. "These people have their heads so far up their asses . . ." My response was always, "All right, Jack, what can we do about it?" We frequently clashed over Jack's bitterness toward the system, and we had some rip-roaring arguments. Through it all, though, I came to realize that Jack had no secret agenda, other than perhaps some personal vow to do the right thing. He truly, sincerely, fiercely, and fundamentally wanted to help the kids who needed help.

Furthermore, and very significantly, he was willing to do it the only way it could really be done—in their element. Jack didn't take on the kids at his convenience, in the institutional safety of a school office or some other closely watched official place; he met them by the lockers and in the neighborhoods. He knew where they lived, and if where they lived was a place white people weren't supposed to go, Jack didn't give a shit. He was one of few people in the city—and maybe the only white person—who could go, with relative impunity, straight from one neighborhood to its geographical enemy; from Sunnydale, for instance, to Hunters Point.

"Jack was known from turf to turf," in the words of one of the Fillmore warriors, Norflis McCullough, better known as Pooh. "You'd be walking in the neighborhood and hear 'beep beep' behind you, and there was Jack."

"Jack would come to pick me up in the neighborhood," recalled Philip Bounds of Hunters Point, which is considered the most dangerous section of the city, "and my friends would ask, 'That the police?' They weren't used to seeing a white man around, and it made them suspicious. But Jack wasn't like any other white man. He'd walk up to me and say, 'Fuck Hunters Point!' He'd do that just to see how I'd react. Then he'd take me to lunch. We went to the Red Java almost every day. We'd just sit on the pier and eat and talk. This is when the turf wars were going real strong, and Jack would say, 'If anybody asks you what turf you come from, tell them Africa.' He loved it when we tried something that he suggested. He'd say, 'Did it work? Did it work?' I'd never say anything about it one way or the other."

Considering his background, Jack's rapport with the street kids was even more remarkable than it appeared, which was remarkable enough. He had grown up in Los Angeles, the son of a Hollywood agent, and had enlisted in the army after graduating from UCLA. Despite the fact that he still looks like one, Jack had never been a flower child; he was too independent for that. But he was always spiritually inclined and always a vigorous champion of those with whom—not *for* whom, the difference, in Jack's case, being everything—he worked. After the army, he became an organizer for the city employees union in Los Angeles. Many of the public workers he represented and recruited were black, and unlike his predecessors and colleagues, he spent a lot of time with them in their homes and their neighborhood, which was basically Watts. He was about three blocks away when the riots broke out in 1965.

When his superior, whom he had trusted, ultimately told him that he was doing too good a job—that too many blacks were joining the union—Jack said "fuck you" and moved to San Francisco. His fundamental opposition to the establishment had crystalized with that experience, and his commitment to the urban predicament had taken hold. Soon after arriving in San Francisco, he caught on with the school district and became loosely involved with the Glide Memorial Church, a famous "church of liberation" of the Methodist denomination, known, among other things, for feeding about three thousand needy people a day. Jack's spirituality, however, is not church-oriented. It's about revolution from within—about saving people from external subversion by reforming them internally.

The bottom line is: I believe in liberation. Sure, I'm anti-system. I always have been. But people try to read me politically and there isn't anything to read because I'm a spiritual person and I'm going with the will and the strength of the people. I do what I do, I am what I am; fuck the labels. Politics isn't going to change anything, anyway, but spirituality might.

Working with black kids is just part of the general struggle of working for black liberation that I've been involved with for years. It's just part of me. I believe that this society is very oppressive to black people, and I'm an activist. I believe in social change. More than anything, I view the situation as a class problem as opposed to a racial problem. Too many people get stuck on the racial issue.

Jack Jacqua

By making it his business, Jack came to know about as much as any adult could know about what went on in the city neighborhoods. He regularly stopped me in the hall or came by my class-room after school to tell me about a kid who was selling crack or another whose name had been spray-painted onto the wall (meaning a contract was out on him) or another who had been killed in a turf battle. He often went to funerals, but I didn't; they upset me too much.

Eventually, through the extracurriculars that I was inevitably involved with (I was director of student activities, ran the student council, put on plays, and so on), I became familiar enough with the kids that I was able to exchange horror stories with Jack. We sat down literally every day—during lunchtime (where Jack could be found outside, supervising the yard) or my prep period or after school, in my classroom or the nurse's office or the main office or anywhere we happened to bump into each other, even a basketball game—and agonized over the young people we knew, putting together an immense and tragic oral compendium, the weight of which we both carried around.

At the same time, we compared notes to identify some of the good kids who were most at risk—the operative word being *most*: because of their environment, all of the PHMS kids were subject to a substantial degree of risk. Many of them were from the Bayview-Hunters Point neighborhood (Potrero Hill is an eclectic residential district—ethnically, the school had a United Nations look—located between the housing-project flatlands of Bayview-Hunters Point and downtown San Francisco), while others came from turfs, such as Sunnydale and Fillmore, that were just as distressed. The children (a term that scarcely seems to apply) whom Jack and I zeroed in on were those already being drawn into "the life," as the gangbanging, dope-dealing street existence was known, but who, by our estimation, would prefer another way if only they knew one.

They were kids like Macio Dickerson, a smooth-talking drug dealer who slept with a twelve-gauge shotgun under his bed; like Marcel Evans, who had recently moved to San Francisco from the South Central neighborhood of the Hoover Crips, and whose house was torn apart by the absence of a father and the presence of relatives who incessantly smoked crack; like Joe Thomas, a stylish athletic kid who somehow managed to keep up with his schoolwork despite spending most of his adolescent years in juvenile prison for various neighborhood offenses; like Jody Daggs, a special education student whose saving grace was basketball; like Emanuel Powell, an angel of a boy whose sweet nature was constantly being harrassed by the temptations of the street; like Edric "Peter Lee" Carr, a smallish inconspicuous Sunnydale kid who was a promising math student on the occasions he actually came to class.

One of the things Jack and I noticed about the kids was that they seemed to do all right when we were around, which, given the enormous amount of trouble they got into when we were not around, impressed upon us the apparent dearth of adult attention in their private lives. The conclusion we arrived at was not a major breakthrough in social science, but it seemed sensible enough: We thought, hey, let's try to keep them around us.

That was easier thought than done, however. We were dealing with kids who had absolutely no structure in their lives, the evidence of which could be witnessed at virtually any moment of the school day at the middle school. It was standard procedure there for kids to run down the hallways screaming at the tops of their lungs, banging on doors along the way. I often sprinted out of the classroom to chase down whoever banged on my door. I considered it my personal responsibility to make the students act like students, which involved breaking up countless fights. One afternoon, I was driving away from school when a riot erupted in the parking lot. Instinctively, I jumped out of my car and jerked baseball bats out of the hands of several kids.

The school itself was powerless to enforce any order. It was also ill equipped to prevent outsiders from entering the building, which meant that the influx of drugs and guns and troublemakers was undisturbed. The teachers tried their best to keep the school together, and when I got there we had an outstanding principal who was making considerable progress, but the situation deteriorated quickly after he and the assistant principal were inexplicably fired over the summer. The faculty and a community group, the

Friends of Potrero Hill Middle School, appealed to the district to let us be involved in selecting the new principal—my name was even brought up—and we were assured that we would be consulted, but it didn't happen. The new principal was a disaster, as was her replacement a year later.

Through all of this, Jack was fighting mightily against the system and becoming increasingly fed up with it. He was so disillusioned with the San Francisco school district that he was thinking seriously of chucking it all and going back to Los Angeles. The only thing that kept him in San Francisco was his loyalty and commitment to the kids whose lives he had entered. He still held out hope that, with or without the school—probably without—we could do something really important for the kids.

Though less consumed than Jack with the failings of the school system, I was on the same page as he when it came to the kids. Jack was still getting out on the streets and volunteering at the Neighborhood House—along with a Neighborhood House secretary, Ruth Passen, and its director, a local institution named Enola Maxwell, he had won an award for his work from the San Francisco Foundation—but it was becoming increasingly urgent that we venture out and do something on our own. We didn't yet know what that would be, but a day seldom passed that we didn't pull each other aside and kick around ways and programs to more effectively reach the kids.

For me, the talking phase ended when Jack walked into my classroom one day as I was working at my desk after school, sat down in the front row, and said, "Mr. Marshall, do you remember Roynell McRae?" Of course I did. I had lost track of Roynell for a few years, but I hadn't stopped thinking about him. Roynell had been in my seventh-grade advanced math class, one of the few black kids who had demonstrated the proficiency and work habits to keep up with the academic-minded Asian and white kids. He was a clean-cut, attentive, athletic boy who was very popular—when the school held a "sweetheart" contest, Roynell was elected king—and he had the college look about him. He even dressed like a preppie. I remember thinking, "This kid is gonna make it to college." There weren't many black kids at Potrero Hill about whom that could be said.

"Hell, yes," I said. "What's up with Roynell?"

"He's messin' up, that's what. He's over in Oakland, selling drugs."

"Naw," I shot back. "Not Roynell. Can't be."

"Yeah, he's out there. You know how it is with these guys, Mr. Marshall. You give 'em your best, but hey, you can't be with 'em all the time. They buy the hype. They get caught up."

"Damn!" I had learned from the Shirley Brown experience not to disbelieve anything about any kid, but I was stunned nevertheless. Knowing Roynell—at least I *thought* I knew him—it seemed like I should have been able to do something to get him back on track.

"I'm gonna go over there to see him," I said. "Just talk to him a little bit."

"You can't do that," Jack answered solemnly, with an authority that I had to accept. "Where he hangs out, you can't just go and visit. Believe me, you can't go there."

This was in the early days of crack, when the dealers around the Bay Area wore designer sweatsuits, and I soon found out through the grapevine that Roynell had a whole line of sweatsuits, along with jewelry and the most expensive tennis shoes, the whole bit. But that was the last I heard of him until several months later, when Jack approached in the hall one day and handed me a letter Roynell had written him from the state prison in Susanville.

That was the last straw. For me, Roynell became the symbol of the failed promise. I'd had enough Roynells and Shirley Browns and Darnell Olivers. I read the letter twice, handed it back to Jack, and said, "Jack, we've got to do it. We've got to do it now."

"All right, then," he replied.

Philmore Graham was a big brother of mine with Omega Psi Phi, a member of the graduate chapter when I was pledging. Later, when I became active with the graduate chapter, he and I attended many of the same functions, which meant that I heard quite a bit about the boys club he had started in his garage in Vallejo, a small but busy city north of Oakland.

Philmore called his club The Continentals of Omega Boys Club, having named it after the fraternity and having intended it to be a national project of Omega Psi Phi. It was an academic and recreational organization that grew tremendously and made Philmore justifiably proud. He frequently invited fraternity brothers out to visit—after the club had moved out of Philmore's garage, we sometimes held our chapter meetings there—and for years I played for and coached the Omega Psi Phi team in the basketball tournament that Philmore's club sponsored every year.

I took Jack to one or two Continentals of Omega meetings over the years, and he was as impressed as I was, but all the while we never thought to transfer the Vallejo concept to our own ambitions in San Francisco. Perhaps it was because we were oriented less toward recreation than toward cultural awareness. Perhaps it was simply because we wanted whatever we did to be uniquely ours. I was intrigued, though, by the club's motto—Brotherhood ★ Scholarship ★ Uplift ★ Perseverance—and the T-shirts its members wore, bearing the declaration I DON'T DO DRUGS. Additionally, the club's tutoring program was highly commendable, and its overall academic performance enviable. Philmore Graham was getting through to the kids of Vallejo.

In December 1986, I attended a Continentals of Omega banquet in Vallejo at which Willie Brown, the speaker of the House of the California State Assembly, was the featured speaker. In the course of his speech, Brown took note of the success that Philmore's club had achieved, and then, scanning the room, his eyes fixed on me—presumably it was only a coincidence—and he said, "You, too, can do this." So powerfully did the words strike me that I wondered if anybody else in the room thought that Brown was talking directly to them.

It was at that moment that I decided to start a boys club in San Francisco. I had been staring at the idea for so long that I couldn't really see it, too blinded by our specific problems and dreams to recognize the solution right in front of my nose. The next day I asked Jack to come by my room after school and then raced the plan by him, suggesting that we use the Vallejo club as a model for our own. He was ready. When I went back to Philmore and told him what we intended, he said, "I've been waiting for years for you to do this."

We had no doubt that, soon enough, our club would assume its own course. Jack being as antisystem as he is, and I being faithful to the agenda I vowed to carry out when I first read Malcolm X, we knew from the beginning that our club, unlike Philmore's (which is now affiliated with the Boys and Girls Clubs of America) and almost every other of any scope, would remain independent, uncompromised by any sort of preexisting structure. Affiliation works wonderfully for Philmore and for Big Brothers and Boy Scouts and any other number of worthy youth organizations, but Jack and I, to be true to our souls, had to go about it differently. It was important to us that we answer to nobody but each other— least of all, a government agency.

Continentals of Omega did, however, give us a name to work with, ideals to strive for, and a framework to build upon. The next order of business was to find a place in which to meet. Jack took care of that by prevailing upon Mrs. Maxwell to let us assemble rent-free at the Potrero Hill Neighborhood House.

With the logistics falling into place, Jack and I proceeded to put together a start-up list of sixteen prospective club members, including Marcel Evans, Jody Daggs, and Emanuel Powell. On February 19, 1987, I drafted the following letter to their parents:

Dear Parents,

Mr. Joe Marshall, *teacher at Potrero Hill Middle School, and Mr. Jack Jacqua, counseling aide at Potrero Hill Middle School, announce the formation of the Omega Boys Club. This club is modeled on a similar organization in Vallejo, California, with which Mr. Marshall is familiar. The purpose of the club is to motivate boys to do their best in life and to enjoy their achievements through academic and recreational* activities. The Boys Club is basically an academic organization. We will ask each member to try to maintain the highest standards possible in school and their social lives. The Boys Club will make a strong effort to find out what it takes to help members develop to their greatest potential.

At club meetings, we will ask members to bring in school report cards and progress reports so that grades can be monitored. Club members will discuss issues of interest to them. The Boys Club will take field trips for sports, sightseeing, and educational interests, and will visit other Boys Clubs. Club members will be involved in civic projects. Most of all career alternatives after high school graduation will be explored, especially a college education. We hope to have some scholarship money available for those Boys Club members who wish to pursue a college degree.

The first meeting of the Club will be Thursday, Feb. 26 at 7 P.M. at the Potrero Hill Neighborhood House, 953 De Haro Street, San Francisco. We encourage a parent to accompany each youngster to the first meeting. If there are any questions, call Joe Marshall or Jack Jacqua at 647-1011. We look forward to seeing you there.

We had absolutely no idea how the club would be received. How could we? We were asking a bunch of cynical street-hardened city kids to belong to an academic oriented, drug-free, nonathletic, basically nonrecreational boys club. We were asking them to not use drugs, and more than that, to wear T-shirts announcing that they didn't use drugs, and more than that, to wear the T-shirts around friends and neighbors who not only used drugs but sold them for a livelihood. Privately, we wondered if we were crazy.

Perhaps out of courtesy at first, or maybe curiosity, the boys came. Jack and I received them in the finished basement of the Neighborhood House—I in my fraternity jacket and Jack in his blue jeans—and more than thirty of them showed up, half of whom we hadn't invited. I can't explain why that happened, except for the one thing I found out that night, the one thing that completed the circuit that would put the juice in our boys club: The kids were as interested in turning their lives around as we were in helping them do it. I could see it in their faces. I can still visualize the alert, even bemused expressions that night of Marcel and Jody and Emanuel and Macio staring up at me plaintively in that flat sprawling room. They weren't sure yet what it was they were getting into, and we weren't sure what we were getting them into, but whatever it was, they were game.

"This is going to be a serious club," I said. "We're not here for fun and games. We're about keeping your grades up and staying away from drugs and learning about black history. You have a lot to be proud of as a black person. We want you to love being black, because if black people loved being black, they wouldn't do the things they're doing to each other. They wouldn't be shooting each other and selling crack to each other. They wouldn't be destroying their own culture—their own people—the way they are. That's why we're going to be serious in here."

"And if any of you have any ideas about going to college," Jack said, "I don't know, but maybe we can help you make that happen."

We told the kids what our motto would be, borrowing from the Vallejo club, and groped our way through an hour and a half or so. We prayed—the debut of Jack's famous rambling, nondenominational, intercultural, five-minute, arm-jerking, finger-in-the-air prayers—informed the guys that dues would be seven dollars, and showed a Bill Moyers documentary, *The Vanishing Black Family*. Suspecting that it was not quite realistic to ask them to join an academic club that didn't do *anything* fun, we also announced that on March 29 we had tickets for Wrestlemania I on closed circuit TV at the Cow Palace (Hulk Hogan versus Andre the Giant).

Finally I said, "You guys know me. You know Jack. You know we care about you guys. We want to have a club here. We want to help you get to where you want to go. Do you think you could go for a club like that?"

They shrugged and said, "Yeah, that sounds pretty good."

After the kids had left, I turned to Jack, shook my head, and said, "Damn, Jack, they said okay. They actually said okay."

3

Homies Anonymous

Because so many homies think they're too cool for school or manage to get kicked out of it, we had been out of touch with some of the kids who needed us most. Joe Thomas, who had been arrested nearly twenty times, was at San Bruno for selling drugs and beating up the undercover cop who busted him. Edric "Peter Lee" Carr, a timid kid when he moved to San Francisco from St. Louis a few years before, was out on the streets making more money than I was. People were telling me that Peter Lee had become a big-time drug dealer. I said, "Who, Edric?" Then he pulled up to school one day in a Suzuki, which at the time was the car of choice for drug dealers, and said, "Hi, Mr. Marshall. What's up?" It looked to me as though Peter Lee was in over his head. I wished we could have gotten him to the club, but the streets had a lock on him.

Macio Dickerson, a grim-looking kid who always wore a baseball cap, had been expelled for bringing a gun to school, but he heard about the club on his own and came, I think, to prove to Jack and me—mostly Jack—that he was worth saving:

I had known Jack since he came to my fifth grade graduation, took me up to Potrero Hill Middle School, and tried to get me plugged into basketball. I never knew what Jack's title was; he was just one of the brothers. I don't think I ever saw Jack with a white person. He was unusual, always telling us how the system was set up for us to fail. He told us things you wouldn't expect to hear from a white man.

I suppose it was mostly because of Jack that I went to that first meeting, just to check it out. In a way, I was hungry. I wanted some help. But on the other hand, I felt that I wasn't their ideal kind of person to work with. My perception was that Jack didn't feel like I was going to make it. So I just walked in with a potna of mine and had the attitude like, "I don't need this."

I was suspended from Mission High School at the time because they had found a gun in my bag. I didn't realize it was there. Jack came with me when I went before the school board—that's the sort of thing he did all the time—and I lied like crazy. I guess I didn't convince anybody, because their decision was to terminate me from public schools in San Francisco. Jack kept bringing me up to the Nabe [the Neighborhood House], and I kept hearing Miss Maxwell preach to me every day. I wasn't a very good listener. All my life, I had been exposed to the projects, the ghetto, big-time drug dealers, gangbangers—all of that—and as a result I had that attitude. I had the clothes. I had the look. I felt that was the way you were supposed to look. Selling drugs was something I didn't think I had a choice about. I had to make some money. So I was always in the life; but just halfway in. My philosophy was that I'm not gonna go out and prove I'm a gangster, but if anybody crosses me or my family or any of my potnas, business was gonna be taken care of. That's just how we did things. I was never interested in being the big man on the block, never wanted to make a name for myself. I just wanted to survive. I didn't know any other way to carry myself and survive. My mother was on crack and I hadn't been with her since I was ten, when she went to Texas to live with her boyfriend. When my mom and dad were together, I was very secure, but when they began to break apart, something in me was torn. I ended up staying with my father. My father tried his best—I don't blame him, because he never had a dad in his house to show him how to be one—but he was an alcoholic. My older brother was always in trouble. So I grew up on the streets, with my potnas, surviving.

I was addicted to surviving. Survival was a matter of peer pressure. I never wanted a lot of money. To me, enough money was, say, five hundred dollars at a time, enough for lunch money, clothes, going places and doing things. And I wanted a car by the time I was seventeen. And you know, we're broke all the time at home, it doesn't look like it's coming from Pops, and all your friends have new clothes, the finest girls. Women are going to the guys with the money. Your role models are the guys who are making hundreds of thousands of dollars on dope. And by that time, crack was real hot. It was the thing. The police weren't hip yet to what was going on—they weren't hip to the guys standing out on the street making money all day long. It was easy then.

The first time I went out and sold dope I made two hundred dollars in fifteen minutes working for my cousin. He bought the rocks, but since I lived in the projects in Potrero Hill, I was more street smart than him, so he gave them to me to sell. I ended up selling them and keeping all the money for myself because there was so much of it. I'd tell myself that I'd buy more dope and pay him back later, but I'd end up spending everything. From then on, I always kept a bag full of rocks. Whenever I needed some extra cash, I took out a couple of rocks and sold them.

I never carried a gun in my pocket. Actually, I always had a fear of carrying guns, but in my business, you had to have one. I kept mine in the house. I had a twelve-gauge, and a friend of mine bought me a .22-pump rifle for my birthday. We made a pact: Whenever either one of us needed it, we'd use it. One time, at a neighborhood gym where some guys were playing ball, my friend got in a fight situation and someone told him, "I'm gonna kill you and your friend Macio." My friend came to me and told me and I put the twelve-gauge in a duffel bag. When I got to the gym, I took out the twelve-gauge and walked straight to the back where this other person was. When he saw me coming, he pulled out his gun and pointed it at me. I cocked the twelve-gauge and squeezed the trigger. The safety was on and I didn't know it. I took the safety off and was about to shoot again when the gym director grabbed me from behind. In my life, there have been many situations like that, when it seemed like somebody was watching over me.

When Jack and Mr. Marshall started the boys club, that was the only place where guys from different turfs could be together and not fight. It was like family there—the family I never had. Until then, Potrero Hill was the only thing in my life. The club opened up my eyes and showed me there's more out there. It was like a slap in the face.

So I made the decision not to sell drugs anymore. It wasn't easy, though. When I ran low of money and started feeling the peer pressure, I slipped again. Jack was working with me the whole time, telling me how much potential I had, and at the club he and Mr. Marshall were giving me a lot to think about. There was a struggle going on inside me. One day I found about three hundred dollars' worth of cocaine on the bus, and

I knew right then that I had to make a decision. When I got home, I flushed it down the toilet. My idea was that I was contributing to the problem. I was killing my own people. I said to myself, "I can't do this anymore," and that was it

I became more and more involved with the Omegas after that. We were reading Malcolm X before it became a fad. For me, it was a discovery. I took in everything that Jack and Mr. Marshall and our speakers had to tell us. For me, there was something about a person standing up in front of everybody speaking from the heart, passing on knowledge. I remember when Willie Brown spoke to us, and I said to him, "It's great for you to come and speak, but when you're through you'll leave and we won't see you on Potrero Hill anymore. There aren't any Willie Browns in this 'hood." I guess I felt like it should be guys from the 'hood up there speaking. That's what we started doing. And that's when I found out I had some speaking ability.

Macio Dickerson

The format for the club evolved as we went along. Macio was an electrifying speaker, and there were other guys, as well, who could hold the room by its throat. As we began to appreciate the value of peer counseling, we relied less and less on outside speakers, although we had some outstanding ones, Willie Brown included. The California speaker talked movingly about the obstacles he had faced coming out of Mineola, Texas, and he took only a glancing blow from Macio's brutally frank observation about the dearth of Willie Browns in Potrero Hill or Hunters Point. Other notables who stood before us were Philmore Graham, who gave us the benefit of his experience starting up the Continentals of Omega; future San Francisco mayor Art Agnos, who seemed to be genuinely startled by what we were doing ("Joe," he said, "this is amazing. We should have a club like this in every neighborhood in

San Francisco."); Dave Stewart of the Oakland A's, an extremely approachable superstar who made the kids feel at ease in his presence (after his visit, he frequently called and left tickets for Omega kids on the nights he pitched, saying, "I want you guys to be there"); and Kevin Johnson, a basketball star at Cal at the time (before moving on to the Phoenix Suns), who talked to the kids about the importance of maintaining good grades.

With respect to the others, though, who were all wonderful, our most memorable speaker had to be Sinbad. A woman who worked at the Circle Star Theater, where well-known entertainers often perform when they come to the Bay Area, was a friend of the boys club and told many of the stars—particularly the black ones—about us, hoping they would consent to pay us a visit. One Wednesday she called unexpectedly and said that Sinbad was coming the next night. We spread the word around as quickly as we could, gathered in the auditorium of the Neighborhood House to accommodate the unusually large crowd (normally, our speakers addressed the club in the basement, where we held our meetings), and around seven-thirty Thursday night Sinbad and his brother, Mark Adkins, strolled through the door as if they were homeboys from Hunters Point.

Rather than putting on a comedy routine—he's naturally funny anyway—Sinbad spoke about growing up as "a high-yellow brother" in Michigan and about black history, in which he was very conversant. "All of this hopelessness we have now is something new," he said. "When they were brought over here from Africa, the brothers were so proud, they would swallow their tongues, jump off the boat, fight the shark, and swim back home. The white man found that he couldn't control the brother. He runs; you cut off his foot, he limps; you cut off his leg, and he rolls off the plantation. Bringing us over here was the biggest mistake the white man ever made. But he did one thing. He instilled self-hatred in us, and self-hatred is killing us now."

It was just the sort of talk that suits us best, and the kids loved him. They gave Sinbad one of our I DON'T DO DRUGS T-shirts and asked him if he would put it on. "I'll do better than that," he said. "I'll wear it on television." He was starring on *A Different World* at the time. Before his last appearance on the show, I received a fax from the program's publicity staff advising me, through a press release, that Sinbad would be sporting his Omega Boys Club T-shirt on his final show. We were all sitting around the TV at the Nabe when the show came on, and sure enough, our man Sinbad walked out in the same shirt that half the guys in the room were wearing. He's never forgotten us and still calls every time he comes to the Bay Area.

We couldn't count on booking a Sinbad every week, however, or a Dave Stewart or a Willie Brown, and after a while we stopped trying. Although speakers were great drawing cards and each one offered something unique, our emphasis was shifting heavily toward the kind of specific naked knowledge that was most pertinent to the teenagers of Hunters Point and Sunnydale and Fillmore. We were discovering, through Macio and other club members just as honest and introspective, that the kids themselves had the best understanding of the complexities in their lives, of the temptations and hardships that made them do the things they did.

Almost every one of them had a demon or two to extract. We were a solution-oriented organization, and consequently our job number one was to identify the problems that needed solving. To that end, we encouraged the kids to take a good look at themselves and tell us what they saw. We asked them to bring their fears out in the open, to talk about the personal circumstances they might have thought were unspeakable, to confess the needs and deeds of which they might have been privately ashamed. "Look into the mirror at four in the morning, when it's just you and God," Jack said, gesturing like an Alabama preacher. "Look in the mirror, ask yourself the tough questions, and tell yourself the truth. Do it when none of your homies are around, when none of your potnas are around. And tell the truth, goddammit. Get your fears out there where you can deal with them. Deal with your pain. Deal with your anger. Take off that mask you're all wearing. You're trying to be so hard, so tough. You think it's weak to show pain. You think your homies will lose respect for you if you show fear. But sooner or later you're gonna have to deal with the fear. You're gonna have to deal with the pain, the anger. You've got to get it out." One by one —not all of them, but some of them, and more each week—the boys would stand up, take a deep breath, stare at the floor underneath the feet that couldn't stay still, and get it out. Our meetings, which in the beginning were held only on two Thursdays a month, were probably not unlike those of Alcoholics Anonymous. We were sort of a Homies Anonymous.

We were also unabashedly academic. We required the kids to bring a written definition of a new word to every meeting, emphasizing language and tying it into history. For an early history lesson, I instructed them to look up the abolitionist John Brown so that they would know what Jack was all about. (I found a picture of John Brown, and he even *looked* like Jack.) We implemented study hall sessions and supplied tutoring, for which we required the kids to bring in their report cards so that we could determine what they needed to concentrate their efforts on. The study halls necessitated that we add Tuesday nights to our schedule.

To lighten the mood at times, we offered diversions. Jack served Cherry 7-Up and played wrestling tapes before the meetings started; he called our Thursday sessions "From Wrestling to Revolution." We showed videos on black sports champions and discussed big games and fights, such as the Leonard-Hagler classic. Jack and I knew that eventually we would pull away from the sports theme, but it was a point of entry for the kids. We went to Giants and Warriors games; we went fishing and sailing. We even played chess.

The Neighborhood House is equipped with an aquarium-sized gym, and occasionally we used it for basketball. When we were serious about the game, though, we used the gym at Potrero Hill Middle School and even played in Vallejo. One evening at Vallejo, Jody Daggs became the first and only club member to beat me one-on-one, best two out of three. I was huffing and puffing by the third game, and Jody didn't often miss with his jumper. He eventually had a nice basketball career at the University of Nevada after making all-city at McAteer High School. With Jody, Marcel

Evans, and a few others, most of whom were college or college-caliber talents, we put together a club team that wasn't half bad and did well in a tournament that the Continental Boys Club put on in Vallejo.

All of that was fun, but fun was not our mission, and before long we eliminated the recreational activities entirely except for those that qualified as fundraisers. We sponsored a few benefit dances and drummed up money with street fairs and car washes and by selling T-shirts, but for the most part our commerce was in the exchange of ideas. Our commodity was knowledge, and consequently we concentrated on the mindset, on getting the young people to think about their lives in a different, critical, constructive manner. The greatest battles they would face in the years ahead would take place not on the basketball court but in the mind.

We soon found that, in the context of sociability, the most meaningful thing we could do for the kids was give them dinner, which was prepared for us free of charge by church and women's auxiliary groups. Meals had not been included in the original master plan. One day Jack just said, "Let's feed them." I wasn't sold on the idea, but it proved to be instrumental in creating a family atmosphere at the club. It was actually more symbolic than anything else—we were an extended family not because we gave the kids mashed potatoes but because we treated them as we would our own and because we were there for them twenty-four hours a day. Dinner was just a time for everybody to sit down together, and before long the tables started getting more crowded. Word was getting out that the Omega Boys Club was for real.

I can't overstate how important that was for us. In terms of reaching the kids, in getting their trust, that was the whole ball game—convincing them that we were for real. The most difficult challenge we faced in the beginning was proving to the young people that we didn't have an angle. Where they came from, everybody had an angle; everybody had a hustle. Especially adults. Individually, Jack and I had both been through the trust gauntlet, but now, with the club, we were throwing around all kinds of new claims and promises. The kids—*those* kids—were wary of adults who made commitments and didn't keep them. Many of them had parents like that. What's more, we were asking them to do something very unpopular, to give up things—drugs, gangs, calling each other "nigger" and "bitch"—that were deeply ingrained in their lives. We had to somehow replace those lost outlets and relationships. The only way we could do that was by proving to the kids that we were real, that we cared, that we were there. If we expected them to jump into unfamiliar waters, they had to trust the lifeguards. But once the word got around that Omega was for real, we were on our way.

Within a year, our membership exploded from sixteen to sixty. Friends of members joined, and kids from school, and kids from the neighborhoods, and kids off the street, and kids from Juvenile Hall. After the first sixteen, we never recruited anybody to the Omega Boys Club; they just walked in and sat down—like the sullen muscular young janitor at the Neighborhood House.

I was working with the San Francisco Public Health Department on a furlough program that Jack Jacqua helped arrange for me while I was locked up at San Bruno. My job was cleaning out the Potrero Hill Neighborhood House. I'd do that during the week and spend the weekends in jail. By that time, I had spent most of my teenage life in jail. I think I was arrested about fifteen times as a juvenile and four more after I turned eighteen. I'd been to the Youth Guidance Center, Log Cabin Ranch, California Youth Authority, two group homes, the 850 big house, and the county prison at San Bruno. When he gave me my furlough, the judge told me that if he ever saw me again, I'd be going to the penitentiary.

Jack had sent me a card about the Omega Boys Club when it first started, but I disregarded it. You have to be ready for something like that. It just sort of turned out later—I guess Jack sort of *made* it turn out—that my furlough was to be served at the Neighborhood House, where the club had its meetings. I tried to sweep down in that area so I could listen to what was going on. I'd sit down and lean my broom up against the table. Up until then, I didn't know anything about Martin Luther King or Marcus Garvey or anybody like that. They were talking about cultural pride, about values, that sort of thing. I was overwhelmed. They told me I could be somebody. Nobody had ever told me that before.

I guess I had hit rock bottom by then. I was in and out of jail. My girl was pregnant. I was confused, contemplating suicide. If I didn't kill myself, I was convinced I would be a criminal for life. I hadn't killed anybody yet, but I figured it was just a matter of time. I was on a train to hell.

The thing that opened my eyes was when I asked a friend of mine what he planned on doing when he was forty. He said, "I don't think I'll be around to see forty." I realized that if he didn't expect to make it to forty, I had no reason to. I had already been shot at several times and witnessed at least three killings.

I had been in the life since I was fourteen. I saw all these guys driving big cars, having money all the time, and I just wanted more. I started selling drugs and running with the wrong crowd. As soon as the money came in, I would buy cars and clothes. My mother knew where it all came from, but she didn't want to accept it. When things got really hard, I'd leave some money in her bed or on her dresser. The little I had left over, my older sister would steal from me. She also stole drugs from me. I saw her getting out of cars with different men, and when people would call her a prostitute, I would have to defend her. But all that time, I kept up with my schoolwork at Balboa High School and did well in basketball and track; won some long jump competitions. I didn't get into any real trouble until one day I got fed up of watching everybody else drive up in big cars and decided to get some money to buy myself one.

At lunchtime that day, I walked over to Mission Street looking for an easy mark. I spotted an old white lady carrying a purse, so I threw her to the ground and snatched the purse. The fall knocked her teeth out, broke her dentures, and hurt her back. Before I could get away, people came running up saying they were going to kill me. The heroes got me and held me until the police came. It seemed like there must have been fifty people gathered around that police car when it got there. The lady almost died. If she had, I'd have been up for murder. Jack and my mother visited me every day at the Youth Guidance Center.

After that, I got deep into the life. My life was selling drugs and fighting. I was in a lot of fights that left me covered with blood. I figured it was just part of my job. If it wasn't over drugs, it was over turf. We couldn't let other guys come on our turf. Some Mexican guys came on our turf once and stole somebody's mini-bike out of the neighborhood. That was the first time I did a drive-by. We went to their neighborhood and saw some Mexicans, boys and girls, sitting on a porch and started shooting. I couldn't tell if we hit anybody; they all started running and scattering. It was terrifying, but I wanted to do it again. One time I did, but I never told anybody. We shot at some people on the street. I really couldn't see what happened; the car was smoky from the gunpowder and my eyes were closed. If I was going to kill somebody, I didn't want to see them fall. I know it would have haunted me the rest of my life.

I didn't enjoy watching people die. There were a couple of twins who lived in the projects who smoked crack, and one time somebody sold them some lemon heads—you know, candy. When you bite off the yellow part, it's white underneath and looks like crack. Well, one of the twins found out it wasn't crack and came back looking for the guy who sold it to them, and there was an argument. One of the twins was beating the guy up, but the guy's girlfriend, who was just out of the penitentiary, pulled out the biggest knife I've ever seen and started stabbing the twin over and over and over in the back. He died. There were little kids watching and everything.

It was common to sell people bogus drugs. Sometimes, when guys wanted to buy marijuana, I would go out to a tree and get some dirt that looked like marijuana and sell that. One time, after I sold some dirt, a guy with a big green overcoat came back to the projects looking for me, wanting his money back. He was at one end of the hallway and I was at the other. I ran, and he let loose shooting. I felt the bullets passing my head, hitting the wall. I got away, but as I ran, I could hear everybody back there screaming. I hid in the basement at first. I heard his footsteps down there looking for me. I was surprised he didn't hear my heart beating and my heavy breathing. I heard him talking to one of my friends, saying he was going to kill me. As soon as he left, I snuck outside and hid under a car for about an hour after I was sure he had left. Later, he fell off and did so much crack that he didn't even know who I was. A lot of guys in the neighborhood used to beat him up.

All that time, my whole teenage life, I'd never been to a prom or a school dance or anything like that. I got most of my school credits at Juvenile Hall and graduated from McAteer High School after attending one semester—cap and gown, the whole thing. I didn't know where I was going after that, though. I was still in the game. I thought college was for Biff and Barbie or somebody on television. I had very low self-esteem. I thought, "I ain't shit," so I just sold drugs.

I was big-time for about a minute back then. I

guess I made a couple hundred thousand dollars, but it came and went. I was the kind who got busted every time I turned around. I was arrested three times for selling crack to undercover officers. One night a short stocky white guy came through the Valencia Gardens housing project where I was staying and tried to buy some crack. I said, "Man, you better not be the police." After we made the exchange, he grabbed me. I can still feel his fingernails ripping into my chest through my jacket. I started beatin' him down. I'd been arrested a week earlier for the same thing, and I swore I wasn't going to jail. A few of my friends came over to help me kick him, and I ran, but he blew his whistle and cops came from everywhere. I guess that pretty much put an end to my career in crime.

Omega came along at the right time for me. For the first few meetings, I just sat there with my broom. Then at one meeting I stood up and said, "I want to go to college." I guess I shocked everybody. Nobody in my family had even graduated from high school.

After that, I started going to all the meetings and talking at a lot of them. They told me I was the first one who really bared my soul in there.

Joe Thomas

The news out of the inner city was all bad—turf wars, drive-bys, crack raids, crack babies, delinquency rates, robberies, funerals—and in 1988, there was a lot of it.

The headlines out of the Bayview-Hunters Point area were so consistently bad, in fact, that in the midst of a series of attacks on Muni buses a news director at San Francisco's Channel 7, Harry Fuller, sent out an unusual call for some *good* news out of that neighborhood. Fuller asked Doris Ward, a San Francisco supervisor (city councilperson) if she could recommend someone or something from the Bayview-Hunters Point district that was worthy of being featured in a positive light. Ward had lived on Potrero Hill and was a longtime friend of Jack and of Mrs. Maxwell, the director of the Neighborhood House, so it was natural that she mention the Omega Boys Club.

While the turf wars raged around us, the boys club had quietly become known as a sort of refuge behind the front lines. The violence of the inner city made us conspicuous by contrast. However, there were numerous other agencies recommended to Channel 7, all deserving, and the station checked out most of them. When it finally settled upon us, it assigned the story to a conscientious, middle-aged reporter named Steve Davis, whose appreciation for what we were doing was genuine.

Our curriculum was expanding at the time. In addition to our study halls at the Neighborhood House, we were holding periodic satellite sessions at various locations around the city of San Francisco—the Mission Recreation Center, the Sunnydale Community Center, the Freedom West housing complex in Western Addition, and Holly Court. We had also begun to benefit enormously from the work of adult volunteers. Tony Alvite, a teacher at Potrero Hill Middle School, ran our Mission study hall, while several other volunteers were becoming fixtures around the club, principally Wilbur Jiggetts, a former military man and part-time coach known to us simply as Coach; Preston Worthy, a popular antidrugs counselor; and Ronnie Hatter, who doubled as a full-time employee of the Neighborhood House. Most of them had been introduced to the club as speakers or counselors and, liking what they saw, stuck around to help out in any way they could. Coach, who had already retired from the military and the grocery business, was an assistant basketball coach at City College when he appeared before the club. The next day, he reported to school and advised the head coach that the current season would be his last; he had decided to devote his energies entirely to the Omega Boys Club. It was apparent right away that he was in for the long haul.

Steve Davis first visited us on a study-hall night in the spring of 1988. He was amazed that so many low-income, hip-hop street kids—the very kind, it seemed, who so often flashed across his station's newscasts for other reasons—would be holed up in the Potrero Hill Neighborhood House learning and studying when they could be out in the spring air kickin' it, or worse. Apparently the viewers were also impressed. The story went over so well that Davis came back the next night, and the next, ultimately running Omega Boys Club segments every evening for two weeks straight. Our phone started ringing with a vengeance. New kids started showing up—some to check us out, some just to be on TV. Jesse Jackson contacted us about riding on our float in San Francisco's Cinco de Mayo parade. Steve Davis and Channel 7 were putting us on the map.

Toward the end of the series, Russ Coughlan, a popular newscaster, got into the act, delivering warm commentaries on the club and requesting that viewers send in donations to aid the cause. "If you like what you see," he said, "send in money." He urged that viewers mail in twenty dollars, ten dollars, five—even a buck, if that's all they had. The checks and bills began rolling in. He went back on the air, held up some of the donations the station had already received, and made the same appeal again. Then Channel 7 executives brought the money over to the Neighborhood House, dumped it on the table, and let the boys play in it for the cameras. The total was $30,000. To this day, some of the contributors still send us ten or twenty dollars every month.

It was not the first time we had been beneficiaries. During our first year, I had appeared on a local television show hosted by the Reverend Cecil Williams, after which a recently widowed woman associated with Stanford University had invited me for a visit. With two club members, Macio Dickerson and Thaddeus Hills, I met her at an office in Marin County and gave her a short course on Omega. As the conversation wound down, she said, "What you people are doing is magic." I said, "It's not magic at all. We're in the business of saving lives." With that, she took out a checkbook and handed me $10,000. We had also received $3,000 from Walgreen's after a *San Francisco Examiner* article mentioned our work in a story about drugs and crime in the housing projects, and another $7,000 had come to us, in conjunction with the Potrero Hill Neighborhood House, from the San Francisco Education Fund for a middle-school intervention project called Potrero Hill Pride.

Our previous good fortune notwithstanding, however, we were awed when Channel 7 dropped its incredible bundle in our laps—awed not only by the public's generosity but also by the fresh possibilities. From the beginning, Jack and I had talked about sending some of the Omega kids to college, and now, suddenly, there was money to help make it happen. But there was no program in place, no realistic starting point. Overwhelmingly, we were dealing with kids who had virtually no academic traditions in their families and for whom college had never been a legitimate prospect. We couldn't simply stuff some tuition in their pockets like it was milk money and pack them off to the quadrangles.

Jack and I, compelled to present college in a special light for our street-raised boys and (in a few cases) girls—one that might allow them to see it not as a slice of the white world but as a grand extension of the club—had for quite a while been intrigued by the notion of enrolling some of them in the black schools of the South. By doing so, we would be distancing them from the familiar tempting urban environment that kept them constantly at risk, and we would also be reinforcing our theme of black culture, black history, and black scholarship. We had set our sights on one day arranging an airline tour of black colleges. The $30,000 raised so unexpectedly by Channel 7 would cover some tuition fees, but we still needed another boost to pull off the tour. We estimated the cost at $8,000 and, perhaps brazenly, took the request back to Channel 7.

With that, Steve Davis went on the air again, informing the public of what we could specifically accomplish with another $8,000. We received not only the necessary funds but two computers and SAT software from Apple. Willie Brown put up money himself to sponsor a kid on the tour, as did Hills Brothers coffee. One viewer donated a 1976 Dodge van in which, among other uses, we could drive our college prospects to the airport.

By this time, the community felt, and rightly so, that it had an investment in us. Our kids had become San Francisco's kids. And so it was with great fanfare that eight Omega Boys Club members—Rudy Draper, Patrick Cooks, Derrick Hogan, Shervon Hunter, Lavaris Hill, Kevin Darvive, Philip Bounds, and Joe Thomas—departed San Francisco International Airport one May evening for Baltimore, where they would visit Howard University, then travel to the tidewater area of Virginia to see Hampton Institute before spending five days in Atlanta touring Clark College, Morehouse, and Morris Brown.

When they returned, there were more cameras and well-wishers at the airport, then more cameras and well-wishers at a giddy Neighborhood House reception, where the eight let it be known that their lives had taken a turn over the past week. They had witnessed young black men and women carrying briefcases, wearing medical smocks, and studying large books over pizza, earnestly preparing for the kinds of futures that none of the Omega kids had previously contemplated. In Atlanta, they had taken in more than that. "The prettiest sight I saw," wrote Derrick Hogan to one of the tour sponsors, "was Martin Luther King's burial ground. It was surrounded by water and had little steps posing as waterfalls. I felt a cold chill that went over me and started to get scared, but I knew if it wasn't for him the black men of the world today wouldn't be FREE!"

Doris Ward, the beaming city supervisor who couldn't have imagined that her offhand recommendation would lead to all of this, told the kids that by going on the college tour, they had forever separated themselves from the gangbangers and crack dealers of the neighborhoods. "The difference between you and them," she said, "is that you have a future."

The eight guests of honor then took brief uneasy turns addressing the happy crowd, and when his arrived, tough-guy Joe Thomas, the cop-beater, said the most important thing of all.

"I'm going to college," he declared.

The next fall, Derrick enrolled at Wiley College in Texas, Shervon accepted a basketball scholarship to Delaware State, and Joe and the other five turned up at Morris Brown.

4

Turf

They never found out who shot Peter Lee.

From the shy keen-minded math student he had been at Potrero Hill Middle School—just one of the homies—Peter Lee had gone on to become an OG, a term that stands loosely for Original Gangster or, more practically, for anyone who has been in the game for an extended time. Peter Lee had the car, the money, the girls. He was popular, likable, and most importantly, respected. He had everything but a future. Jack and I had been aware of that for some time and in fact had gone to see Peter Lee in Sunnydale shortly before he was killed. We talked to him and his cousin, Passion, trying to advise them of what lay ahead. We suggested that they come to the boys club. They weren't ready to listen.

Peter Lee was gunned down at the age of nineteen while riding in a car beneath an underpass in Hunters Point. It was in March 1989, not long after the movie *Colors* came out, with Sean Penn as a tough young urban cop hell-bent on breaking up the gangs. *Colors* was one of the many recent films capitalizing on the violence and sensationalism of street life—the sort of films that make black people very angry and sometimes set them off. After *Colors,* the turf wars escalated sharply in the Bay Area. After Peter Lee was killed, they went crazy.

Jack and I had hoped, as we often do, that this murder would be the one to bring everybody to their senses and stop the madness. The opposite happened. The teenagers who lived in the immense graffiti-stained Sunnydale projects, located in the Visitacion Valley section of San Francisco's southeast corner, received the news of Peter Lee's unsolved homicide as a call to arms. Peter Lee had been an active player in the turf wars between Sunnydale and Hunters Point, and word was that Hunters Point got him. That was all Sunnydale needed to hear.

Sunnydale's gunmen were so notorious that the San Francisco Police Department had identified one Sunnydale clique, known as the Swampy Desert Gang, as the most violent crack outfit in the city. The authorities tended to regard the youth violence that came out of Sunnydale as economically motivated, but that was a very narrow perspective. The marketing of crack represented just one front in a much larger, deeper conflict based on turf. Whether or not Peter Lee's murder was precipitated by a drug-sale dispute, its reverberations shook the San Francisco turf like the earthquake that brought down buildings and highways later that year.

From Sunnydale's standpoint, Peter Lee was a banner that the street warriors could carry purposefully into battle. After the funeral, they started wearing San Diego Padres baseball caps (with the SD representing Sunnydale) and writing "Peter Lee, R.I.P." on the inside. Hunters Point replied by special-ordering HP hats and sewing each kid's street name onto the sleeve of his Starter jacket. The gauntlet had been dropped. A month after Peter Lee was buried, two Hunters Point kids were taken out in a retaliatory double murder. Back and forth it went, killing after killing. For more than a year, turf murders dominated both the streets and the news. Players spent their evenings watching for homies and cars that didn't belong in their 'hoods, waiting to catch an enemy "slippin' " so they could blow him away with provincial justification.

Others dressed in black and sneaked into hostile territory on night-time murder missions. Sunnydale and the sprawling central-city Fillmore district were both at war with Hunters Point, and for a time they joined up. Some of the 'hoods became identified by personalized turf jackets, and so many people were killed over them that the police declared them illegal. If a player from one turf so much as saw a player from another turf—anytime, anywhere—it was on.

Until the late 1980s, most of the turf fighting in the Bay Area had been with fists and bats—the battle was coming from the shoulder, as the kids liked to say—but after *Colors* came out and crack took over the scene and Peter Lee was killed, guns became standard equipment. They were as common as loose change in the hands of street warriors like Little Disease, a dark good-looking kid from the Lakeview district of southwest San Francisco who referred to himself as "a cold piece of work" and whose nickname was bestowed as a tribute to the creative disorder that he was so consistently capable of effecting.

> The turf wars really weren't that intense around San Francisco until *Colors* and Peter Lee and all of that. But *Colors* pumped up the whole L.A. scene as far as drive by shootings. People started shooting people over basically nothing. Before that, if somebody had a personal beef with somebody, they might pull out a gun, but there had to be some serious disrespect involved for that to happen.
>
> Out here, the way it was, if I see you at school and we got a beef, I might hit you in the head with a bumper jack. If I want to shoot you, I'm not gonna come by in a car and shoot up ten people. I'm gonna kick down your door. If I want to shoot you with your homeboys, I'm gettin' out of the car, me and my homies or whatever, and we gonna make everybody lie down. And I'm gonna tell you, get up, get up. And if you don't get up I'm gonna pistol-whip you. We gonna tear you or

put you in the trunk and go wherever we got to go and do whatever we got to do. If we got to kill you, we gonna kill you. Or torture you. Or leave you in the trunk and shoot up the car. Or shoot a person twice, in the back of each elbow, shoot you in the kneecap, take you out to the pier, throw you in the freezing water, and make you swim back, and if you can't, you die. It was only forty or fifty feet to the shore, but nine times out of ten they didn't make it. That was something that was a specialty of a lot of people where I grew up.

It was all turf wars. We didn't call it gangbanging. We thought of ourselves as cliques. Or posses. Mobs. Family. It was respect involved. I don't want to shoot your mama. I don't want to shoot your daughter. I want you. We really never heard about drive-bys. So when the drive-by scene came on, the respect as far as the gang was concerned was lost. It got to the point you could get a M.A.C.-10 that shot sixty rounds and just go shoot up the whole block. It was no longer, "I want you." It was whoever was out there on the corner. Whoever you see that ain't with your turf, you get with 'em. If there goes Fillmore, or there goes Sunnydale, it was, "Let's get 'em." It was shoot on sight.

A car would come up to you and start shooting into your car. Somebody would pull up and say, "What's up? Where you from?" You'd get to having words, then get to letting off out the window. If we were going somewhere, we'd have two in front and one in back with a shotgun in his lap. Normally I was the driver, because I was calm under pressure. Out of thirteen high-speed chases, I was only caught twice. But that's how we always rode, with a shotgun in the lap. You shoot, you shoot to kill.

If we gonna commit a shooting, we stop the car, let two people out, and they'll walk in the other guy's neighborhood. They over there gamblin', maybe, not trippin'—what we call slippin'. We come walkin' by, "Hey, what's up?" They turn around and look, see what's going on. Then, "Boom! Boom!" A lot of times we come back in another car an hour later, see how many ambulances there, what the scene looks like. We might even get out.

I been shot three times—twice by brothers out of Fillmore, once by police. I probably hit over ten people. It's got to be over ten. People say they don't know, but they know. They just don't want to say because they don't want no backlash. I'm pretty sure somebody has died at my hands. When you walk up to them and stick the barrel in their heart and shoot . . . well, I've seen it done.

Little Disease

From about 1988 to 1990 or so, it seemed that the entire city was fractured into teenage guerrilla nations. I happened to be sitting with our counselor Preston Worthy at the 1989 city basketball tournament, which was held in the allegedly demilitarized district of Haight-Ashbury, when a full-scale brawl between Fillmore and Hunters Point broke out on the floor between games. Worthy and I ran around the gym pulling people out of the fight, ultimately gathering up about a half-dozen Omegas and shepherding them into our donated Dodge van outside. At the time, it didn't occur to us that Worthy or I could easily have been killed.

In the Bay Area, that level of violence was by no means restricted to the turfs of San Francisco. At one of the annual Martin Luther King holiday celebrations at the San Francisco Civic Center, where Omega kids sold I DON'T DO DRUGS T-shirts, a fatal fight broke out between cliques from San Francisco and East Palo Alto—which has a serious ghetto and in 1992 became the deadliest city in America, with forty-two homicides in a town of 23,000—resulting in one of the Omegas being charged with murder (for which he was later acquitted). At McClymonds High School in

Oakland, a group of students moved swiftly to the exit doors after a 1989 basketball game with Oakland High, removed chains and padlocks from underneath their leather jackets, sealed the gym, and proceeded to beat the hell out of anybody from the other school. Turf was one thing the entire metropolitan area had in common.

I liked to think of our kids as alumni of the turf—young people who had been there, served their time, earned their stripes, and then, by virtue of their Omega Boys Club education, graduated to a higher level of citizenship. However, I harbored no illusions about their sainthood, or even their clean breaks from the life; it's a rare thing when a kid can pull out of the game cold turkey. Some of our members slipped back into drugs and gangbanging. Some of them went to jail. At least one was convicted of shooting somebody, and it's possible that a few of them may have been involved when gunplay flared up in Sunnydale and Hunters Point exactly a year after Peter Lee was killed (the timing was considered by most, including the police, to be no coincidence).

An example of a guy who kept one foot in the club during those years was Frank Newcombe, a handsome Fillmore teenager —I called him Billy Dee—who had been back and forth to YGC from the time he was nine years old. His parents were drug dealers and users, and Frank almost never had a home-cooked meal; they would throw him twenty dollars every day and tell him to get himself something to eat. He used most of the money to buy cocaine, which he snorted in imitation of his mother and father. When he was about twelve, Frank and his friends walked over to Castro Street and beat up gay men until the gays began equipping themselves with whistles. Then it was into stealing cars and weapons. When we came to know him, Frank was heavily involved in turf. It seemed like he lived for parties and fights, and his best nights were the ones in which he could find both in the same location. When four disk jockeys sponsored a series of rap concerts in the ballrooms of San Francisco hotels, Frank Newcombe was always sure to be there.

One night the party was at the Hyatt on Van Ness. The guys onstage were from Richmond. They were okay, but one of the brothers with us was a rapper, and we started chanting his name, to get him up there doing his thing. Then the dude, the rapper on the stage, said fuck him. All hell broke loose. We ran on the stage, picking up mikes, beating guys up. Then we heard an Uzi going off. Security had scanned us with metal detectors so we couldn't bring any weapons in, but the band could because it was their security. It was like in the movies, where everybody is running out of the room, jumping over tables, stomping on people. There were people stuck on the escalator, getting stepped on. When we got outside, we all picked up the guns we had left outside by trees or in cars, and then about twenty-five of us tried to jump into a Delta 88.

Frank Newcombe

Once, as he was standing on Fillmore Street, a minivan pulled up, the side door slid open, and Frank was hit in the arm as a barrage of bullets was let loose from automatic weapons. Newcombe thought the shooters were from Hunters Point, but he couldn't be certain. "It could have been brothers from another project in Fillmore just shouting Hunters Point," he said later. On principle, and after a couple of months had elapsed, revenge was exacted against Hunters Point in a larger rented van, with the help of two girls who engaged the targets in conversation until Frank and his buddy opened fire from the rear. "I don't know what kind of damage we did. When people go down, you never know if they've been hit or if they're just ducking or just falling to the ground."

Although I was surrounded by people, including Jack, who were intimate with the subplots of the streets—Omega's membership by then was well over a hundred—my closest link to the game in those days was probably Jermaine King, an ornery but profoundly likable teenager from Hunters Point who, despite his efforts to distance himself from the neighborhood posses, somehow managed to get in the middle of just about every dispute that came down. I supplied Jermaine with rides to and from our meetings, and after he realized he had a car and driver at his disposal, he began to call me in all sorts of dire straits. One time, when he was beefing with Sunnydale, he was waiting for a bus when a carload of Sunnydale kids rolled past. Jermaine sprinted over to a pay phone and implored me to come pick him up immediately, saying, "Marshall, they're lookin' at me crazy." I drove over to where he said he was, but I didn't see anybody. All of a sudden, here comes Jermaine sprinting out from behind a trash can.

Jermaine stayed with friends in Oakland after he was kicked out of the San Francisco school district—not just his school but the whole *district*—for bringing a gun to class, and as a result I spent a hell of a lot of time ferrying him back and forth. The hours were crazy, and when I was finally alone in the car, I would fall into total exhaustion, but there was no way I could drift off as long as Jermaine was around. His street stories tuned me in to the countless temptations and activities that were there for virtually all of the young people—Jermaine and I were simultaneously educating each other—and many of them left me speechless. The kids in Jermaine's world lost their virginity before their voices dropped, bought and sold guns in the schoolyard, and played at death the way kids in my day played tag. After Jermaine's crash course in street reality, I had a better feel for what was going on and began to pick up information from any number of Omegas and assorted homies. Crazy things were going on in the neighborhoods, like kidnaping an enemy from another 'hood, carrying him to a vacant building, and playing Russian Roulette—placing a bullet in one chamber of a .38 and taking turns pulling the trigger until one of the brothers was a murderer. An Omega kid whom I knew very well found himself holding the gun once when it went off. It's a hell of a way for one kid to die, and a hell of a thing for another to live with.

A longtime club member told me once about a time when his potna was shot in the stomach, after which they caught the dude who did it, tortured him, then put him in the trunk of a car for a couple of days. About the third day the homie who had been shot decided it was time to kill the one who had tried to kill him. The Omega brother was reluctant, but his potna checked him on that, as potnas customarily do. The potna went ahead and did the deed, then put the body in a car, set a flare to it, and burned it up right there in the projects. The incident never even made the newspapers.

The thing that staggered me most about Jermaine's world—and his world was little different from the one the other homies lived in—was that he took it all for granted. At the age of sixteen, Jermaine had already left home and pocketed more money selling drugs than I would make in six or eight years of teaching. He also told me that he had met the right woman. When I suggested that he couldn't possibly know that at sixteen, he said, "Shit, man, I been messin' with women since I was nine." By the time he was old enough to drive, Jermaine had experienced not only an eventful life but more death than he had any right to see. He once watched five friends die in the course of a month.

Jermaine's homes and haunts in Oakland were more or less —actually, less than more—on the way to my house in Pittsburg, and after a few months of nocturnal commuting I made the acquaintance of several third-shift patrolmen on Highway 24. One officer pulled me over for driving too slow, recognized my purple Omega Boys Club jacket, and said, "Didn't I stop you out here last week?" Others, unfortunately, were not quite as cordial.

After dropping off Jermaine one late night, with my son Malcolm in the car, I was cutting through Berkeley, taking a back road to Highway 24, when one of the Berkeley policemen mistook me for a drunk driver. He obviously didn't believe my story that I was just very tired, and he gave me a sobriety test. When the sobriety test came up negative, he said I must have been on drugs. With that, Malcolm, who is normally pretty dignified, went nuts. "Drugs?!" he screamed. "Are you crazy? My dad runs the Omega Boys Club! He doesn't use drugs!" Then the guy shined a light in my eyes and proceeded to slap on the handcuffs, saying that my pupils had not dilated properly or some garbage. "What do you mean, my pupils?" I shouted. "What kind of shit is that?"

By this time, the officer had called in backups. I was gradually becoming as angry as Malcolm. Finally the guy hauled us off to the Berkeley jail, gave me a urine test, and said, "When it wears off, we'll let you out." My response was, "You must do this to all the brothers." I stayed in jail, and Malcolm waited downstairs in a hard chair until five A.M., when another cop unlocked the cell and handed me my car keys. The car, however, was still across town, and we had to walk to it. A couple of weeks later, concerned that the department might have dummied up the urine test, I called for the results. "Oh, it was negative," I was told. My buddy Jack wrote an appropriately scathing letter to the Berkeley PD on my behalf.

As humiliating as that long evening was, I have to note here that it was not unique in my experience, nor was it substantially different from experiences shared by most black men in this country. I learned very early in life that policemen are some of the worst enemies I'll run into along the way. When a black person has an encounter with an officer of the law, he can only pray that he has come across a decent human being. From the black perspective, the cop's motto "to protect and to serve" often seems as though it should be "to accuse and to abuse." The good cops can't seem to do a damn thing about the bad ones, who tend to enhance their authority through a gang mentality. Black people were well aware of this fact long before the Rodney King beating or Mark Fuhrman's racist comments were caught on tape.

In many instances, if a crime is allegedly committed by someone black, it's open season on all black people in the area. There's not a black person I know who doesn't see the police as an occupying force in the community. At the same time, though, I'm convinced that if black folks stopped blowing each other's brains out, they'd be in a much better position to deal with police issues. If Crips and Bloods weren't constantly at war with each other, for instance, then the cops in Los Angeles wouldn't pick up Bloods and drop them off deep in Crip territory. The police are happy to let black people do their work for them, and we're too damn happy to do it. What's more, when it comes to siding with either the police or the homie, the community is often compelled to fall in with the police. And that's the homie's fault, because he's been menacing the very neighborhood that he needs for nurturing and support. As far as I'm concerned, the homie and the bad cop play the same game. As I tell the kids when they complain about the harassment they get from the cops, if police banging isn't right, then gangbanging sure as hell isn't, either.

There's no question that my several brushes with policemen over the past few years have been predicated largely on the fact that I was black. In the majority of cases, if I had been a white person under the same circumstances, I probably wouldn't have even been approached. A couple of months after the Berkeley incident, for instance, I was so sleepy driving home one night that I pulled off the highway and turned into a convenience store parking lot to lie down for a while. The next thing I knew, there were lights shining through the back window of the car. When I sat up, a cop was holding a gun on me. He dragged me out of the car, and when I asked what the hell was going on, he said, "I got word of a robbery around here." I said, "Look, I'm tired. I've just been lying in the car trying to get some rest before I drive home." With that, the cop went into his Bull Conner thing and snarled, "Fella, you want this easy or you want it hard?" I could play that game, too, and lapsed into my "yes sir, no sir, whatever you say sir" mode. He harassed me a little more, looked over my license, checked my story with the clerks in the store, and reluctantly let me go. Just to get in the last word, he looked at my Malcolm X cap, smiled, and said, "Nice hat." What an asshole.

As I was leaving the Neighborhood House at about four in the morning on another occasion, a cop pulled up next to my Ford Taurus, checked out my sweatshirt and baseball cap, and asked, "Where'd you steal that car from?" My crime, I suppose—in addition to being black—was working late. I do a lot of that. A few times at that hour, I've turned on the engine and fallen asleep before I could get the car out of park; I'll wake up about two hours later, the car still running, and drive home. If I know I can't make it home—it's a long drive—I'll stop at a San Francisco bed and break-fast owned by Elaine Silverman, a loyal friend who was the English teacher on my staff at the Guidance Service Center. Elaine kindly gave me a key to the B&B, and when I need to crash in the middle of the night, I just look around for an empty bed.

There have been occasions when, after staying late at school or speaking somewhere or visiting kids, I've pulled up to the Nabe at some small hour of the morning and nodded off before I could get the car door open. When that happens, the janitor comes out and wakes me up. Somehow, though, I've managed to almost never fall asleep while driving, the one notable exception being the time I zonked out on Highway 24, hit the road divider, and totaled my Nissan Sentra.

Fatigue has been an inevitable by-product of my work with the boys club, but given that, I've never attributed it to my work with the *boys*. It's the paperwork that wears me out, the mundane business of operating the club—applying for grants, recommending members for scholarships, soliciting donations, maintaining the budget, writing letters. In the early years, I did all of that myself after the kids and everybody else had left for the night. Chauffeuring Jermaine and his friends was the fun part.

It also proved to be eminently worthwhile. One of the places to which I drove Jermaine was a black history class being offered in Fillmore. I had encouraged him to enroll in the course, but he refused at first, insisting that he couldn't get there without being shot at; the situation was so intense that a friend of Jermaine's, who happened to live in Fillmore, couldn't even go home many nights because of their assocation. When I offered to take Jermaine to the class, he reluctantly agreed to go, and he did, every day. I think he felt that if I was willing to go the extra mile for him, the least he could do was take the damn class. He had a hard time believing that somebody outside of his family or his posse would look after him in that manner.

Jermaine desperately needed somebody—an adult—on his side. He was a rambunctious, mischievous kid, a rabble-rouser, and as a result it seemed as though he got blamed for everything that

Hunters Point did, even after he had moved to Oakland. His name was written all over walls in Fillmore and Sunnydale, which meant that there were numerous contracts out on his life. Often in those days, if there was a lull in the action, somebody would start a rumor, saying that so-and-so had been dissed or that so-and-so had said they were looking for so-and-so. That may or may not have been true, but it was usually enough to put the concerned parties on edge and get them shooting at each other. It was because of rumors that Jermaine had thought it necessary to carry a gun to school.

Jermaine's fear for his life was not imagined. An enemy once put a shotgun to the head of one of Jermaine's buddies and told him to pass along the news that Jermaine would be killed. Several times, he nearly was. At one of the hotel parties, he was beaten by anywhere from forty to eighty Fillmore kids, depending on the eyewitness.

About eight of us had caught the bus to a party at the Hyatt downtown. We had our little Hunters Point caps on, and we were just there chillin'. There were a bunch of Hunters Point people there, and I thought, good, we'll get a ride home. On the way out, though, we were having a good time and somehow got split up. I was walking with this girl I went to high school with, and then I saw a friend of mine from Sunnydale. At this stage of the game, Hunters Point and Sunnydale were working together against Fillmore. My friend pushed me into the street and said, run, because they were coming after me. They caught me about three blocks later. I felt some pipes hitting me, some chains. They were stretching me out, playing World Wrestling Federation with me. I was waiting for somebody to shoot me in the head. I knew it was coming. The next morning, when I woke up and looked in the mirror, I had the insignia of a tennis shoe under my right eye.

A while later there was a party at the Meridian

Hotel. A lot of Fillmore people were there, and they were expecting a fistfight. They didn't know we left guns outside the hotel in bushes and on the tires of cars. We rushed the party with some friends from Sunnydale, and when everybody was kicked out of the party, the fight jumped off in the street. It was a big old one-way street where you could block the traffic, and you could kill each other all night. That's practically what we did. There must have been fifteen carloads of gang members. A lot of people were wounded. The police saved some lives that night. They came with twelve-gauges, dogs, riot gear, the whole thing. It was wild.

We won that round. Then Fillmore came back to our turf, thinking we would be celebrating. If they had waited about another ten minutes, we would have. But we were ready for them. Hunters Point stayed ready. If anything ever jumped off in Hunters Point, everybody would be there.

At first, our battles were always against Fillmore, but then we split with Sunnydale and we had to take them on, too. We got it on big-time with Sunnydale. One time, up on Potrero Hill, everybody was outside kickin' it and some guys from Sunnydale came through and did a drive-by. A good buddy of mine got shot in the head and died immediately. When Sunnydale came through, they came through sick. They came through crazy. I wasn't there when the payback came that time, but I think three people died that night.

One of my best friends who was like a brother to me stayed out of that stuff, and he asked me why didn't I get out. I said, "Man, you're from Hunters Point, how can you stay out of it?" He said, "Naw, it's not for me." One day when Sunnydale came through the 'hood, they hopped out with guns and my buddy didn't run 'cause he didn't have nothin' to do with it. They cracked a shotgun over his head and he was unconscious for four hours.

I knew about twelve people from Hunters Point who died at the hands of Sunnydale. So many of my good friends died. We were filled with so much anger. One night, when the drama had been building for about nine months straight, we went through Sunnydale and touched it up. There were three cars of us. Two people died that night. I don't know if I killed anybody, but I tried. There were about seven of them standing around in the projects, and we just started busting on them. At the time, I was hoping it was one of my bullets that killed somebody. That's just the way your mind worked when the turf wars were goin' strong.

Jermaine King

While we knew all too well that many of the Omegas were still involved in turf in those days—some voluntarily, some by association, and some, like Jermaine, by inertia—the club itself remained a safe haven. The word they use on the streets of San Francisco for gunplay and other deadly violence is "drama," and there has never been any of it at the Omega Boys Club. We don't allow it.

On the occasions that drama has seemed close at hand—with our clientele, it's never far away—we've always managed to avert it, which testifies to our uncompromising position on gunplay. A couple of rival gangbangers, Demetrius Williams and Antoine Bird, got into a fistfight outside the Neighborhood House one evening as the meeting was breaking up, and I had to drag them back inside to calm them down before the situation escalated, as situations such as that often do. They were contrite, respecting the atmosphere of vigilant nonviolence that we had painstakingly developed.

Our most volatile situations have generally occurred when the club has been visited by those relatively unfamiliar with it—which, of course, we encourage as a rule. Now and then, Jack would set up ad hoc meetings with kids who needed some specific attention, often because they had just been released from the Youth Guidance Center or some other penal institution. The two he called in one particular night in 1989 were Sam Robinson, a handsome, soft-spoken teenager from Fillmore, and Danny Boy Williams, a spirited turf warrior from Hunters Point, who were involved in a trivial beef that could easily have ended up with one of them dead.

The meeting took place in the theater room of the Potrero Hill Neighborhood House, and only Sam came alone. Danny Boy was accompanied by a rock of a kid named Bernard Temple, widely known as the toughest gangbanger in Hunters Point. Bernard was a legend. His nickname was Mani, for Maniac. There was nothing on two legs—and probably four—that Bernard couldn't beat up. He was the kind of kid who would walk up to you and knock you out just because he felt like it, the classic "crazy nigger."

As Jack and I and Coach, whose calm wisdom was very effective in tense situations, talked to Danny Boy and Sam, Bernard looked on quietly until he could contain himself no longer. "Yeah, I been sittin' here listenin' to you," he bellowed at last, standing up to pace and point. "No matter what you say, man, there will always be turf. That's just the way it is. You guys, with all your talk, peace and nonviolence and all that shit, you can't do nothin' about it because no matter what you say, turf will be there forever. These motherfuckers are gonna have to fight, and that's all there is to it. That's the only way."

Danny Boy, of course, was under pressure to live up to whatever Bernard said, and Sam was ready to go, too. He said, "Let's do it." I said, "You're not doing anything. There ain't gonna be no fightin' here."

Finally, while Jack tried to talk down Bernard, Coach and I took Sam and Danny Boy into the office, where I was able to lay into them without Bernard's persuasive specter lurking over my shoulder. "Sam, sit down," I said sharply. "Danny Boy, sit down. Look, both of you guys, this is the Neighborhood House. This is the Omega Boys Club. No matter what you feel like, or what Bernard says, or what you think you have to do, you can't fight here. Now, I don't know what the hell your problem is, but we're not gonna have it here. If you're gonna fight, fight somewhere else. But as long as you're here, you're gonna listen to me. Now, what's the deal here? What's really the problem here?"

The real problem was that Danny Boy had some kind of grudge against Sam going way back—he thought Sam was coming at him one time, which he may or may not have been, the truth of which wasn't important because Danny Boy *thought* he was and there were probably other people who thought it, too—and the last time he saw Sam, because of that thing way back when and because, you know, he had to protect his reputation, Danny Boy dissed Sam, and of course Sam had to answer because he, too, had to protect his reputation, which wouldn't be worth a shit in the 'hood if he allowed Danny Boy to dis him that way. Or something like that.

"I don't want to disgrace the club, Mr. Marshall," Sam said, apologizing in advance for what he thought he had to do. "I don't want to mess up the club or nothin', but you understand   "

The two of them were downright sheepish back there in the office, especially Sam. I suspect it was because they had to explain to Coach and me why it was they had to fight, and when they tried to explain, it sounded so damn silly. The fact was, neither one of them had actually *done* anything to the other. They understood that. They understood that fighting didn't make any sense. Ultimately, they admitted it and grudgingly agreed—for the time being, anyway—to let the whole thing slide. But at the same time they understood, as we did, that no matter what we decided in that office, when we stepped out of it, there would be the matter of Bernard to contend with.

When he heard that Sam and Danny Boy had agreed not to fight—at least not there and not then—Bernard became very angry. He became, in fact, a very angry, mean, bad-ass brother with a gun, which he was never without. But Coach and Jack and I held our ground and made good on our claim that there would be no bloodshed at the boys club; to his credit, Bernard ultimately—if grudgingly—honored that tradition. Sam and Danny Boy and Bernard finally left without an incident. Such was Bernard's reputation that when word got around that he had been to the Omega Boys Club and nothing happened, we were suddenly legitimized in many parts of the 'hood. (A few days later, Bernard was shot in the stomach, but his stomach was so tough that the bullet didn't make it all the way through. I called him in the hospital, and he thanked me for thinking of him.)

For his part, Sam Robinson was sincere about upholding the integrity of the boys club and turned to us increasingly after his flirtation with Danny Boy, who proved to be more impressed by the 'hood. Danny Boy was eventually killed taking a bullet intended for his brother. Bernard, meanwhile, was hardly slowed by the slug in his gut. He fully recovered, then, going somewhat straight, became a professional boxer.

Through the episode with Bernard and others like it, we were able time and again to get a close look at a phenomenon observed by virtually every urban youth worker in America—that the violence practiced by so many city kids is very often the result of encouragement from their peers. Nothing new here; but beyond the proverbial bad influence of friends, it's startling how many boys and girls are brought into gangbanging and drug dealing by their brothers or their cousins—or in some cases, their parents. In the same way that Frank Newcombe inherited a drug legacy from his mother and father, I've seen the tradition of violence handed down ceremoniously to kids like Lamerle Johnson, a criminally minded teenager from the depressed, gang-infested industrial town of Richmond, located between Oakland and Vallejo.

Lamerle Johnson came from a family of hustlers. We met him through Juvenile Hall, where Coach had been the first to take him under his wing. I joined the fray when Lamerle started coming to Omega meetings, and I spent a lot of time with him, much of it in my car with Jermaine. The knowledge he picked up at the club made sense to him, which is why he continued to listen, but he was reluctant to embrace it. There were stronger pressures pushing him from the other side, which I learned firsthand one evening in

1989 when I was working alone in the office and Lamerle walked in with a message.

I sat on the desk facing him as Lamerle pulled up a rolling office chair and, choosing his words carefully but without showing the slightest bit of discomfort, informed me that his family did not appreciate my interference in his life. Lamerle told me that some of his family had trained him to be a criminal, and from where they stood, I was trying to lead him out of the life they had groomed him for. The bottom line was that if I didn't back off, the family would have to handle the situation in its own way, which meant that anything could happen. "Marshall," Lamerle said smugly, relishing the opportunity to reverse the roles and play teacher, "there are things out there that go on that you just don't know about. This shit here is nice, but you got to think about the real world. You don't know who's calling the shots out there—it might be some dude in prison, and he don't care what happen to you. Out in the real world, people don't play around."

"Bullshit," I said. "Do you think this is a game, Lamerle? Don't you know this shit is for real? I'm talkin' about our history, our heritage. What I'm talkin' about is bigger than any of that shit you're talkin' about. Don't you understand how important this is? Haven't you learned anything from Martin Luther King, from Malcolm X? This is about doing things for the people. It's not just about you. It's not just about me. This is about the people. It's a hell of a lot bigger than you and me. So don't give me that shit."

Lamerle just shook his head, and with that I pushed my foot against his chair and sent it spinning across the room. I was hot. I don't think I've ever been as mad at anybody as I was at Lamerle that night. This was a kid whom I had carted all over the Bay Area, from San Francisco to Richmond to Oakland to Vallejo, at all hours of the night. I was trying to get him into college. I had helped him find an apartment. I was trying to get him out of the gang. I was trying like hell to save him from himself. And in return, he was threatening my life.

Nothing ever came of Lamerle's warning, but I never forgot it, either. Even when he was attending club meetings and contributing to them positively, there was a restless, hard-edged under-current in his manner. I wasn't ready to write off Lamerle as incorrigible, but it was obvious that his corruption was much deeper-seated than that of most of the kids we dealt with. It was largely because of Lamerle, in fact, that I worried about Jermaine. The two of them became close friends after they joined the club, and by gravitating toward Lamerle, Jermaine made it apparent to me that part of him was still out there on the street.

At the same time, though, Jermaine was becoming equally tight with a short, unimposing kid from Oakland named Andre Aikins who was practically the antithesis of Lamerle. Andre was perhaps the most honorable, positive kid in the Omega Boys Club. I had met him while speaking at a high school in Oakland, and he indicated from the beginning that he was searching for the very sort of thing that we had to offer. Once he began attending the meetings, he immediately fell in with our principles. And because he, too, needed rides to Potrero Hill and back, he also fell in with Jermaine and Lamerle.

Just as Jermaine's attraction toward Lamerle was cause for concern, his friendship with Andre was extremely promising. When Jermaine and Andre were together, they traded stories about their past and present lives, supported each other, and celebrated the changes they were both making. Andre and Lamerle, on the other hand, argued constantly about right and wrong, morals and money, the ideal and the practical. But it was interesting, all the while, that as much as Lamerle resisted and fought with Andre, he nonetheless hung with him, the same way he hung with the club in spite of the attitude he copped with me. Obviously, part of Lamerle wanted to be somebody else. That was the part that he tried to cover up with attitude. Having been raised on guns and crime, Lamerle just couldn't seem to get comfortable with his other self.

Andre, meanwhile, reveled in the fact that he was turning his life around. In contrast to Lamerle, he was a kid who had started out good and gone bad grudgingly. For him, the street life was not a birthright but an alternative that he had been driven to against his better judgment. Once in the life, though, he had acquircd a tastc for it; an addiction, in fact, that was no casicr to break than an addiction to drugs or alcohol.

When I was a seventh grader in Oakland, I was what you might call the perfect image of a nerd. I didn't have the opportunity to get out in the 'hood and be cool like the other kids. My mother and father were both at home, which right off the bat made me different than most of the kids I knew. I also have a younger sister and a younger brother who is a slow learner, so I had a lot of household responsibilities. I wasn't a street kid. And where I came from, if you're not a street kid, you're a victim.

I used to get beat up a lot. People in school would come up to me and say, "If you don't want to get whupped on, give us some money." I gave them money and they the ones that whupped on me. One guy in particular used to beat me up all the time. Finally, one day in the seventh grade, I decided enough is enough. He had beaten me up again that day, and I went home and cried. I sat in my room crying and thinking about it, and I decided right then that I was going to change. I was not going to let it happen again. I got myself a new attitude.

For school the next day, I put on different clothes than the kind I had been wearing, changed my look completely. That didn't keep the same guy from picking on me again. But this time, I put all the pressures and frustrations of the past years into that one fight and knocked this guy around the school. I tore him up.

Just like that, I was suddenly known. It was a trip. My whole life flip-flopped with that one fight. People started hanging around with me and calling me "little cousin." I started getting, "Hey, what's up, what's goin' on? You need anything, let me know." Being able to fight opened up a lot of doors. People wanted me on their team. And I got off on all of that. From then on, I got real mean. I found that being mean brought me respect. It was a shame I had to whup up on somebody to get God's natural gift of respect, but that's the way it was.

At that point, I was still reluctant to get involved with drugs and the things that were going on in the streets, but it didn't take long before I learned a different lifestyle. Then the game changed and you needed money to get respect. Respect is a lot like money anyway —the more you get, the more you want. All of a sudden, I had to sell drugs to keep my respect.

I started selling around 1985. I got some money and I thought, "Man, this is good!" At first I just sold for another guy, and I would get between twenty and thirty-five dollars out of a hundred. Then I got to where I bought the whole bundle and sold it for myself. I'd buy a half zip for about four hundred or four-fifty. I could make about two-fifty or three hundred a week. I wasn't no baller or high roller, but I was into the life. When I left the house, I would dress one way, then go to my potna's house, change my clothes, get my jewelry, then go and do my thing. Then I'd go back to his house, change clothes again, and go home. That way, I kept all the dirt away from my house.

I was in the ninth grade when I stopped going to school. I went for a while just for a place to kick it, but I wasn't taking care of business when I was there, so I said, "Fuck this." There was a new thing coming on around then. When you're on the streets, you get tired of the same old. I had a potna who was a hit man, an enforcer. I started hanging with him, and me and my potna got a reputation for being tough guys. One day my potna walked up and shot somebody in the back of the head, then buried him.

There were two potnas of mine who did that type of thing for a living. It was all business, and that was cool. They said to me, "You won't never get caught 'cause you're doin' it for somebody else." So I lent a hand. I was there a few times when they made the hit. There was money in it.

This was when I was about fifteen-sixteen years old. After that I got into stealing cars and beating people up. We had a game called Let the Slaughter Begin. We'd go out and whup up on people. Sometimes there would be eight or nine of us; sometimes it was just me and my potna. Anybody we'd see, we'd whup up on 'em. If we didn't see anybody, we'd take a baseball bat and whup up on some cars.

After a while you get numb to the violence. It just becomes a part of your life that you take for granted, like watching soap operas. Drinkin', kickin', whuppin' up and robbin' people—it was as natural as breathing to me. Some guys even get used to going to jail. I didn't do much of that. I had been in Juvenile Hall a little bit for stealing a car, and there were many nights when I was chased by the police, but I got to where I could just sense if they were around. I'd walk out, everything would be quiet, and I'd say, "Man, this feels like a task-force night." A little while later you'd hear the sirens coming from every direction. I was gone by then. One time I punched a hole through a wooden fence escaping from the police.

I tried to get myself together after my close friend Monkey was killed. We were grindin' together one night, and it was cold. Things were rollin' slow. I had a little more crack to get off, but I said, "Naw, fuck it, I'm goin' to the house." Monkey wanted to keep grindin', so I went to the house and he went out by himself. Later that night, he got killed. He was fifteen. There wasn't even an investigation that I know of. That was the thing that made me look at what was goin' on. Around that same time there was a story on TV about kids and violence or kids and drugs or something. My mother was watching it, and she said, "I'm glad my kids are not involved in that kind of stuff." I was like, "Oh, man." I thought to myself, "Fuck it, I'm gettin' out."

I was like at a crossroads. It was like, "Why is this shit happenin'? Is this all that life has for me?" I was at the stage where I needed some help to get out. I tried to do it myself, but it didn't work. I couldn't get out. I didn't have any money; my potnas were wondering what was goin' on with me; it all felt real funny. Finally, I thought, "Man, fuck this half-ass shit. I'm gonna be in it to win it."

The day I decided that, I went to school with a game plan to go for turf. And that was the very day I met Marshall. The principal or somebody at my school had seen something about the Omega Boys Club on TV and invited them out to talk to the kids. I went to the assembly and there were all these guys on the stage with yellow and purple T-shirts. They looked like some kind of basketball team, and I'm short, so I thought, "Shit, this ain't for me."

Jack Jacqua was the first one to come out and speak, and when he came out we all went, "Oh, shit! It's a white dude!" Jack walked out there and said, "What's up, brothers?" We listened, and he started talkin' some deep shit we never heard before—about how we all got to stick together and how the white man tryin' to keep us down. He said we got to stop killin' ourselves. He was kickin' so much shit, I thought, "Damn, this is some good shit." After Jack, some of the members got up there. That was the first time I ever heard somebody my age talk about college. Jermaine was there, Joe Thomas, some of them.

Marshall was the last one to talk. I'll never forget the first thing he said. He said, "If you knew what I knew, you wouldn't do the shit you're doing." Then he said it again. "If you knew what I knew, you wouldn't do the shit you're doing." He was layin' some deep shit on us. After it was over, I walked up to Marshall and said, "Man, what is it you know that I don't know?"

He said, "Do you really want to know?"

I said, "Yeah."

He said, "No, you don't."

I said, "Yeah, I do."

He said, "You say you want to know, but you don't really want to know."

I said, "I do. I want to know."

When I convinced him that I really wanted to know what he knew, he went off about how black people gave up so much for us over history. He was telling me about all the black people who invented things and did great things and about how black people could be burned if they tried to read. He said, "They did all of that, and *you* don't even *want* to read!" He was talkin' about the struggles of black people over history and how they worked so hard to get to the point where we are today, and we throwin' it all away. That was some deep shit. He got me thinkin' with that shit.

Then he invited me to a meeting of the Omega Boys Club in San Francisco. A parole officer gave me a ride over there. But the whole way goin' there, I was thinkin', "Man, why am I goin' to San Francisco?" I thought for sure those guys in San Francisco would be eyein' me. I said to myself, "If one of those fools looks at me crazy or says somethin' out of pocket, it's goin' to be on." But when I got there, it wasn't like that at all. They were talkin' about real shit—about history and drugs and violence and college and shit like that. I thought, "Damn, this is deep. They sittin' here talkin' this shit, and we standin' around in Oakland bullshittin' on the corner!"

I was interested in what the guys in the club were saying and I wanted to join, but it wasn't that easy to change. I had been programmed into the hustle mode. You can probably tell by my dialect that I'm still deprogramming. At that time, I was going through a lot of things in my personal life and having a hard time with school. It wasn't long after I met Marshall that I got kicked out of high school. Later, I went to another high school in Oakland and got kicked out again. After that, I couldn't get in school. At the same time, I was constantly fighting with myself over my transition. It was tearing me up inside. I was trying to think the right things and do the right things for a change, but all the outside pressures were still there—the money, my potnas, all of it. Even after I joined the boys club, there were many days when I failed, when I went back to the neighborhood and fell in. There were many days I would have probably gone under if Marshall hadn't called.

I spent many, many hours in the backseat of Mr. Marshall's car with Jermaine, going to and from the boys club and talking to Mr. Marshall. From being a teacher, and from being around kids so much, I think he knew I was at the point where I could have gone either way. I listened to what he was telling me, but only when I was ready to hear it. It took him a long time to break it down to me—why I was doin' what I was doin'; all the frustrations I had. I was trying to solve my problems by being a tough guy, but after I did my little thing, the old problems were still there and I had more problems on top of them.

All this time, I was also finding out that once you're in the life, you're never truly out of it. You make lifelong enemies, and any one of them might try to take you out at any time. At the same time that I was trying to start over, my past was trying to catch up with me.

My potnas were rejecting me. My enemies were hunting me down. There were problems in my home between me and my father. Stress was hitting me from all sides. I finally decided the only thing I could do was get out of Dodge.

I had been going to GED school—the teacher somehow bypassed a long-ass waiting list and let me in because I had been going to the class anyway, just sitting there listening—but I dropped out of it and tried to join the army. Then I was told I had to have a high school degree to get the kind of job I wanted in the army, so I went ahead took the GED (General Educational Development) test. I couldn't believe I passed it. When that happened, I thought I was all clear for assignment in satellite repair, but when the army recruiter was interviewing me, he asked if I had ever used drugs. I said that I had sold them but never used them. They rejected me because of that answer. I would have probably been accepted if I hadn't said that, but I was trying to do the right thing. That was hard for me to take: I had stopped doing the wrong thing because that way was a dead end, and when I tried to do the right thing, I ran into a dead end that way, too. It seemed like I had nowhere to turn at that point, but I had the GED and I was still determined to get out of town, so I said, "Fuck it, I'm goin' to college!"

I went on the Omega Boys Club college tour, and I saw a whole different world. The next fall I enrolled at Morris Brown, and it still seemed like a different world. I was sitting in my room reading Franz Kafka one night when it occurred to me that all I ever read back in Oakland was comic books and the sports section. I said to myself, "How the hell did I get here?"

I had a lot of questions like that. Another question I've asked myself a lot of times is how come, out of that whole day at my high school when Mr. Marshall and those guys came and talked about the Omega Boys Club, I was the only one who joined?

Andre Aikins

5

Throwaway Kids

All along, Jack and I presumed that our work with the boys club complemented our full-time roles within the school system. Many people seemed to agree with this assessment, but predictably, it was not unanimous.

"One of the principals at Potrero Hill Middle School came to me once," recalled Mrs. Maxwell, our champion at the Neighborhood House, "and told me that I ought to quit worrying about what was going on at the school and have a word with Jack. He said that Jack talked to the kids like he was their father.

"Well, I knew he did, but I had always thought that was an asset. I never dreamed that talking to kids like a father was a problem. I was shocked beyond words. You would have thought a principal would be delighted to have somebody on his staff that related to the kids that way. The kids and everybody else knew that Jack was extremely committed to his counseling, the same way Joe was committed to academics. Their commitment is the thing they had in common. Otherwise, they were completely different. I called them Mutt and Jeff. Or Whitey and Blacky."

On another occasion, a teacher at the middle school filed a

complaint that Jack and I were using school time and materials for our boys club work—a charge that was patently untrue. We knew that Omega's publicity made us very conspicuous, and consequently we went out of our way to avoid any appearance of wrongdoing or conflict of interest. Thankfully, the school administration backed us when the allegation was carried to the superintendent. Had it not, Jack very conceivably might have moved on—he had been poised to do so for quite a while—after I left Potrero Hill to accept a position as assistant principal at San Francisco's James Lick Middle School.

As it was, Jack's continued presence at Potrero Hill enabled him to maintain strong ties with Mrs. Maxwell and the Potrero Hill Neighborhood House. The Neighborhood House served as our fiscal agent in those years, which meant that Mrs. Maxwell's staff handled our bookkeeping and channeled the funds that came our way. Until we officially declared our own independent nonprofit status, it was necessary that donations and grant money be processed through an agency such as the Neighborhood House. The considerable advantage to us was that we didn't have to busy ourselves with government paperwork, a burden that Mrs. Maxwell shouldered charitably on our behalf. Additionally, by virtue of this arrangement, we were not answerable to the government, United Way, or anybody else.

Jack and I were very comfortable with the accommodations at the Nabe, and so were the kids. It became a home away from home for those who actually *had* a home; if they didn't, they had us and each other. While Jack and I had tried to fashion the boys club into an extended family, the kids themselves went about the same task unwittingly. Their fraternalism held them together not only at the club but in their social lives as well. Young people like Macio and Jermaine and Lamerle and Andre and Philip Bounds and Corey Monroe and Marcel Evans and Zachary Donald and Norflis McCullough and Joe Thomas and Shervon Hunter had so much in common, so much to talk about, that they drew close inevitably, spending much of their free time kickin' it in large groups at the Nabe or one of their houses.

While Mrs. Maxwell and Jack and I were immensely pleased by the sight of black kids from all over the Bay Area congregating peaceably at the Nabe, the folks of Potrero Hill were not so thrilled. Often, the kids were in a boisterous mood as they headed to their cars and the bus stops after our meeting broke up, and the resulting commotion, harmless as it was, sometimes prompted the DeHaro Street neighbors to call the police and complain. On one occasion I stepped outside to find a couple of cops examining registrations and driver's licenses while our kids leaned against their cars spread-eagled. When I informed the officers that the young men were members of the Omega Boys Club on their way home, I was told to back off. The temptation was to lash out, but my role, at that point, became one of calming down the kids. "Let the cops do their thing," I said. "You know how they are."

I felt as though we were walking on eggshells in that mostly white neighborhood, that the slightest impropriety would bring down the wrath of either the residents or the police. I momentarily double-parked one time so that one of our guys could run up and knock on the door of another member who was to accompany us on an errand, and while I waited, a cop pulled up and instructed me to get my car out of the street. So I pulled up about fifteen feet and parked, whereupon the officer walked up and gave me a ticket for not wearing my seat belt. I said, "The only reason I moved was because you told me to." His response was the typical "Are you getting smart with me?" How many times do I have to hear that one?

As a fundraiser to raise scholarship money, we attempted one time to promote a Casino Night and publicized it locally as such. Two days before the event, I got a call from a police officer informing me that casino activities were illegal. So I clipped some advertisements from the *San Francisco Chronicle* about big political fundraisers that were being billed as Casino Nights and took them in to the precinct captain. "Well," he snarled, "none of those are in my precinct. If they were, I'd shut 'em down just like I'm gonna shut down yours if you try to have it." It was just another warm reminder of the special relationship between policemen and black men.

For all of the resistance to us, though, we were not entirely without allies in Potrero Hill. Mrs. Maxwell witnessed a couple of incidents in which neighborhood residents stood up for our guys and helped them avoid confrontations with less sympathetic local people. "Leave those kids alone," they would shout. "Those are the Omegas!"

For the most part, the community distractions were relatively insignificant—they were certainly no greater than we would have encountered most anywhere else—and were overridden by the hospitality we enjoyed at the Nabe. If anything, it would have been easy to become *too* comfortable on Potrero Hill, and that was part of the reason why Jack and I felt it important to extend our reach. We had done that to an extent by setting up the satellite study halls, but we sensed that we were still lacking contact with many of the neediest, most desperate young people in the Bay Area. We believed strongly that the next step was carrying our message to the kids being held at the Youth Guidance Center and other juvenile corrections facilities.

In addition to the counseling possibilities at the juvenile institutions, we were motivated by the fact that many of our members had friends in lockup with whom they wished to visit and share their new knowledge. Prior to that point, however, only family members had been allowed to enter facilities such as YGC, where we concentrated our initial efforts. Since the pools of young people served by Omega and the juvenile justice system overlapped extensively, Jack and I reasoned that it wasn't sensible to prohibit the boys club from visiting some of the kids who needed us most. With that logic working for us, we approached the juvenile justice authorities and requested unprecedented access to the detention centers.

One of the principal officials we had to win over was the county's chief juvenile probation officer at the time, Dennis Sweeney, who regarded the issue as one of confidentiality. Sweeney was reluctant but reasonable, and when Jack asked him, "What are you trying to hide?" he realized he was hard pressed to come up with a satisfactory answer. Jack was able to persuade him that we already knew most of the kids at YGC from the streets, knew that they were being held there, and knew what they were being held for, so what was the difference? Sweeney was also influenced by the fact that when many of the delinquent kids were at home in their neighborhoods, Jack was their most devoted advocate and champion. The chips were stacked in our favor. Preston Worthy, who conducted a volunteer drug education program at YGC and the Log Cabin juvenile facility, also testified effectively in our behalf. The great publicity that Omega had received in the media didn't hurt, either.

When our counseling privileges were granted, they came with the obligatory condition that the juvenile authorities would monitor our sessions for security reasons. But in spite of the fact that our continued presence at YGC was at the mercy of the system—juvenile justice personnel were always on hand to listen in on our meetings—Jack didn't back off in his rhetoric. From day one, he was quick to inform the inmates that their enemy has never been the kid in the next 'hood or the next cell, but the multifaceted establishment—the rich guys who put the drugs in the neighborhoods and the authorities who operate the juvenile justice system, among numerous others. In his soul-stirring John Brown rhetoric, Jack is fond of referring to the penal system as the new-age plantation and those detained there as the new-age slaves. "It's genocide!" he roars as the teenagers, in their blue pajamas, sit motionless at their minidesks, not knowing quite what to make of this raging white man. "The system is trying like hell to break you down! The Man is trying to take you from your families, to tear you apart, just like he did in slavery times. He is trying to wipe you out!"

This, obviously, is more than enough to make the authorities squirm. It is revolutionary oratory, but it is no less than they could have expected out of Jack. Thankfully, they didn't attempt to censor us. That would have been unacceptable to the club and anathema to Jack, who would be the very last to temper his remarks for political considerations. The juvenile officials understood from the outset that while Jack speaks brutally of the system, he is every bit as candid with the kids about their own responsibilities. The message that Jack totes through the doors that lock behind him is not pie-in-the-sky idealism but rugged, scrupulously honest reality.

A lot of community groups and counselors and social workers and the like don't tell the truth. If a kid is messing up, they let it go. I tell the truth. I'm hard on them. I think that's why the judges and the probation officers trust me. I tell the kids they either do the right thing or, hey, basically, "Fuck you. I love you, but I'm gonna try to save your life." I go to funerals all the time; I don't need any more of that.

One reason we're successful is that we're tough. This is not bleeding-heartism. It's not stupid liberalism. This is toughness. We're not afraid to tell it the way it is. You go from the heart. I'm always telling young people, "You might not want to hear this, but I'm telling you out of love—you're an asshole. You're acting wrong." That's the way it is, and the young people appreciate the integrity, the honesty of that. I've never been hit by any of them. I've never had a fight while telling any of the worst guys the worst word at the proper time. There's no problem in telling the truth. They might say, "Fuck you," and walk out and stay away for two weeks, but the next time you see them it'll be, "How you doin', man?" "It's cool. I'm fine."

So you gotta tell the truth. You gotta be hard on the kids. You gotta tell 'em what's up. Adults don't do that because either they're scared or they don't know what's up themselves. I'll tell 'em, "Fuck you," but I'll never give up on them, and they know that. The other side of it is, while being tough and giving discipline, you gotta reach out and love 'em. It's part of the whole process of being an extended family. You hug them, you tell them you love 'em. You do both. You mix 'em up, put it

in the blender, and sometimes it comes out good, sometimes not.

Jack Jacqua

Jack's frankness set the tone for our YGC sessions, and on
his cue, club members like Joe Thomas and Macio Dickerson carried forth eloquently in the same spirit. Peer counseling, as presented by the Omega Boys Club, was not taken out of any social
service handbook or drug education manual. It came from the front
lines—often from club members who were in the throes of the
same temptations that ultimately had dressed the audience in baby
blue. The authenticity—that is, the street credentials—of the club
members was not in dispute; many of them were peers of the
inmates in the truest sense.

We soon found that, while effective, this could also be an
uncertain proposition. When Joe Thomas spoke at YGC during his
first summer home from Morris Brown, he was accompanied by an
infrequent club member from a rival neighborhood who had been
feuding with one of Joe's best friends. Joe had reasoned with his
friend to let go of the feud, and he made the same appeal to the
other teenager on the night they spoke together at YGC. The other
kid opened a vein that night, describing the tensions that darkened
his life and telling everybody in the crowded room that he was
ready to "leave all that bullshit behind." The next day he gunned
down Joe's buddy at the Valencia Gardens housing projects.

Because a spirited peer counseling session can take on some
of the qualities of a revival meeting, the young testifiers (the one
who killed Joe's pal being a vivid example) often make professions
of redemption that are easily forgotten on the street. That is why
Jack and Omega keep coming back with the same message week
after week after month after year; the seeds of reformation must be
planted deep and the shoots tended relentlessly. To successfully
counsel and rehabilitate city kids, the bottom line is, you've got to
be there, and be there, and be there.

Owing largely to the selfless efforts of Jack and club members like Joe and Macio, our peer counseling program quickly became an integral and increasingly prominent part of what we did. After gaining a foothold at YGC, we were able to extend our outreach to include Log Cabin and, for a while, San Bruno County Jail (until the administrators there began to fear that we were putting too many ideas into the heads of the inmates). Then, through the auspices of the Neighborhood House and under the supervision of the San Francisco Police Department, we received a grant from the Office of Criminal Justice to expand our presence at YGC. The purpose of the grant, as stated in the official description, was to discourage the buildup of gangs:

> The problem of gang activity associated with drug use, delinquency and violence in the San Francisco area has escalated over the past several years to near epidemic proportions. Recent efforts to cope with this growing problem have failed to produce any far-reaching effects that might prevent the young people from eventually entering the juvenile justice system.
>
> Particular groups seem to be more susceptible to these current problems than others. For example, Black and Samoan youth who are severely affected by high unemployment, family instability, alcoholism and drug abuse appear to be among those most at risk. . . .
>
> Omega will conduct ongoing drug information seminars for member youth, including what services are available for youth that are related to gangs, drugs, and gang-related problems. The OBC will establish referral relationships with the San Francisco Youth Guidance Center in order that YGC may refer designated youth in need of service to the Boys Club. OBC will also provide information to youth incarcerated at the YGC through its youth membership. Information will focus on the hazards, risks and potential outcomes of gang affiliation and drug use.

The working relationship with Criminal Justice meant more to us than the several thousand dollars it gave our staff to work with. It was another step in the very important public validation of the club, evidence that our work was being acknowledged by both the community and the authorities. Additional validation came when Macio and Jermaine and a couple other members spoke before the California legislature's Joint Committee on Organized Crime and Gang Violence, and when I was named to Mayor Agnos's task force on dependent children. Meanwhile, Preston Worthy, whose rueful personal experience as a former drug abuser made him an ace counselor, was making headway at Log Cabin Ranch in much the same manner that Jack reached kids at the Youth Guidance Center.

Through trial, error, and the opportunities that resulted from public awareness, the club was spreading its wings. In this regard, it was apparent that the momentum from the Channel 7 series had been sustained. And like the financial fruitage resulting from the television newscasts, there were monetary repercussions that went along with our growing reputation.

A new level of funding for the boys club was attained when a charitable organization called the Spinsters decided to virtually adopt us as its own. The Spinsters, made up of young unmarried professional women, each year designate a community recipient for their sizable philanthropic contribution. When they first anointed us, the windfall was $46,000. The next year, the Spinsters selected us again—the first time a beneficiary had been named twice—to the tune of another $26,000, and on it continued for four straight years.

Most of this growth and relative prosperity could be tracked back to the Channel 7 series, which in turn underscored in no uncertain terms, (1) how rare it was for inner-city blacks to receive favorable media coverage, and (2) the enormous potential that such coverage carries with it. It's staggering to think of the public good that could be realized if television stations around the country demonstrated the initiative and civic-mindedness that was exercised by KGO-TV in San Francisco.

Channel 7 was not finished with us, either. While reporting the original Omega series, Steve Davis had encountered and taken an interest in Lamerle Johnson. Like everybody who met him, Davis had recognized a spark and a charisma about Lamerle, who was every bit as charming as he was corrupt. Through an Omega scholarship, Lamerle had managed to get accepted into Morris Brown College for the following fall, and in the meantime Davis talked his KGO bosses into hiring Lamerle as a summer intern. He had one principal assignment: to create a series on drug dealing in the Bay Area.

It was a memorable series that aired in the fall of 1989. Lamerle interviewed dealers, counselors, cops, and friends from the Omega Boys Club. The star, though, was Lamerle himself, who impressed all who watched as earnest, capable, and camera-friendly. The anchorpeople gushed over him, remarking that college was certain to bring his obvious talents to the surface.

I was encouraged by Lamerle's progress but knew, at the same time, that ability and opportunity weren't always enough to transform a street kid—and complete transformation was what it would take for someone like Lamerle to turn his life around. Lamerle, who after watching *Menace II Society* commented that somebody must have been following him around for a couple of years with a movie camera, had been a habitual delinquent on the scale of Joe Thomas. Even while attending college, their customs and inner struggles keep guys like that constantly at risk; they are still lying in beds that they made. Although Lamerle was able to convince the Channel 7 people and the public that he had separated himself from the drug world and the lawless lifestyle that goes with it, his partners from the 'hood weren't buying it in the same quantity. They *knew* Lamerle, and knew, also, that in his world the con was part of the game.

Many of the Omega kids ran into the same sort of skepticism from their homeboys and acquaintances. When Jermaine King wore his I DON'T DO DRUGS T-shirt, guys on the street would say, "I don't care what your shirt says, man—I know you." More than once, dealers walked up to Corey Monroe, a clean, sincere brother from Hunters Point (and a first cousin of O. J. Simpson, who came from the same neighborhood), and said things like, "Hey, man, can I have a shirt like that? I don't do drugs, either. I just sell them."

Back in the neighborhoods, Omegas were called "future kids," a label derived from the comment—that unlike the gangbangers and crack dealers, they had a future—made by Doris Ward, the city supervisor, to the eight club members who participated in our first college tour. Our emphasis on academics was also an object of sarcasm. The gangbangers would desecrate a slogan like "Reading Is Fundamental" by changing it to "Reading Is for the Mental." And when our guys would speak up about citizenship or black history or saving the race, or speak out against guns and drugs, invariably the homies would say, "Don't give me that black shit. Don't give me that Omega shit. And don't go around telling about things that don't need to be told." For trying to change their lives, Omega kids were called punks and sellouts and hypocrites and squares.

Winfred McDowell was another of our boys whose reputation—whose identity—had been invested entirely in the streets. "When I joined the club," said Winfred, "I was called every name in the book by my old potnas. They were saying, 'You don't want to roll with us no more.' I said, 'Hey, I'm still me. I can still fight. I can still cuss. I still like women.'" Winfred stuck with us, but at the same time he felt the need to keep answering his critics, to keep proving himself on the turf. When he showed up at our Christmas party in 1989, he had with him several neighborhood friends who weren't familiar with the boys club or the kids who attended it. He also had with him a gun, just in case. That was when we stopped having Christmas parties.

Mindful of the temptations and challenges that the kids encountered the moment they left the Neighborhood House, we tried to prepare them by rehearsing responses to various entrapments and insults—what to do, for instance, when a gangbanger from another turf sauntered up with the mad-dog look on his face and said, "What's up, nigga?" Those words mean that the gauntlet has been dropped. "What happens after that," I said, "depends on your reaction. Instead of mad-doggin' him back, try putting out your hand. Say, 'How you doin', brother?' Or, 'How you doin', black man?' That's all you got to say. You can diffuse the whole situation by the way you respond, based on your words and your body language. You can say with your reaction that you're not with what they're tryin' to do.

"Brothers in the Nation do it all the time," I told the guys, referring to the buttoned-down, self-respecting Nation of Islam members. "That's why nobody messes with them. That's why guys in the Nation can go anywhere. They make a statement by the way they look, the way they talk, the way they carry themselves. It's not just the tie and the suit. It's the manner. By their manner, they tell people that they answer to a higher power. They deliver a message about themselves and about their race. And nobody calls them a punk. Why is it that they're able to go anywhere in the city even though turf is on? Why can they go places you can't go? What does that tell you? So why don't you try it next time? Just stick out your hand and say, 'How you doin', brother?' "

Often, after receiving that advice, the kids would come back a week or two later and say, "Hey, Mr. Marshall, I tried what you said and it worked." Of course it worked. At the same time, though, we realized that not all the answers could be rehearsed. The city street is an improvisational stage, and the Omega kids, for all their knowledge and good intentions, would have to deal with it spontaneously or else surrender to it and melt back into the asphalt.

That's why Joe Thomas was so important to us. Joe was older than most of our other members, and he had their respect for any number of reasons. For one, he had a longer record than most of them. He had made more money. He had beaten up more cops. He was a good athlete (a basketball and track star). He looked good. And more than anything, Joe could handle himself in any situation. When the cameras and interviewers came around, they regularly wanted Joe, and Joe capably dealt with it all—not only with the cameras and the interviewers but with the fallout.

One guy from the *Chronicle* talked to me for a story and said he was going to put a small picture of me in the paper. I didn't think much of it. The next morning, a little kid comes running up to my house and shows me a giant picture of myself in the *Chronicle* with a story at the bottom of the page. It took up almost the whole page. A little while later I left my house and went out into the projects, and all my friends were saying, "You're a punk, man. You playin' the 'hood out. You goin' square on us, nigga?" All I could say was, "Naw, man, that ain't me. I didn't say any of that. They made that shit up."

I went back to Mr. Marshall and said, "Man, I can't do this. They called me a punk." Mr. Marshall said that next time it happens, tell them, "Don't call me a punk just because I don't want to hang around losers all my life." He said to tell them, "I'm doing this because I want to be somebody. I want to make something out of my life." I did what he said, and it worked. After I went off to college and came back in the summer, those guys who called me a punk were standing around the hallways asking, "Hey, man, how do I get up with the Omega Boys Club? Can I go to college, man? Hey, man, the money's dried up around here, it's played out, I'm ready to get out of this shit myself."

Joe Thomas

Joe Thomas provided a case in point for a compelling theory in which Jack had come to believe after years of working closely with troubled teenagers. It was Jack's observation and enduring opinion that the kids who can be found at one time or another locked up in a juvenile detention center are, generally speaking, more alert and promising than most of their peers. They are there because of excessive, conspicuous street activity, and while some may regard those kids as being among the most depraved characters in a morally decrepit culture, they can also be viewed as the most ambitious, hardest-working players in the game that has become the national pastime of the inner-city neighborhoods. Consequently, when the Omega Boys Club began casting about for young street people with college potential, Jack turned straight to the juvenile justice system.

In the ensuing years, the achievement that has brought the club the most acclaim is our record for sending kids from jail to college. This has often been called a remarkable thing, and although I won't say that it isn't, from our perspective the remarkable aspect of it has much more to do with the kids themselves than with the club. They are remarkable kids. Many of them have gone to college without ever graduating from high school (through the mechanism of the GED), some having dropped out in the ninth grade.

The enormous worth of these kids is accentuated by the contrast it represents with public perception and social stereotyping. Many of the young people we have placed at Tuskegee or Howard or Grambling or local junior colleges are the very ones on whom society had essentially given up—the "throwaway kids." They are the kids on whom the San Francisco Unified School District had given up when they were sent to me at the Guidance Service Center. They are the kids on whom the juvenile justice system had given up when they were sent to Log Cabin or the California Youth Authority or YGC for the umpteenth time. They are the kids whose parents had long before given up. They are the kids whom the inner-city statistics had already written off. They are the kids of whom so many white people were so deathly afraid.

And yet through some unseen inner reserve, many of these kids have fought off the prevailing opinion and refused to give up on themselves—even after being shot several times; even after being arrested over and over; even after being kicked out of school; even after being neglected by their families; even after being told time and again, in countless different ways, that their life didn't and never would amount to anything.

But for his undauntable desire to make it into college, Joe

Thomas would have been a throwaway kid. But for his fierce sense of integrity, Andre Aikins would have been one. But for his faith in God, Macio Dickerson would have been one. But for Jack Jacqua, any number of Omegas would have been tossed aside by society. But for the boys club itself, I believe, Jermaine King almost certainly would have been a throwaway kid.

Even *with* the help of Omega, not to mention friends like Andre, Jermaine might have become another tragic urban statistic if he, like so many others mired in the city neighborhoods, hadn't been so proud and resilient, so damn talented, so absolutely remarkable. First, after being banished from San Francisco schools, he finagled his way into a local alternative school and managed to graduate in two weeks despite the harrowing pressure of a contract out on his life. It was unsafe for him to actually *go* to the school—Sunnydale went there looking for him and had it out with some of his friends—so Jack and I picked up Jermaine's homework every day and delivered it to him. We told him that if he graduated, we would do what we could to get him into college. But even as he willed his way to a high school degree, college life was something Jermaine had a hard time imagining.

I didn't think I was college material. I went on the college tour with the boys club, and it got me thinking about college, but I still had the contract out on me and I thought that even if I received aid and got accepted, I'd never actually make it there in the fall.

It came to the point where I was walking down Third Avenue one day, thinking about all the stuff going on, and I thought if I killed myself, nobody would have to trip anymore. I wouldn't have to worry about me or anybody else getting hurt. So I took my gun out and put it to my head. But before I pulled the trigger I thought, "Naw, I can't do that. I can't be a coward." Marshall and Jack always said that when I felt like that, I needed to open my heart to God, to put myself in His hands. I said, "Lord, put me in Your hands." It's by the grace of God that I'm here.

Jermaine King

It was by the grace of God, also, along with financial support from contributions to the Omega Boys Club, that Jermaine enrolled at Morris Brown in the fall of 1989, majoring in criminal psychology. And when he returned safely home in the summer, he was proud to share his experience and knowledge with young brothers and sisters at the boys club and the juvenile detention centers, where many more unlikely college prospects were in waiting—some who would eventually pursue a higher education, and some who wouldn't.

They were teenagers like Frank Newcombe, Sam Robinson, Zachary Donald—a Sunnydale kid who was uncomfortable with the drug life that engulfed him—and Little Disease, who had been incarcerated for attempted murder of a police officer, a charge that resulted from an automobile duel during which he was serenaded by bullets buzzing past his head. Little Disease managed to earn his GED while at Corcoran State Prison, one of many institutional stopovers during which he had plenty of time to reappraise his life and values. It was that self-driven reevaulation process that brought him to us. Little Disease represented a formidable challenge for the club. Having a natural moral and intellectual curiosity, he had always asked the right questions; he just didn't have much faith in the usual answers.

I'd heard about Just Say No and Operation Push and all that, but those people don't know what it's like in my neighborhood. They don't know what it's like to be awakened by gunshots and see ambulances all over the neighborhood, to get up in the morning and see dead bodies on the street and firemen hosing the blood off the concrete. How are these people who live outside the city somewhere in a nice house gonna tell me to just say no? Show me something, don't just tell me. Show me another alternative.

Mr. Marshall and Jack showed me something different. They brought people in front of me who had changed their lives. They used to be people I knew when I was doin' dirt on the street. Now they were doin' good things, they had good self-esteem, good values, a better love for themselves and their community. I didn't have no love for myself. I didn't know who I was as an individual. All I knew about myself was the negative stuff about me that I saw on TV. When they talk about welfare, they show black. When they talk about homeless, they show black. When I see a police show, it's a black man doing the robbery.

Then I go out in the neighborhood, and it's another black man doing a robbery. When I go to school, all I learn about about black people is that Martin Luther King won a Nobel Peace Prize and we used to pick cotton. I don't think that's enough for an individual to feel positive about himself as a human being. Instead of being taught the right way, I was taught the white way.

If I hate myself, I'm gonna hate somebody who looks like me; but if I love myself and who I am, I love my complexion, I love my nose, I love the texture of my hair. Why should I want to hurt this brother who looks just like me, who looks just like the son or daughter my mother might have? It took me a long time to realize all of that—a long time listening to Jack and Mr. Marshall and reading books and thinking.

After kicking back and thinking about the situation, reading the Bible and the Koran and listening to God in Juvenile Hall and Corcoran and Vacaville and San Quentin, I realized I wasn't goin' nowhere. I needed to find out who I was, because for so long I had worn a mask. I had portrayed the attitude, "Fuck you! Fuck you! I'll take your life just like I eat food! It don't matter to me! I don't give a fuck about you!" I can still walk down the street and scare any of these young cats by just the way I look at them. It's the mask. The mask was permanently there. But it was portraying something I really wasn't.

I'm not no gangster. I'm not no killer. These are images that sublimity fed into me. It was all so much of my life. I saw death in my neighborhood the same way I saw Elmer Fudd on TV trying to blow away Porky Pig with a shotgun. Then Porky Pig gets up and talks to him, like it's no big deal. I see Terminator, he's killing. I see Rambo, he's killing. Goddamn, I guess this is what the world is about when I'm ten years old. How do I know any different? I go to the store for my mother, there's somebody runnin' down the street, hollerin' for his life, with somebody else chasin' him and shooting. I got to get down on the ground so I don't get shot. Then I get up and go buy the bread. I had never seen anything different. They come on TV and say, "Hey, brother, don't do this or don't do that . . ." But that didn't mean nothin' to me. That's not real life. That's not what I see every day.

I first started hearing word of the Omega Boys Club when I was at Log Cabin Ranch when I was fifteen. I wasn't ready at that time to take off my mask and find out who I was. I was just trippin' on gettin' home, sellin' my dope. When it got to the point where I seen my homeboys were not really my homeboys and I might not have no more life out on the street, that was when I was ready to turn my life over to something. I'm not gonna dis the gang because the gang was good to me, but a lot of those cats on the street who are always talkin' about how real they are were snitchin' when the pressure was on. I needed somebody who was gonna be there for me.

Jack was the first brother I met from Omega. The

next time, Mr. Marshall came to see me. Then Preston Worthy. They all said that if I wanted to do something for myself, they could help me. If I didn't want to do anything for myself, there was nothin' they could do. They identified that I was serious about rectifying my I-don't-give-a-fuck attitude. That was my problem. That's why I was doing a lot of the things I was doing—because I didn't care. If I don't care about myself, how could I care about you? I really didn't know what I was angry about. Growing up, I'd always heard to blame white people for this or that, but I really couldn't tell if it was white people doin' shit to me indirectly or my own people doin' shit to me directly. I think I was more mad at myself than anything.

I knew there was gonna come a time when I would have to choose between Omega and my homeboys. When I first got home from prison, the lights would go out at night and I would call my homeboy and he's tellin' me, "Yeah, come on, we got a lick goin' down, we're about to kick somebody's door down and pull about ten keys up out of there." That's money. You get to thinking, shit.

"You gonna throw me a gun?"

"Yeah, I got a gun. I got everything. We got it goin' down right now. All you gotta do is come. It's gonna be around four-five thousand for you."

Then I started really thinkin' about it and I said, "Fuck, nah."

I got these pooh-butts comin' up to me, they want to rob their own homeboys. They're comin' up to me because they know I'm a soldier. That means I put the work in when I was out on the street. So they know their own homeboy's got $45,000 at the house and they're afraid to go by themselves, so they call me. Man, these cats are growin' up with each other and then tryin' to rob the cats they grew up with. It's scandalous out there.

That was the difference with the club. They showed me they cared. They would help me without getting anything in return. When I decided I might want to go to college, they helped me with things like learning how to write again. My spelling was bad and they helped me with that. It's a support system. They gave me books. They were there every step of the way, including helping with my tuition. That itself shows love, which was what I needed.

All my life, I never thought about goin' to college, but I figured that the same way I was a hustler selling drugs and robbing, I could hustle on the legal side. I was so good at hustlin' that I'd quit school when I was fourteen because the time at school was costin' me money. I was making $700 a night after school, and I figured I could make that much more if I didn't waste my time sitting in class all day. When I finally decided to get out, I knew damn well that if I could survive and make money in the game, I could do it the other way. The other way is much easier. All you got to do is wake up, study, learn. I'm willing to get an education, work two or three jobs, do whatever it takes.

Eventually I want to go to a school that specializes in marine biology. I have a love for all kinds of animals.

Little Disease

6

Norris U.

Lamerle Johnson had been at Morris Brown for a little less than a semester when I received a call from the dean of students informing me that, because of Lamerle's fighting, they were going to buy him a bus ticket and send him back to San Francisco. I suggested that since it was so close to the end of the semester, they might as well let him finish and pick up a few credits. They agreed, under the condition that Lamerle not return to Morris Brown.

As disappointed as I was in and for Lamerle, the problem was by no means restricted to him. A year or two after we had so proudly sent off Omega's first class of college students, we began to realize that they were woefully unprepared for the pursuit of higher education. One by one, they started dropping out. Some of them simply weren't good students, and others were so overwhelmed by freedom and temptation that they partied away their scholarships. The only ones who seemed to have the combination of discipline, maturity, and determination required to stick it out were Shervon Hunter, who would eventually become a basketball All-American at Delaware State, and Joe Thomas, who was older than the others and better able to cope with the transitions and temptations.

It was apparent, though, that even Joe was wrestling with an identity crisis. Every time he came home, he sported a different haircut—which may have seemed only cosmetic but actually was a symptom of the changes he was going through. When he arrived at Morris Brown, he wore long gheri curls and a perpetual mean-mug expression that prompted other students to inquire what gang he belonged to. He looked so worldly that he was asked, more than once, if he had been through Vietnam. Joe preserved his street look for a while as a defense against the strange new environment, but gradually relaxed it, haircut by haircut, and became, as he called it, "a schoolboy." He pursued a major in communications, carried a briefcase, and triple-jumped for the track team. But even as he tried to blend into the grassy plazas of the A.U. Center (the Atlanta complex that includes Morris Brown, Morehouse, Clark, and Spelman colleges), he could never quite escape the streets of San Francisco. He was robbed. He rumbled with the football team. He fought with a guy who fought with Jermaine. He found himself perpetually defending California.

So many Omega kids had collected at Morris Brown that they came to be regarded as the heart of a California clique. Club members like Joe and Jermaine and Andre and Philip Bounds—a Hunters Point street veteran who was one of our original eight collegians—thought they had left the turf wars of the Bay Area far behind when they arrived in Atlanta but soon found themselves banding together to ward off verbal and physical assaults from the representatives of other cities and turfs.

> We went down there thinking we didn't have to worry anymore about what's going on at home—the fighting, the shooting. We can be at peace. Then fights started breaking out in the dorms. There were groups from New York City, Jersey, Miami, Washington, D.C. We weren't San Francisco or Oakland because the guys from the East just saw us as being California. So we developed

what we called Cali Love. Every city had its own club. We had a Cali Club. Everybody from California was mixed into it. We were so far away from home, it seemed like all we had was each other.

One time I had on a Houston Oilers hat because it matched the clothes I was wearing, and some guy came up to me and said, "Take off that hat. You're not from Houston." I walked away from him. I was down there trying to get away from turf, so I walked away from it whenever I could. By the second semester, I could listen and find out that the fools from New York were taking a certain class on a certain day, so I'd sign up for the class on a different day. But still, there were a lot of fights. It was just like the turf back home: If somebody on your side got beat up, you had to retaliate with something stronger.

In the Cali Club, we were trying to avoid all of that, so we started doing more traditional college things like panty raids. After a while, we got the whole dorm involved in the things we did. We started playing dominoes together, cards, anything. We tried hard to keep the peace. We kept in constant contact with Mr. Marshall or Jack back at Omega, so we were always being reminded about why we were there and how we were supposed to act.

I don't know if we had chips on our shoulders— maybe we did, being so far from home and not being the preppy types, like so many of the other students seemed to be—but we felt like the underdogs. I remember I had been hyped on going to Morehouse at first, but it intimidated me when I walked into the parking lot and there were all these BMWs. I thought, "I can't compete with this." Morris Brown had more of a sense of realness about it, but I still felt like I was out of my league at first.

That feeling lasted until the second semester,

when I was talking in the hallway one day with a guy from Cleveland named Eddie. I had gotten a call about a friend from high school who had been shot and killed, and I was talking to Eddie about that, trippin' about when I was on the street doing things and almost killed somebody. This guy Eddie looked like Theo Huxtable. He drove a BMW and everything. He was the kind of guy that intimidated me because it seemed like money always meant favoritism, but when we got to talking he started telling me about being a drug dealer. It turned out that was how he got the car. I started looking at people differently after that. I started to branch out. I went home with a friend from South Carolina and another one from Tennessee, and I found out that they weren't much different than I was.

Philip Bounds

It was important that, when they were back in the Bay Area on breaks, college guys like Joe, Philip, Jermaine, and even Lamerle would relive their campus experiences for the younger members. It made college seem real to kids who felt they existed in a world apart from all of that. More to the point, it made college seem attainable to kids whose futures appeared as hopeless as Joe's and Philip's and Jermaine's and Lamerle's had appeared only a year or two before. It also prepared the next class of Omega college students much more specifically than the first two waves had been prepared.

Some of the talks that the college guys delivered to the club in those years—as well as random remarks that other members made spontaneously—were so effective that we began taping our Thursday meetings and transcribing the tapes for a written record. We wanted to be able to refer, for instance, to the message Lamerle had for the club after the eventful completion of his first and only semester at Morris Brown:

"First, I'm gonna tell you all a little something about college," he said, neglecting to mention that he had been kicked out. "It's kind of hard. Like, I got there and had to adapt. First I had to adapt to southern attitudes, and after I adapted to that I had to adapt to northern attitudes, who I thought were going to welcome us with open arms but they didn't. At first you experienced a lot of jealousy and stuff like that and brothers didn't like you because, you know, all they see about California is the stereotypes. You know what I'm sayin'? First of all I didn't swing right. Brother said, 'You don't know how to swing you stay in California.'

"But you know, the best thing that happened to me in college is that I got closer to all my brothers. You know what I'm sayin'? You know, I found out what true love amongst brothers was all about. There was nights, you know what I'm sayin', when we didn't have nuthin' to eat. I swear to God we'd be walkin' around eatin' Spam and stuff like that. You think I'm lyin'? There was nights when you'd be bowin' your head, you'd be lonely, you'd be hungry, you got to study for a test the next day, and you like, 'Damn, I can't make this.' Then somebody like Joe or Jermaine will come in there and talk to you, and something will pop open for you and inspire you all over again. You know what I'm sayin'? I got a love for my brothers all over again. I love all my brothers, ain't no punkish way about it.

"Now I'm gonna tell you about reality. The same problems they got here, they got out there in Atlanta. You know what I'm sayin'? It just slaps you in the face. They got so many projects it ain't even funny. Atlanta University surrounded by projects. They just like a pit of hopelessness. A pit of hell. You know what I'm sayin'? And I know it's my job to pull my brothers up out of there. And then somebody gonna say, 'Well, how you gonna pull your brothers up out of there?' You gotta have determination. You gotta think. But most of all, you got to be willing to give yourself.

"Right here," Lamerle went on, picking up steam, "a lot of people come up here every Thursday real faithful like, come to the meeting and everything, and they doin' the same old same old. And they come up here smilin' in everybody's face like they really changed or somethin'. But to me you need to get in beat. You know what I'm sayin'? It has to look real, 'cause you put the image in my little brother's head that, hey, it's okay to come up here on Thursday and say the good things and go out on Friday and sell the bad things. To me that's bunk. You know what I'm sayin'? And what's worse, brothers out there sellin' dope and stuff, and sisters gettin' impressed with him. What's the deal? Are you impressed by this sucker selling poison to your brother? You know what I'm sayin'?

"You see all these little knuckleheads out there cussin' and sayin' 'nigga' and 'bitch' and all that shit? You think that came from what, overnight? We taught them that. Who you think they learnin' from? They learnin' from us. And if it's goin' to get right, we the only ones to teach it to 'em. A lot of us, we'll be out there in the projects and stuff and we'll be wherever we'll be, and we walk on by little brothers and sisters and you see 'em messin' up. And yet you keep on walkin'. And you ask where the problem is. You the damn problem! You ain't man or woman enough to stop and say, boom, this this this and this. That may not be your job, but that's the problem.

"All the black kids are my kids, and I'm only nineteen. Who gonna love 'em like we gonna love 'em? We don't even love our own people! What's wrong with us? Man, you get some of these clowns out there, you wanna get yours and run. Get yours and be gone. You need to get where you comin' from. You still black. The white man, what he gonna do? I don't care what neighborhood you live in or how intelligent you sound, when that white man come get me, he gonna get your black ass too!"

The force of Lamerle's apparent commitment to the black struggle—to doing the right thing—made it all the more difficult to reconcile the fact that he had proven unfit for college. But by then it was an old story. The heady promise that had seemed so tangible when our first eight kids returned from their college tour had been aborted by cold objective academic reality. Derrick Hogan was out of school. Rudy Draper was out of school. Patrick Cooks was out of school. Philip Bounds wouldn't make it through his second year, either.

It was becoming painfully obvious that if the Omega Boys

Club was serious about operating a college program, we had to be *serious* about it. We had to be thorough. We had to be unflinchingly honest with ourselves. We had to squarely and humbly confront the fact that our mean-street, gangbanging, turf-fighting, high-school-dropout, YGC, GED teenagers, for all of their intelligence and resolve, were simply not ready for a consecrated life of scholarship.

That was the tough truth we were wrestling with when Margaret Norris came to us.

I faintly remembered Margaret from the University of San Francisco. She had been a freshman member of the Black Student Union when I was the former chairman and sixth-year senior being tried for inciting a riot. Since then, she had been raising three sons and teaching English at Westmoor High School in Daly City. We hadn't been in touch since college, but early in 1990 she happened to be attending a conference on crack cocaine, sponsored by Glide Memorial Church, at which I spoke and conducted a workshop. When she realized that I was her old BSU guru, Margaret came up and reintroduced herself. I told her a little about the boys club, and she allowed as how she'd like to come by and see what it was all about. Once she got there, she recognized immediately what she could do to help us—specifically, she wanted to encourage the kids to read and teach them how to write—and she jumped right in.

Coach had joined our ranks in much the same way, rolling up his sleeves, defining his own task, and getting about it. We've had dozens, maybe hundreds of callers and visitors over the years who have offered to serve the club on a volunteer basis, but the club doesn't operate that way. It's not practical for me to spend my time organizing volunteers and creating jobs for them. I suppose I've alienated some people by telling them we can't use their help, but it's important that we remain true to what works for us. The volunteers who have become part of Omega are those who have simply shown up, carved out their own niches, and started contributing whatever it was they had to contribute.

It helped immensely that Ms. Norris—I call her Doc because of her considerable intelligence—was a resourceful, creative teacher and a student of African-American culture as well. In our discussions about the problems our college students were experiencing, Jack and I had agreed that we needed to punch up our academic curriculum without forfeiting our emphasis on black awareness. Unwittingly, we had been prescribing Doc.

Within a very short time, she became our academic director. It happened so quickly, in fact, that some of the senior members resented the intrusion. They might also have been deceived by Ms. Norris's elegance, which at first blush obscured an iron toughness that the club members hadn't expected. When Doc began conducting Tuesday night sessions at the club, Shervon Hunter, for one, didn't try to hide her annoyance. "Who is she, Mr. Marshall?" she asked.

I said, "Ms. Norris is our academic director."

"Well, I don't want to talk to her. I want to talk to you."

"That's too bad."

"Damn, Mr. Marshall, she's too mean. She makes us read all this shit and write all this shit. It didn't used to be that way. What was wrong with the way we were doin' before?"

"What's wrong," I said, "is that too many of you knuckleheads are goin' off to college and having a good ol' time and burning up our scholarship money and comin' home before you even have a chance to learn anything!"

With Doc in place, we discontinued our study-hall program, for which the grant money had expired, and changed our emphasis to academic preparation—both for college and for mainstream life.

She picked up on the fact that most of our young people were deficient in the skills required for a continuing education, particularly those pertaining to writing and research, and to get them on track she diligently schooled the Omega kids on how to take notes, how to organize thoughts, how to synthesize ideas, how to analyze a concept, how to draw from personal experience, how to expand their vocabularies, and how to convert all of that into coherent sentences. She taught them how to communicate as well as how to write. Doc was dragging our kids into corners of academia that they'd never before visited. It was a castor-oil education for many of them, but if they could get it down—if they could survive Ms. Norris—they could make it in college or anywhere else.

To ensure that her students were truly ready for college when they enrolled, Ms. Norris revised and tightened our scholarship requirements. If a kid didn't pass the Norris test, he didn't get any money for school. Even when our members graduated from Norris U. and made it to a college campus, Doc wasn't finished with them. Omegas reported to her by telephone on a regular basis so that she could monitor their progress and, if necessary, help them write papers or study for tests. When she received a worthy term paper from Joe Thomas or Andre Aikins, she would read it to the kids at the Neighborhood House on Tuesday night and say, "This is the type of work you will have to turn out if you want to get into Grambling," or, "This is what it takes to make it at UCLA." Of all the remarkable things that happen at the Omega Boys Club, nothing makes a bigger impression on me than the sight of twenty-five boys (and a few girls) from the 'hood studying with Ms. Norris on a beautiful Tuesday night.

Doc's emphasis on reading and writing, in addition to raising our kids to new levels of scholarship, also offered benefits that far exceeded the solely academic considerations. As they exercised the communication skills promoted in their Tuesday sessions, the students naturally engaged each other in sensitive, firsthand topics concerning a lifestyle that not only impeded their academic growth but severely jeopardized their futures. Margaret's reading list placed a premium on relevance. We weren't studying *Moby Dick*. The kids were reading about themselves—through black history, black literature, and their own heartfelt essays.

As in any good literature class, the material gave rise to passionate discussion. Ms. Norris addressed the subjects of manhood, friendship, death, family, prejudice, education—all of the things on which an adolescent's life can turn. It's said that the way to learn to write is to start with things one is familiar with, and our kids were intimate way beyond their years with the prickliest social issues. They had not *read* about them previously, however, or dealt with them openly. They certainly had not written about them, pondered them, or talked about them in front of thirty other teenagers. Ms. Norris's ambitious, self-defined challenge was to teach academics through self-awareness in a setting where self-awareness was considered an unacceptable and even punishable weakness. She was breaking ground.

It was to our advantage—and hers, and her students'—that Doc was able to practice this technique simultaneously at Westmoor High. One of her students there was a drug dealer named Ron Foxx who had grown up in the wasted streets of Richmond and had never spent a full year out of jail since becoming a teenager. In English class, Ron sat impassively with his baseball cap pulled down over his eyes and his Starter jacket zipped up to his chin. Unable to reach him while lecturing to the class, Margaret pulled a chair up next to his desk and showed him a copy of Richard Wright's *Native Son*. She talked about it a little bit, and when he showed the first signs of responding, she began asking him, without prying, about his life on the streets, using *Native Son* as a basis of comparison. Then she moved on to *The Autobiography of Malcolm X*. Within a couple of weeks, Ron was genuinely interested in what Richard Wright, Malcolm X, and Margaret Norris could teach him. When he started coming to her classroom after school to keep the dialogue going, she asked if he would write down some of his experiences, or maybe some of his thoughts about being a teenager in Richmond. Timidly at first, and then with more confidence, he told her and wrote about the twentysomething times he had been locked up; about grinding on the turf; about running from the cops; about being stabbed; about holding a shotgun to his temple. Somewhere along the way, he made up his mind to become a professional writer.

Doc achieved the same type of results with the tough nuts at the club. Her method worked because, for one, she is a gifted teacher—I've watched her compare *Romeo and Juliet* with *Boyz 'n the Hood* and have the kids thinking of Shakespeare as practically a brother from Fillmore—and also, perhaps more important, because the boys and girls were thirsting for it, just as I had been thirsting for self-knowledge when I started reading Malcolm X a quarter of a century before. In the same way that I learned from Malcolm why I did the things I did and why certain things had happened in my life, the Omega kids, through reading and writing and dialogue, began to intellectually examine their own histories, their own behaviors, their own mentalities. They began to look at things differently, to reevaluate their galaxies. The failures of our first college students had made it clear that this was imperative.

I had felt from the beginning that if we gave the kids knowledge, got them into books, everything else would fall into place. But as the kids who dropped out of college demonstrated, I had underestimated the crushing weight of the baggage they carried with them every day. Being ill equipped for higher education was hardly the whole of it. It startled me that, even with the knowledge Jack and I had given them, some of the Omega kids still gangbanged and sold drugs and shot at each other.

The fellow who really brought home this reality was Martin Jackson, a Potrero Hill resident whom I had met on a visit to San Bruno County Jail. Martin was a little older than most of the Omegas and considerably ahead of the others in historical knowledge. Like Malcolm X and so many other black men who had been confined to prison cells, Martin had taken advantage of his time in jail to become a voracious reader of African-American history and a devoted student of it. It was at his behest, in fact, that we opened the club on Fridays for Knowledge Night, an evening dedicated strictly to books, films, and discussions on black culture. We did that for a year or so, and Martin helped me conduct the sessions. He was a walking bibliophile.

At the same time, though, Martin had his own personal demon to deal with. In his case, it was drugs. For all of his knowledge, he couldn't resist the lifestyle, the prestige, and the action that went along with selling drugs. Martin was a huge disappointment to me, and when he ended up back in prison for parole violations and drug convictions, I began to understand that knowledge itself was not enough; that the lessons of history and culture alone were insufficient to bring about the fundamental penetrating changes that our members so desperately required.

Gradually it became evident to me—and to Jack and Margaret and Coach—that the knowledge we gave them could take hold only as the baggage was stripped away. While offering the kids knowledge, we also had to deal with their anger. We had to deal with their fear. We had to deal with their pain. Because of the family and educational advantages I'd enjoyed as a child, that lesson came to me slowly. It comes slowly, I suppose, to anyone who hasn't been where today's city kid has been.

My own learning process was helped along by the fact that the boys club was like a laboratory wherein I could study the impulses and sociodynamics of young black urban males. Ms. Norris was an accomplice in this endeavor. Exchanging observations, listening to the kids, preparing agendas, Doc and I examined the young people in her class at the same time they were examining themselves. On Tuesday and sometimes Thursday nights, after everybody else had left the Neighborhood House, we would sink into chairs and review everything we had seen and heard in search of patterns, of commonalities. Why was it, for instance, that Joe Thomas and Andre Aikins had changed but Lamerle Johnson and Martin Jackson really hadn't? Which way was Jermaine headed? Why were some of the kids moving forward with their lives while others were stuck in transition?

By analyzing the boys and girls we knew so well, we were able to recognize, among other things, that the ones who had turned their lives around were those who had looked in the mirror and come to grips with what they saw. Almost without exception, they were the ones who had acknowledged their problems and dealt frankly with them. They had spoken publicly about their lifestyles and made it personal, confessing their mistakes and criminality. More than that, though, they had challenged their anger and allowed their pain to show. Joe was the first to do that. Macio and Jermaine and Andre had done it memorably. They had searched inside themselves until they found what it was that made them so angry, what it was that had made them inflict their own pain on everybody else.

More often that not with our kids, the pain had to do with their family situation. Andre Aikins was probably the best example of that. My admiration for Andre is tremendous because he, as much as any kid I've ever worked with, dove headlong into his reformation. He was completely willing to reveal himself, to let his private anxieties come to the surface and admit that it hurt like hell to do so. Andre's anger was about being small and being picked on when he was a kid, but his pain came from his relationship with his father. There was a searing absence of communication in their relationship. Andre was raised in a stronger, more traditional family than most of our kids, but that alone is no guarantee of anything. His father was a go-to-work, come-home, leave-me-alone kind of dad with whom Andre couldn't share his problems and feelings. So 'Dre took out his frustrations—his pain—on other people. Then, when he made the decision to create for himself a separate life outside the home, he became a victim of bad friends and bad advice. In simplistic terms, his pain sent him to the streets and his anger took over from there.

By the time he came to us, Andre had built up quite a reservoir of anger and pain and also fear. He was afraid to give up the gangster life because he thought it meant giving up the respect he had ostensibly earned among his peers. On a more tangible level, he was afraid that if he let down his guard—if he pulled back the hard street veneer—he would be at the mercy of his enemies and even his homeboys. He had a lot to work through, but once he truly made up his mind to start over again, the old Andre didn't have a chance. He was that strong.

By observing how Andre and some of the others fought through the layers of their past, Ms. Norris and I began to identify some of the steps that are indigenous to the rehabilitative process. To start off, it was plain to see that we had to provide the kids with the information they required to recognize the wrong in what they were doing. That is, we had to familiarize them—as obvious as it might seem to anyone outside the 'hood—with the self-destruction and the community destruction that was fundamental to the trafficking of drugs and the abuse of guns and the disdain for education and the disrespect for black people, including themselves. That was the educational part of our job.

We had learned, though, by studying the patterns of their successes and failures, that education was not practical for our gangbangers and criminals until they started to clear out their internal residues of anger, fear, and pain. They had to deal with their rage. They had to expose their deepest psychological sores. They had to exorcise their demons in the manner that Martin Jackson had failed to do.

We found that the ones who were able to do this did it mostly by talking. Writing helped. Writing organized their thoughts and recorded them, but talking made the process cathartic. The kids who bogged down in the process were those who couldn't negotiate this step. It was a painful exercise for them, and risky as well. The young homies had to not only expose their intestines but pass them around to be appraised and analyzed by their peers.

Guys like Joe Thomas and Andre Aikins and Macio Dickerson virtually stood naked before us at the Nabe. They hid nothing. As a result, Ms. Norris and Jack and Coach and I were able to custom-clothe them with an entire wardrobe of alternative behaviors. Once they confronted their own psychological hangups, they were free to absorb and implement the new information they needed to counteract the misinformation they had been living by.

That misinformation, in their cases and virtually all others, took the form of what the homies call rules for survival, which in fact are behaviors that make survival highly unlikely. The so-called rules for survival really amount to so many self-imposed gottas:

> *Gotta handle my business.*
> *Gotta do what I gotta do.*
> *Gotta get my money on.*
> *Gotta be down for my set.*
> *Gotta be down for my 'hood.*

Gotta get my respect.
Gotta pack a gun to watch my back.
Gotta pack a gun to watch my homie's back.
Gotta be with my potna, right or wrong.

I can't tell you how many times we've heard all of those things, and heard them declared with passion. Our challenge was to refute them with the same passion and much sounder logic. No matter how sincere they were about wanting to change their behavior, if the young brothers and sisters were going to make it to the finish line, they had to discover—we had to provide them with—new ways of doing things that removed them from the perils inherent in their lifestyles. They had to adopt new rules for living to replace their old rules for survival.

Doc and I numbered the new rules, or principles to live by, to four:

1. Life is the most precious thing an individual will ever have;
2. A friend will never lead a friend to danger;
3. Change starts with oneself;
4. Respect comes from within.

The first rule is a basic principle that has been twisted beyond recognition by the savagery of the streets. Life is *not* precious in the death games that the city players play, and death is not the answer that they seem to think it is. They don't understand that you can never kill an enemy; a homie might waste a warrior from the other turf, but there is always a brother or a potna who will rise up in the dead one's place as an enemy with mortal designs of his own.

We focused the next rule on friendship, refashioning the concept as so many of the brothers know it. Their definition of a friend is someone who watches their back or will be there for them when it all comes down. The problem is that their notions of friendship and danger are all jumbled up together. We redefine a friend as someone who will lead a friend *away* from danger, not into it.

Our third principle for living takes on the complicated process of change. Doc and I were enlightened on the dynamics of change through the book, *Assata,* by Assata Shakur, who faced up to it when she realized that her reefer habit was counterproductive to her mission as a revolutionary. "Revolution is about change," she said and then wrote, "and the first place the change begins is in yourself." As far as the homies are concerned, the bottom line is that if they want things to change in their lives, they must first change their lives. Changing themselves might and probably does mean that they have to separate themselves from the clique. They have to understand—and it's hard for them—that it doesn't matter what the other homies are doing. We preach that, when it comes to doing the right thing, a real man or woman stands alone.

The final point of emphasis has to do with the thing that all the homies covet: respect. I have no problem with lusting for respect as long as one is after the proper type of respect—that which, like change, comes from within. It is the materialistic pursuit of respect from other sources that warps the brothers' values. They think that the right clothes and jewelry will bring them respect from others. They think that the right car and a fat roll of bills in their pocket will do it. They think that guns and a rep and making babies will do it. They are constantly chasing respect and are baffled when they accumulate all the trappings and it still remains elusive. They don't understand that they can't *earn* respect, because if they're dependent upon someone else to give it to them, then someone else can also take it away. They don't understand that respect is something they have to give to themselves. If they do that, no one can take it away.

Doc and I figured that if our guys could deal with life, friendship, change, and respect, they could deal with the streets. What we focused on, consequently, was the mindset of each young man and young woman in the club. The things that Omega has tried and essentially abandoned—the ball games, the basketball teams, the parties, the study groups, Big Brothers and Big Sisters—

were chucked because they didn't focus on the mindset and consequently weren't critical to what we were trying to accomplish.

Although I don't underestimate the value of athletics and healthy socializing, our fundamental task at the Omega Boys Club is to get our kids in a healthy *mental* condition. This entails preparation for ACT and SAT tests and college-level academics along with simultaneous preparation for the madness that awaits them the moment they rise up from their long tables, collect their books, and close the Neighborhood House door behind them. Ms. Norris and Jack and Coach and I are not unlike football coaches, building up the mental endurance of the Omega students, conditioning them to deal with the anger, fear, pain, term papers, and street realities that lay ahead.

And like football coaches, we can never be sure what will happen when our guys take the field; when they hit DeHaro Street. The streets don't care what goes on at the Nabe. They don't care how Jermaine is dealing with the anger of not having a real home, or how Andre is coping with the pain of being held at arm's length by his father. Oblivious to all of that, the ball takes some unpredictable bounces on the city street; some damn cruel bounces; some inexplicable twists and turns that can cut off one person's life and tear another's heart out. The streets are ruthless to the point of being insane. This I know from painful experience.

After a Thursday night meeting in the early summer of 1990, a couple of club members from Hunters Point, Corey Monroe and Omar Butler, both of whom were back from college until the fall semester—Corey from Morris Brown, Omar from Tuskegee Institute in Alabama—caught a ride home with some neighborhood friends in a car driven by a known gangbanger named Toriano Brown. As they turned off DeHaro Street, where the Neighborhood House is located, and headed down the steep inclines of Potrero Hill toward the lowlands of Hunters Point, a car packed with teenagers from Sunnydale slipped in behind them. At Third and Palou, the Hunters Point car stopped to let a couple of passengers out, at which point the Sunnydale kids—a group that included an infamous gangbanger named Ernest Hill—got out of their vehicle, walked up to Toriano's, and started firing into it. Corey and Omar were both hit.

I was still at the club, going over strategy with Doc, when they phoned me from the hospital. I burst through the door of the emergency room and somehow (not even their families had been allowed in at that point) wrangled permission to see them. From the desk, I was led through the emergency room and around some corners, where, lying on a couple of gurneys in a small open area, I found my guys covered with hospital robes and a sickening amount of blood.

I can't describe how I felt when I saw them. The anger and the grief were competing inside of me, but I could submit to neither. I had to say something, but what the hell could I say? I was accustomed to speaking to the guys in terms of lessons, but this was not the occasion for a lesson. It wouldn't help to tell Corey and Omar that they had been caught in that famous wrong-place, wrong-time situation. It wouldn't help to tell them to stay out of cars with the Toriano Browns of their acquaintance; they would be able to figure that much out for themselves when a little time had passed and they'd had a chance to think about it. But that wasn't what they were thinking about as they lay on those gurneys with blood all over their arms and faces.

I knew what was going through their minds: They were pissed as hell. Here they were, college students on summer vacation, trying to do the right thing by coming to the club, and they get blasted on their way home. They had nothing to do with turf, and more than that, they *deliberately* had nothing to do with turf. In their eyes, they had earned the right to be safe by turning away from the turf, which had taken all the strength they had, and those goddamned bullets—those goddamned motherfuckers from Sunnydale—had violated all of that. Corey and Omar were happy to be alive, but happiness was not the emotion that consumed them as they looked up at me through the drying blood.

My concern was the form that their anger would take. According to the laws of the street, a shooting such as this would demand an automatic retaliation—especially with a reputation like

Toriano Brown's at stake. If that retaliation came down, there would almost certainly be casualties, and one of them could well be the Omega Boys Club. With Corey and Omar involved, suddenly, in one tragic moment of senselessness, our policy—all that the boys club stood for—was on the line. We had cleared a big hurdle when we managed to keep Bernard Temple's gun in his pocket, but this was the ultimate test. It was as if Omega's manhood had been challenged. Our stop-the-violence talk was cool, and so far the kids had been willing to play along, but this was not the Neighborhood House; this was not a game. The homies would be coming at Corey and Omar from both sides, egging them on for revenge.

"You know, you can't retaliate," I said finally. "It's gonna be hard. It might be the hardest thing you've ever had to do. Your best friends are gonna say you ain't shit if you don't retaliate. They're gonna say you aren't a man if you don't take somebody out for this. And if *you* don't do it, they're gonna wanna do it for you. They're gonna say, 'Man, *somebody's* got to do it.' And they're gonna throw you a gun, and if you don't take it, they're gonna look at you like you're nobody, and they're gonna get in the car without you, and they're gonna drive off lookin' for Sunnydale. But you can't let that happen. You got to call it off. You got to make sure there is no retaliation."

I'll never forget the look on Corey's face when I said that, God bless him. He was staring straight up at the ceiling the whole time I was talking, and when I was finished, he waited, as if to make sure I really *was* finished, and then he turned to me and he said, "Nah, Mr. Marshall, we ain't thinkin' about that. I just want to get the hell out of here. I just want to go back to Atlanta, and when I get there, I'm never coming back to San Francisco again. Fuck this place."

He stuck to his word, too, except for the part about never coming back to San Francisco, for which I'm eternally grateful. After regaining his strength, Corey became a central figure at the boys club, a trusted volunteer and one of our best spokesmen. Omar also held to the bargain, although we didn't hear as much

135

from him as we did Corey. I still see Corey on a regular basis, and every time, I think of him lying on that gurney. He still carries a bullet in his hand; the doctors would have had to sever a nerve to get it out.

When Corey assured me there would be no retaliation, I wishfully thought that perhaps the moment had passed. But it's never that clean and simple on the streets. The same night Corey and Omar were hit, a pregnant girl named Muffin was randomly shot and killed while standing alongside Third Street. The Sunnydale homies had just kept rolling after shooting up Toriano's car, and they got her, too. Ernest Hill was later convicted of shooting all three.

What happened to Corey and Omar and Muffin was naturally a hot topic at subsequent club meetings, which were charged with turf warriors from both sides, including, unbeknownst to me at first, Ernest Hill's brother. He was not a regular at the club and came to my attention only because he was grumbling and generally disrupting me as I spoke emotionally about the events that were still fresh and painful in most of our minds. "Now, I'd like for you to identify yourself," I called out to the other Hill in vain, after several interruptions, " 'cause sometimes I can't really tell the good from the bad. At least when the Klan was runnin' around I could tell 'cause they had sheets on. But sometimes I can't tell who's on the side of saving us and who's on the side of destroying us. 'Cause all of you look like me, you see? So maybe you need a mark, or maybe you should be honest and put your sheet on. All you gangbangers in here, all you brothers who want to destroy brothers, put the sheet on so when I drive my kids down the street . . . Maybe if Ernest Hill had put his sheet on, Corey Monroe and Omar Butler might have known he was comin'. And maybe the lady he went and shot later would have known so she could get out of his way. But he didn't have that kind of guts, did he?

"No, he hid behind that black skin and banged two innocent brothers, and then gonna kill a woman who lives in Sunnydale. Oh, yeah. Uh huh, uh huh, nod your heads. What you gonna do about it? He ain't been caught. He ain't been tried. And he's not the only one, 'cause they never get these people that kill our people. Black people get killed all the time, and they never arrest any black people. They'll let you kill each other all day. And you can come up with reasons for doin' it. You can say, 'Well, this happened back then, and he did this, and they said that.' Yeah, you can come up with every reason to justify blowin' your own brains out. So what you gonna do now? You gonna go out now and blow somebody else's brains out? You gonna do the Man's work for him? That what you're gonna do?

"Where's Omar?" Omar had managed to make it up and around a little quicker than Corey, and he had courageously attended a meeting that he knew might be explosive. "Raise your hand, Omar," I said. "Stand up for a minute. I hope you don't mind this. See, I love this brother. But you see, this brother come home from college, come home from Tuskegee Institute, where he's makin' a 2.6 grade average, ain't mad at nobody, and he come to our meeting and left our meeting clean, good. And the sickness almost killed him. Thank you, Omar, for puttin' yourself on the spot.

"Come up with a plan, people!"

At times that night, the dialogue degenerated into turf talk, but mostly the kids—the Omega kids, at least—were defiant about putting an end to the vicious violence, about making it stop right here, right now, with Corey and Omar and Muffin. It was inspiring to hear them—the very turf warriors and potnas and dropouts we had been so concerned about—speak with such knowledge and conviction.

"You know, a lot of times I think back to the day when I used to be involved with the stuff that, you know, I could never get out of," said Jermaine King, who, while not as free of the gangster life as he might have thought, had begun to put his energy and charisma to good use. "Me and Mr. Marshall used to have talks all the time, and he always used to tell me, 'You can. You just gotta want it for yourself.' And so, you know, it was like it came to a point where I really wanted to get out. One day I sat there and said, 'Okay, I'm gonna change.' But I fucked up and took a gun to school and got kicked out. But I said, 'I ain't worried about it,' 'cause I understood finally who I was and where I was in my life.

"So I watched some of my buddies get killed, and I understood that I couldn't do nothin' because I was makin' a change for myself. They had put theyself in that situation at the time, and I couldn't do nothin' about it. If I'd a did somethin' back then, I wouldn't be here today. It hurt not to do nothin'. Believe me, it hurt. But it woulda hurt more people if I'd a did somethin' and died too. Or if I'd a killed somebody. See, does everybody understand, when you read in the Bible that God made man in his own image, do you understand that? Do you all understand that the first man on this planet was a black man? See, understanding is a key to life. Knowledge is a key to life. Trying is also a key. You use all those keys, and you ready to open the lock, turn and open the door. When you open that door, you gonna see a new and better you, and you gonna love you and you gonna love all your brothers.

"You know, this man right here," Jermaine went on, pointing to Ernest Hill's brother, "he said somethin' a little while ago I didn't like. But see, I understand because I came from there. See what I'm sayin'? I ain't puttin' him down or nothin' like that because I understand how he's feelin'. I understand that he is my brother. So now I'm not gonna stand up here and defend doin' somethin' to get back for somethin' else that may or may not be true, because I understand. See what I'm sayin'? It hurts me because, you know, he from Sunnydale and I'm from Hunters Point. But see, you got to understand. That's the key to it all."

I was proud.

7

A Warm Thursday Night

As a hardcore aficionado of jazz, it was difficult for me to appreciate rap. In fact, I hated rap.

I had many heated discussions about rap with my son, Malcolm, who was a disk jockey and rap fanatic. I contended it wasn't music. "Music has melody," I would argue, showing my prejudice for jazz. "Music has harmony. I don't know what this is, but it ain't music." Where was the piano? The trumpet? The saxophone? To me, rap was rhythm and noise. I didn't want to hear it.

Jazz, on the other hand, I could listen to all night and often did. I can't count the times that I've dozed off to Oscar Peterson or Ahmad Jamal or Miles Davis or Thelonius Monk or Herbie Hancock. I was so enamored of jazz that at the age of twenty-seven I bought a piano, set it up in the garage of our little house in Concord (where we lived before moving to Pittsburg) so that I wouldn't disturb the family with my banging, and vowed to become the next Herbie Hancock. When I was in the city, Elaine Silverman let me practice anytime I wanted on the piano at her B&B, which I did many nights until one A.M. I read books, studied chord structures, practiced scales, and finally got serious enough to buy a Fender Rhodes electric keyboard, a synthesizer, and a Peavey amplifier. Then I put together a little pickup band called Two Shoes and played gigs around the Bay Area. We copyrighted about half a dozen songs and for a while I flirted with the notion of dropping everything (mind you, this was before the Omega Boys Club came along) and giving myself to music full time, but ultimately I had to face the fact that I wasn't Herbie Hancock—which only deepened my admiration for jazz and the people who play it well.

I have to concede that my loyalty to jazz might have made me somewhat intolerant of other forms of music (with exceptions made for the likes of Stevie Wonder, whose every song I swallowed whole). With all respect for my son, whose knowledge of rap is encyclopedic, I suspect that the only person alive who could have talked me into actually liking nonmusical music was Macio Dickerson.

Macio could talk anybody into anything. He was very skilled at expressing his thoughts in persuasive words and speeches, and he was never lacking for thoughts to express because he was an uncommonly serious kid—serious about putting in work on the streets when that was what he lived for, and serious about going straight when he decided to turn his life around. Macio even *looked* serious, his penetrating eyes and a Fu Manchu moustache characterizing a fairly humorless face.

Macio was certainly serious about the boys club, and as a result he was the first member to be named a junior director. It's a title we've since done away with, along with many of our early customs and gimmicks. For instance, as much as I admired our guys for wearing the I DON'T DO DRUGS T-shirts, we don't wear them much anymore, one of the reasons being that young people see right through a person who is trying to portray something that he's not—they don't like it at all—and a few of the guys wearing ID shirts were still out there selling dope. In addition to that, the T-shirts might have scared off some of the kids who needed us most. That wasn't the effect we desired at all. In the same way that a church tries to attract sinners, one of our functions was to share

Omega's knowledge with the brothers and sisters who were trapped in the drug life. Our T-shirt message ultimately became a question of exclusivity, which also turned out to be an issue in the practice of naming junior directors.

Concerning the latter, the problem arose when Macio was named a junior director. The sticking point was that Jermaine King thought he should have been selected, too. Calling on his untiring capacity for stirring people up, Jermaine ranted and pouted until he had succeeded in rallying together a sympathetic posse that turned on Jack and momentarily split the club into factions. Jack, of course, thrives on a good argument, and the feud intensified until my partner stormed out of the Neighborhood House one night in a righteous rage. Some of the kids feared that the club had sustained a mortal wound, but Jack and I realized that it was only growing pains.

Macio was usually a calming influence in those situations, the level head, taking things in stride and not hesitating to point out the flaws in the other fellow's logic or to inform him that he was out of line. Nonetheless, he, too, was not above losing his inhibitions and/or his temper from time to time. At a party in Vallejo one night with a group of our kids and some of Philmore Graham's Continentals of Omega, Macio, in his inebriated enthusiasm, began thrusting his fist into the air and shouting, "Omegas! Omegas!" He had assumed that everybody at the party was an Omega, but that wasn't the case. Inevitably, one of the outsiders thought Macio was calling out his turf and took exception. He also took the firearm from his pocket and pointed it at Macio's chin while pushing him up against the wall. On that occasion, it was the other club members who were called upon to calm things down on Macio's behalf.

The Vallejo incident turned out to be one of several in which Macio came away with the feeling that his life had been inexplicably spared. Collectively, those episodes, along with other signs and messages, began to alter his perspective and to make him believe that someone or something was intervening in his life for the purpose of redirecting it. At the time of the party in Vallejo, Macio had attended one semester at Tuskegee Institute and returned home with the realization that he lacked the discipline required for college. When he joined back up with Omega, one of his objectives was to acquire that discipline and use it for whatever means his unseen protector seemed to have in store for him.

Another of his objectives, apparently, was to break down my resistance to rap music. At the club one day, he came to me with a compact disk and said, "Marsh Man, I think you'll like these guys. They're talking about Malcolm X and Martin Luther King." The group was Public Enemy, the album was *It Takes a Nation of Millions to Hold Us Back,* and Macio was right. To my surprise, Public Enemy had something to say that I wanted to hear. They had a message that related to culture, to freedom, to history, to knowledge—to the things black people needed to do in order to change our lot—and I found it riveting. One of my problems (in addition to the absence of instrumentation) with the gangster rap I'd heard so much of from groups like NWA was that it told me things I already knew. I knew how bad life was in the 'hood. I knew how angry the brothers were. The gangster rappers were street reporters, but what I wanted was answers. When Public Enemy gave me answers, I was hooked.

After that, I became a comparative expert on rap; at least I could distinguish the good from the bad, anyway. Public Enemy also became Omega's rapper of choice. When they visited Oakland in 1990 for a Saturday night performance at the Henry J. Kaiser Convention Center, they agreed to put on a benefit for us the night before at a San Francisco club called City Nights. At the benefit, which was attended well and enjoyed enormously, the rappers didn't rap; they just talked to the people and signed autographs. It was a great occasion. Prior to the benefit, we spent the whole day with Chuck D, Flav a Flav, Terminator, and Professor Griff, among others. Professor Griff confirmed my opinion about PE when he told me that they had all worked with kids back in New York and formed the rap group as a vehicle to get their message out to more young people.

Since having my head turned by PE, I've come to regard rap

as another source of material for the club, and one that obviously gets the attention of the kids. Because of its incredible hold on black youth, it's important to be discriminating in our selection of rap, because the wrong sort—the gangster rap—can perpetuate the urban problem by glorifying the type of conduct and mentality that we're trying so hard to reform. Positive, constructive rap, however, can put the right sort of thoughts between a teenager's headphones as he tours through the 'hood. For good or bad, rap is one of the most powerful communicators in the inner city. In retrospect, I think that if my ignorance of rap had continued, I would have found it increasingly difficult to understand the kids I work with.

While I thank Macio for enlightening me about rap and credit him for making it part of Omega, his biggest contribution to the club was made as a speaker. As he articulated his goals and feelings on many memorable Tuesday and Thursday nights, we could all see that he had a calling in that regard. His language was nothing special, but his sincerity came through unmistakably in his voice and his earnest eyes. Macio delivered the unvarnished, tough-love truth in a way that made him our unofficial spokesman. Fortunately —for purposes of this book as well as the good of the club—we captured many of his and other members' speeches on the tapes and transcripts we started making when our original college students came back to the Nabe.

"You know, brothers," Macio told the club one warm Thursday night in 1990, "I hate to say this, but it seems like we ain't doin' nothin'. We not giving back enough, 'cause we know what it is to succeed in a sense. So I'm a little disappointed in myself and in some members of the family, 'cause we ain't doin' enough. Ain't enough brothers goin' to YGC. Ain't enough brothers goin' to Log Cabin. Ain't enough brothers goin' to San Bruno. The thing you gotta ask is how the hell can you live with yourself? Brothers out there shootin' each other, and you ain't doin' a damn thing. And I want you to know that I'm straight from the heart right now. There's a lot of things that I have to get straight with myself as far as the differences I've had with other people. That's something we don't have time for. We don't have time to have differences among one and another.

"And all I want to say to y'all is I love everybody in this room, and I mean it from the heart. I love everybody in this room. And I want to see everybody succeed with me. And I want to see everybody help somebody else succeed. And that's from the heart. I can't get no more truthful than that. I can't say no more than that.

"All you need is dedication. All you need is to get this straight up here and get your heart straight. To be dedicated to one another. That's all that matters. It don't matter if you get up here and speak. It don't matter if you go to college. All that don't matter. It don't mean shit, 'cause you got a lot of crackers, you got a lot of Uncle Toms out there that done been to college and got degrees and ain't doin' a damn thing. It starts in here. I'm serious as hell. This club is the most important thing in San Francisco for blacks. It's real important. And I don't think some of you in here understand how important it is."

When Macio lectured the other members about "giving back" to the community, portraying it as a responsibility that went along with their knowledge, he was saying, in essence, what my grandmother said to me and I said to the Omega kids so many times: "The more you know, the more you owe." It was apparent that the Omega spirit was being passed down, and in that light I often followed Macio's speeches, or Jermaine's or Andre's or Joe Thomas's, with lessons straight from Gue Gue. After Macio's little talk on that June evening, I told the club, once again, "The greatest person in my life is my grandmother.

"My grandmother is eighty-three years old," I said, "and she set me down and told me about everything—stories about my people, about what she couldn't do and what she saw in the South. Lynchings. Lynchings—something you ain't got to deal with, but it's your history. And the only thing that got them out of that was one thing: unity. Black folks took care of black folks. 'Cause they had to. 'Cause the Klan was riding right there in front of them. 'Cause the rope was hanging right there in front of them. And that's the only thing that's going to deliver you out of this dope, out of this gangbanging, and out of all this other mess we're in: unity. That's all; it's that simple. The only thing that's going to deliver you out of this is unity. And if you ever find that out . . .

"That's what they're really afraid of—you're going to find out what you can do if you stick together. They're really afraid that you're going to get hip. 'Cause when you get hip, see, you're going to stop blowing people's brains out. You're going to stop selling dope to each other. You're doing their job for them right now, you know. You've got to get hip and start loving black people instead of hating them. If black people loved black people, there wouldn't be no turf. Let me say that again. If black people loved black people, there wouldn't be no turf. There wouldn't be no Sunnydale, no Fillmore, no HP. There wouldn't be no Crips and there wouldn't be no Bloods if black people loved black people. You wouldn't think of pulling a gun on a black person because he wears a different color of clothes. I still can't get over that. You wouldn't think of shooting a black man or woman that wears a different color if black people loved black people. And you see, that's the thing they taught you to do. They taught you to hate yourself.

"Don't tell me you don't hate yourself. If you didn't hate yourself, you wouldn't call a woman a bitch. You wouldn't say he's too black, she's too light. If black people loved black people, you couldn't invent a reason to sell drugs to each other. You couldn't invent a reason to sell to a pregnant mother. Once you really understand that—once you understand what hate does, and what love can do—then you can put a stop to the turf and the drugs and all the other things that are killing our people. It's a real simple step. Just love black people. It'll fuck up every plan the Man has. And when you love black people instead of hating them, then you can start giving back to the black community instead of taking from it. Because the more you know, the more you owe."

As the kids listened patiently, slouched in hard chairs and sprawled before me on the floor and against the basement walls of the Neighborhood House, I explained to them that knowing and owing operate in a geometric relationship—that satisfying your social debt is a learning experience unto itself, and as a result you owe much more in year six than you did in year one. I also explained to the boys and girls—often—(and Jack and Margaret and Coach did the same) how subtle habitual customs, such as the use of the terms *nigger* (or more commonly, *nigga*) and *bitch* snipe relentlessly at our people's self-image. Self-image was and is a major theme at the Omega Boys Club.

With that in mind, I mentioned to the Thursday crowd that I had spoken at San Bruno the night before, along with a revolutionary sister from the neighborhood named Yasmin Sayeed, and on the way home I had stopped at a little soul food restaurant, where I was approached by a young black woman who said she was hungry and needed fifty cents. When I gave her the fifty cents, she looked at me and asked, "You wanna spend some time together?"

"Now, this is how far gone I am," I said. "I actually thought she wanted to get in the car and talk to me. I really did. I thought she was lonely and needed somebody to talk to. Then she looked at me again and said, 'You wanna spend some time? I need some money.' I said, 'Wait, sister. Hold on.' I said, 'Sister, you're disrespecting yourself. You're somebody's child. You want some money? Here's some money. Take it.' She looked at me like I was crazy because, first, I didn't want to get with her, and also because I took the time to say, 'No, you're better than this. Don't treat yourself like this.'

"I knew that she was just going to go down the street and proposition somebody else, but I had to let her know that she was a better person than that. Somebody has poisoned that woman. Somebody has tainted her to the point that she can only view herself as a whore and view me as somebody who can't see anything but a whore. But that woman ain't no whore by nature. She ain't no bitch. I got a mother; I got five sisters; I got two daughters —ain't none of them bitches. Cassandra there, I know her mother —she ain't no bitch. I know Yolanda's mother—she ain't no bitch. You gonna call your mother a bitch? Somebody, somewhere, is calling that woman a bitch."

On that subject, however, I was not nearly as eloquent as

Yasmin, a teacher, writer, and mother who, in addition to accompanying me and Jack and Worthy to places like San Bruno County Jail, had volunteered to work with some of our kids in math and to share with them the power of her knowledge. Yasmin had become acquainted with the club through her son, who attended our meetings, and when she had something to say—as she did that warm Thursday night—the floor was hers.

"I like to talk about how, in slavery times, they often took the strongest woman and mated her with the biggest man," Yasmin advised the tough young audience at the Nabe. "Nobody said, 'Do you love this man?' Or, 'Would you like to enter into an intimate relationship?' Nobody asked us that. They said, 'You're my property. Get together and make us some strong properties.' Then they took these babies when they got older, and they made the sons mate with the mothers. They made fathers mate with their daughters. These were breeding farms. And we run around today and call each other motherfuckers! Ain't that deep? Ain't it deep? But we say it so much till it lost the disgust in it.

"You call someone a motherfucker, what are you saying? What are you saying about that person's mother? But we say it so often, we forget how wicked and despicable the system of slavery was. Sisters, could you imagine someone telling you to lay with your child and make a baby? And when that baby gets big enough, rip that baby from you and sell it to somebody else? Sometimes they would make these big sons lay with their sisters. You see? And we are only a hundred and twenty-five years up from slavery. It's not that long ago. Brothers and sisters, we still act like slaves.

"The whole idea of not having respect for black women is a carryover from slavery. When we do this, we act out the master's plan. What we say is, 'Thank you, white folks, we know you're right. We're trash. Our women are whores and bitches, and we're motherfuckers.' Y'all see something funny in that? I find it disgusting. I ain't no bitch. I'm somebody's mother. I'm somebody's daughter. I'm somebody's granddaughter. These sisters ain't bitches. These sisters ain't whores. Somebody ask you to toss up for drugs, I say the same thing. I say, 'You put your thing in a meat grinder first.

And if you do that, I'll toss up for drugs.' 'Cause how anybody gonna ask me to do something so foul and disgusting? I'm your sister, brother. I'm your sister! Don't look at me like I'm a walking breathing pussy! It's not who I am! I'm a woman! I'm a black woman and I'm your sister, and you exist because you came from between the legs of some black woman. That's the only reason you're here."

By this time the kids were no longer slumping and slouching but straight-backed and wide-eyed as they glanced around at each other without moving their heads. "We need to stop acting like slaves," Yasmin continued. "And to the sisters, you need to carry yourselves in a certain way. You understand what I'm saying? We can't walk around with our asses hanging out and get upset because somebody wants to touch it! I sent a young woman home from my class today, fine young sister, seventeen years old, very nice kid. She had a skirt on this short, you know. She couldn't have bent over and picked up a pencil. The world—it would have been flappin' in the wind. I said, 'No, girl, you need to take that home.' And she said, 'What's wrong?' I said, 'You forgot the other half of your clothes. You must have been in a rush and left them at home. Go home and get the other half of your clothes.'

"Now if you run around here acting like your legs gonna flap open like window shades, you can't get upset 'cause the brothers wanna sniff it. I don't want no brother to come up to me and act like I'm some *thing*. And I don't want to see young women acting like they believe it. You see, because what happened in slavery, we took that in and we're acting like it's true. Like we all heard this lie so much, and because people treated black women like that's all we're good for—for breeding—we act like it. That's why a sister can walk up to a brother, and he give her fifty cents, and she ready to just flap it open. Somewhere along the line, this sister believed that what they said about her was true. That she was a whore and that's all she was good for. And anything that anybody ever wanted to do for her, she had to repay them sexually.

"This is not just about sisterhood and brotherhood," she said. "It's about building a nation. They didn't wipe us out in slavery. The Knights of the White Chameleons and the Ku Klux Klan didn't wipe us out. But we doin' a pretty good job wiping ourselves out! And they say, 'Oh, yeah, okay. We've hit them with everything we've got and that's not successful; let's hit them with them. Let them do it! They can wipe each other out!' We wipe ourselves out by disrespecting our women. We wipe ourselves out by not taking care of our children.

"If we knew who we were, we wouldn't even think of acting like that. You'd turn to your brother and say, 'I'm a queen. What's your problem? I am a queen, and you better go get yourself together and remember that you are a king and come back here and walk and act like a man and not treat me like I'm trash, not treat me like I'm a whore, because I'm a queen!' You understand? We need to stop acting like slaves. We need to stop acting like it!"

There's no doubt in my mind—and Jack and I have repeatedly hammered on this theme—that the pernicious lack of respect black people have for themselves has been fostered by the lack of respect with which white people have, for ages, treated black people. The problem has forever been the slavemaster's ability, way back when, to convince black people that there was something wrong with them. Conspiring with this serpentlike fable has been the historically unique phenomenon in which black people were systematically cut off from their native culture, then educated to dismiss that culture as heathen and unimportant.

As a whole, African-Americans have perpetually been straining for respect from the larger society—on its terms—all the while failing to see through the institutional bigotry and understand that there was nothing wrong with them in the first place. The moment our people bought the idea, even subconsciously, that there was something wrong with them, the black man's epic quest to validate his worth was under way. The colossal struggle of the race, in turn, manifests itself individually, from cotton field to crack house, from college to Congress, in the visceral plea that is common to every black male in America: "I'm a man; respect me, too."

This of itself is not inherently deadly, but in the desperate effort to declare his manhood—to assert his presence and prove his worth; to be *somebody's* master—the black man, and especially the young black man, has turned fiercely on his own. He has whirled on his black brothers and his black sisters with different but equally destructive forms of violence. His apparent contempt for the color black is something he has in common, ironically, with the embattled redneck and with the white cracker who wears a hooded sheet as a way to feel superior to somebody, anybody. It's human nature, it seems, that every group must have its nigger.

Fortunately, human nature can often be surmounted by knowledge. This is one of the principles upon which the Omega Boys Club is predicated, and if our members don't recognize this, they haven't been paying attention—not to me, to Jack, to Margaret, to Coach, or to each other. Not, for instance, to guys like Jermaine on nights like that warm Thursday in June 1990, when Macio and Yasmin and I preceded him.

"You know, everybody come in here every week to get the knowledge," Jermaine said, "and a lot of us, we stand up here in front of everybody and say we gettin' the knowledge, and we give you the knowledge here, but what the hell you do with it? You know what I'm sayin'? Motherfuckers get tired—excuse my language, I'm sorry for sayin' that word—everybody gets tired, I get tired, of sayin' and hearin' the same shit every damn week. You know what I'm sayin'? Every motherfuckin' week! (See, they got me bad; they still got me bad. I can't hardly talk without usin' words like that.) But every damn week we come up here sayin' the same shit, and what the hell you doin' with it? I mean, if you ain't goin' to go out there and help the next man, at least get off your ass and help yourself. No joke! I know this shit is hard. I mean, there's still places in the city I can't go to. You know what I'm sayin'? I don't go around those places 'cause I'm not gettin' back involved. If I go there, I know I'll get involved again with my potnas. I got what Jack calls a buddy sickness. You know I love my buddies. I love my buddies to death, and that's the problem. If they put theyself in a wrong situation, I ain't gonna die for 'em. That's a hella hard thing to say 'cause there was a day when I woulda died for 'em no matter what, but that's what a buddy sickness is.

"Everybody needs a plan to make it through life. But your number-one plan starts right here with you. 'Cause if you can't start a plan off for yourself, how do you expect somebody else to do it for you? You know what I'm sayin'? We was brought over here with a plan. We been raised, we been taught in this country with a plan. Our death is nothin' but a plan. Down at twenty-five is a plan. Gettin' shot by your brother is a plan. Smokin' crack is a plan. Snortin' coke is a plan. You know what I'm sayin'? So if you want a plan for yourself, you better start it with yourself.

"Me and my boy Lamerle was talkin' the other day and he was sayin' it's a damn shame that black people in this city, black people in this country, don't hardly have nowhere to go but the damn ghetto. And you can't even go over there 'cause another brother gonna shoot you in your back. It's a motherfuckin'—damn, I said it again—it's a damn shame. But once you get some knowledge, once you see something, as Coach told me, make it yours and understand it. Know it inside out, back and forth. Then you can make your decision. Then you will get somewhere in life."

It was a memorable meeting that night, and I was still feeling good about it the next day when word arrived that two guys who had been coming to our meetings, D.C. Stiles and Maurice Paige, had been shot in the back of the head and found dead in a van.

The streets never rest, and they don't permit us the luxury, either. There is never an opportunity for complacency in a situation like Omega's, in a place like the inner city. Every morning, when Jack shows up in the probation offices of the YGC, there is a good chance that he will hear bad news about some kid with whom he has worked long and hard and grown fond of. Every morning, when I open the newspaper, there is a good chance that I will read bad news out of the neighborhoods that house the young men and women of the boys club. The best source of bad news, though, is the kids themselves. Every one of them has a good friend or brother or cousin who has been killed in the neighborhoods. Some of them have a dozen or more.

D.C. Stiles and Maurice Paige were middle-class kids. D.C.'s mother was a juvenile guidance counselor, and with a little assistance from us—the club had helped send D.C. to a local college—she seemed to be succeeding in weaning him off the drug life. D.C., in turn, was trying to help his friend Maurice turn things around for himself. Maurice's mother and relatives were very successful merchants with a chain of stores in the Bay Area, but their relative prosperity didn't lessen the temptations Maurice encountered in the Fillmore district, where he lived. D.C. also lived in Fillmore, and in the end it was their proximity to drugs and bad guys that proved fatal. I really don't know whether D.C. had made any progress in leading Maurice away from drugs, and it might not have mattered in their demise; murderers seldom take rehabilitation into consideration. Maurice and D.C. were killed execution style.

By our next meeting five days later, the kids were well aware of what had happened. Our job was to put it all in perspective for them—to find a moral in the senseless murders of two teenagers.

"I don't have a lot to say," I started off. After having dealt with the same sort of thing time and again, at school and in the club, it still wasn't easy. It will never be easy. "I just want to dedicate . . . I really don't . . . I want to . . . I'm very upset. I'm still sad about D.C. and Maurice being murdered, and actually I wanted to dedicate this meeting to them because, well, despite what they may have been doing, which of course I didn't like, their murders only point up, you know, the same old same old, same old, same old, tired old, years old, day in, day out, century old, aeons old problems that we as black people have.

"So I guess I'm more sorry for D.C.'s mother, whom I've talked to a thousand times on the phone, who did everything certainly that she knew how to do for her son. She was pushin' and pushin' and pushin' for that boy. Bailed him out time and time again even when maybe she shouldn't have. But you know how mothers are. Mothers, you know, they always want to do whatever they can, as long as they can, as hard as they can, in the hope that somehow their sons will turn around and be saved. I almost wish

D.C. could look back from the grave and see his mom. A mother's anguished cry is about the worst thing you can hear. It's a horrible scream. It starts at birth when they scream when the baby is being born, and it goes out in a scream when their son dies, especially in the way that those two boys died.

"The day before he died, D.C. was up here. Many of you know he had eighty hours of community service to do after being in jail, and he was working the community service off. And he was up here at the end, every day. The day before D.C. got shot, he took a bunch of kids from the Neighborhood House to the zoo. Of course, one of those kids was my eleven-year-old daughter, Sydney. And I guess I'm just thankful that this murdering fool didn't pick a crazier time to do this evil deed and somehow in the crossfire pick off my daughter or some innocent bystanders in this whole madness.

"I can't tell you how or why this all happened. Somehow, somewhere, they took Maurice's soul. They took D.C.'s soul. A rock took his soul; he sold out. He didn't sell out like the Uncle Toms sell out, but he sold out. Sold his soul! Sold his heart! I don't know if it was for money or for fame, but he sold himself down the river. I mean, it's like you make a bargain with the devil, and the devil, he's made a bargain with that drug. I know Jack is hard on you, and I'm hard on you, but anytime something like this happens, it just shows that the more things change, the more they stay the same. Like, we may have saved all of you, I don't know, but somebody's gonna die. We don't know when and we don't know who, like we didn't know it would be Maurice and D.C., but we know it's gonna happen.

"So we have to move on now, and the point is, can I count on you? If you're not thinking first and foremost about the liberation of black people, God help us. 'Cause if we trained you just to go off and get your own, it's gonna continue. It's gonna continue. God, I hope I can count on you. We're trying to build a nation, and in nationhood, the number-one thing is the education of its young. We're not trying to build a group of college people to go out and party in the fraternity. And I am a fraternity brother to my heart, you see? And the reason I love the fraternity so much was because it was the first group of young men that I was ever in that wasn't trying to kill each other. 'Cause I'm from South Central Los Angeles, and all the black boys down there was beatin' the hell out of each other. So when I got to college and I found a group that wanted to be together in friendship, I couldn't believe it. But it doesn't stop there. One of the reasons I don't sell my own fraternity now is it doesn't do enough. They're a bunch of guys with big fat cars who don't do anything else for anybody but themselves. And they just let this continue. Because they have the wherewithal to help young men all over the United States, and they're not doing it. I can't count on them, so can I count on you? I don't know.

"D.C., can we count on somebody? Maurice, can we? I don't know. God, I don't know.

"So now, I'm askin' you to do one thing," I said. "And then I'm gonna stop 'cause we got to go on. I only want you to point one finger. I want you to take this finger—you don't have to do it publicly, you can do it in your mind—and I want you to point it at one person: yourself. And I want you to ask yourself, where do you stand? What are your values? Am I doin' the right thing? Don't worry about the person next to you. Don't worry about the club. What am I doin'? How am I livin' my life? Where's my heart? That's how you cure turf in the first place.

"Well, all of this wasn't for you, really. This was for Fanny Stiles, whom I know very well and can't understand how her manchild got ripped off. Never thought it would happen to her. Think about it. Don't applaud. Think about it."

I was eager to turn over the floor that night. It was an occasion that called for peer counseling; the Neighborhood House was packed with kids, and they needed to hear from each other. "Shawn," I called, motioning to a friend of Maurice's named Shawn Richard, a young Fillmore man who had been a basketball star at Balboa High School, where, under the category of business supplies (he was an entrepreneur of the streets), he carried a gun in his backpack. After a stretch in prison, Shawn was trying hard to make the transition from illegitimate to legitimate businessman—soon thereafter he would open up his own "hip-hop sportswear" shop on

San Bruno Avenue—and our job was to help him graduate from parole. "Do you have something to say?"

It wasn't easy for him to talk, either. "I'm not here to give you all no sad shit and talk to you all about all this, 'cause I'm being up front with you all," Shawn said, pacing and gesturing in the rhythmic self-conscious manner that many of our members do.

"I know my language is heavy, but that's why I'm comin' at you all, 'cause we brothers and sisters, and if we don't stick together, who gonna stick with us? It's about touchin' each other's heart. It's like you always hear your mom and your daddy's the only thing you got. Okay, outside of that, this is the Omega family. This is all we got. See what I'm sayin'? Just like we got the HP gang and the Fillmore gang—this is the Omega gang. We gotta run together, spittin' knowledge. You wanna do a drive-by? Do a drive-by spittin' knowledge. You know, like when Jack said go up to Lakeview [a rival turf] and sit out there, and all you all laughed. That shit wasn't funny. That shit wasn't funny. All you all laughed, huh? Go out in Lakeview and sit down. What he was sayin', he meant it. Go out there, sit down and spit fuckin' knowledge. Straight up. Talk to them brothers. You know what I'm sayin'?

"Last night in Fillmore there was a drive-by. You know, my little brother was down there, and my mama came runnin' out of the house. She scared, she cryin', she wonderin' if her son got shot. You know? I mean, just trip off of it. I mean, I know you don't want you all mothers runnin' out of no house wonderin' if one of you all got killed or if they son or daughter got shot. See, that shit hurt . . . like Maurice. I knew Maurice real well. I grew up with Maurice. Maurice was under when he was eighteen years old. I used to take Maurice to the show—you know we grew up together, we hung out. You know, when I found out he was dead, it hurt me, you know.

"I took his mother flowers and she said, 'Shawn, don't give me any flowers. Take them to your mother for what she does for you.' You see? And when she told me that, it hurt. But she accepted the flowers finally because I brought 'em to her. But it hurt for her to say it. You know, this lady looked, when I used to go over there and see her, she lookin' good. Always keep herself up. This lady look now like she ain't slept in three years, three years. Shakin', cleanin' up, bundle of nerves, I mean a trip.

"Just trip and think about it. If one of you all should die, you all wouldn't know how your mom, your parents would go through it. Just think about it, that's all."

8

Street Soldiers

In the fall of 1991, the hottest rap star in the galaxy was Hammer, who by that time had dropped the MC from his name. Being from Oakland, Hammer stayed in touch with the rap world the same way most of the teenagers in the Bay Area did, through radio station KMEL, which was far and away the number-one music station in town. It was KMEL, in fact, that had first put Hammer's songs on the air, and even after he became a pop icon, he invariably dropped off his new material at the studio in order to get airplay and feedback.

When he stopped by that October to see Keith Naftaly, KMEL's program director, Hammer had with him his new album, *Please Hammer, Don't Hurt 'Em.* He also had a little problem. Having attained megasuccess on the pop charts and crossed into the American mainstream as a result, Hammer was fearful that he might have lost some of his credibility on the streets. *Please Hammer* was his attempt to gain back his urban integrity, to reconnect with his roots. The songs on the album were lyrical but more hardhitting than his previous works, and one of them in particular moved Naftaly. It was a cut called "Street Soldiers." When Naftaly commented on its effective portrayal of the pitfalls of the inner city, Hammer swiveled in his chair and said, "You know, that song would be great as a basis for a program on KMEL."

His idea was to add a twist to a popular late-night show on KMEL called *The Love Zone,* which was hosted by a disk jockey named Kevin Nash. *The Love Zone* revolved around callers who dedicated songs to their boyfriends and girlfriends and so on, and Hammer suggested that, once a week or so, instead of phoning in on behalf of their lovers, the listeners could pay tribute to those for whom they were deeply concerned. Moms could call to dedicate songs to their sons who were running in gangs, and girls could send out messages to brothers and boyfriends who had been out with their potnas for days without checking in. The show would still be predicated on music, but it would be driven by reality rather than romance.

Naftaly and the KMEL management bought into the idea and promoted it heavily on the air. The new show would be called *Street Soldiers,* and for the first installment, at least, Hammer would be on hand to assist Kevin Nash from ten to two o'clock on a Friday night in early November. When ten o'clock arrived that Friday night, however, Hammer was nowhere in sight. Nash nervously put on some socially conscious songs, such as "What's Goin' On" by Marvin Gaye, and a few minutes later Hammer called from his cellular phone to inform Naftaly that he was stuck in traffic on the Bay Bridge. At about 10:15, Nash invited the listeners to call in if they wished to dedicate a song to somebody on the streets, and at about 10:16 mayhem descended upon KMEL. Naftaly had to round up virtually everybody in the building to help him answer the phones.

The first call to Nash came from a teenage girl who wanted to know what to do about her twelve-year-old brother on crack. Kevin told her to hold on. The next one was just like it, and the next and the next. Please hold the phone, Kevin said; please hold; please hold. Meanwhile, Naftaly was frantically dialing all the clinics and emergency numbers in the Bay Area, trying to come up with places to which the callers could be referred. He and Nash had gathered mountains of music to be readily available upon request, but not a single referral number.

Hammer heard all of this as he followed bumpers toward the station, and when he finally arrived, he was wise to the situation. Actually, it was right up his alley, affording him the opportunity to help the community and at the same time reestablish his neighborhood credentials. "Streets of San Francisco," he said, "what's goin' on?" As the listeners lamented the brothers and sisters and potnas they had lost, Hammer and Nash played songs like "It's So Hard to Say Goodbye," by Boyz II Men and dedicated them to the fallen. Then Hammer would say, "Streets of Oakland, what's goin' on?" and the cycle would turn over, one poignant tragic story after another, with an occasional chest-thumping, cock-a-doodle, crack-slangin' knucklehead for a change of pace.

By the second week, the station had a long list of referral numbers on hand. It was obvious by then that the show was not going to center on dedications, and that the music would be only peripheral. Hammer, back for another round, capitalized effectively on his experience in posing as a role model, while Nash, who was a sympathetic listener but never purported to be an authority on social problems outside the realm of romance, confined himself pretty much to greeting the callers and referring them to get-straight places such as the Real Alternative Program in the Mission District, Friday Night Live in East Bay, and the Omega Boys Club.

The club had established a relationship with KMEL through the station's annual Summer Jam concert, some of the proceeds of which went to our scholarship fund. We teamed with KMEL on other community projects as well, and I was at the station talking with Naftaly about one of them when he happened to mention the *Street Soldiers* shows. I hadn't heard them and was aware of them only because we had agreed to have our phone number read over the air by Kevin Nash. I was astonished when Naftaly told me about the response that Hammer's shows had elicited. It sounded like an extremely promising phenomenon, the only problem being that Hammer had never intended to make a regular commitment toward the show. He was about to go on tour to promote his new album, and after that there were the usual demands of super-stardom. For him, it was two-and-out.

Determined to somehow perpetuate what Hammer had started, Naftaly and his KMEL cohorts were playing around with the concept of revolving guest hosts. The guest hosts would be authorities in the youth crisis area, some of whom had already been lined up. He mentioned to me that day at the station that I might like to be one of them, but the prospects in that regard did not seem particularly outstanding. I had been on the air a few times to promote our various community service events, and while I was not intimidated by the microphone, I was no Wolfman Jack. I did have some expertise in dealing with street kids, however, and for that reason Naftaly asked me if I would take the show on the Friday after Thanksgiving.

I spent Thanksgiving Day with my family in Los Angeles and caught a flight back to San Francisco on Friday night. Hurrying to the studio and arriving just before ten o'clock, I banged on the front door for somebody to let me in. Nobody came. I checked every entrance. They were all locked, with no security guards in sight. Finally, just before I took out my frustration on the door, Kevin Nash showed up to let me in. I was steaming and let him know about it. "I'm sorry about that," he said calmly, "but are we gonna do this show or not?" He then led me to the fourth floor, I put the headphones over my ears, and off we went. It was a night I'll never forget.

> I had heard Joe speak on the air and at benefits around the city, and although he was very cordial, obviously articulate, and a good communicator, I never saw him stepping to the plate as a host. I saw him as more shy and introverted than not. Boy, was I wrong.
>
> When his voice came over KMEL, something magical happened. To me, it was like either he had been like this all along and I'd missed it, or what he felt inside and the potential magnitude of the show overwhelmed him to such a degree that it brought out a side of him

that even he never knew about. In the radio business, you hear moments on the air now and then that just click, that just make sense, that you know are going to be win-win situations for everybody. When Joe came on as our guest host, it was immediately clear that this was the future of the show. It became clear that the show would be an on-air reflection of what the Omega Boys Club is all about.

Keith Naftaly

I thought the show went well, but to me, except for the size of the audience—I couldn't imagine fifty thousand people out there listening, anyway—it wasn't that much different than a Tuesday night at the Nabe. My responses were the same. I had talked that talk often enough to be confident that, no matter what excuses a young street person could give for bangin' or slangin' or hangin' with his homies, I could dial up an answer. Some of my answers were unrefined at that point, but my ace in the hole was the fact that whatever they said and however much money they had in their pockets, their way wasn't working. "Man," they would moan, "you don't understand. It's the way it is out here. It's the life." "No," I would say, "*you* don't understand. You say it's the life; I say it's the death." Virtually every caller had brothers or cousins or potnas who were dead and brothers or cousins or potnas who were in jail. Over and over, the homies would talk about surviving, and I would show them, again and again, that no matter what they thought, no matter what their potnas told them, they weren't really surviving, and if it seemed that they were, it wouldn't seem that way for long. Somebody has been perpetuating a cruel hoax to call that lifestyle surviving.

After the first Friday night, Kevin told me, "I like the way you talk to them." I liked talking to them and hoped I would get the chance to do it again. Keith Naftaly was quick to assure me that I would. The station was still toying around with various authorities and personalities, however, and through the month of December I shared the show with guys like Chil E.B., a local rapper, and a Samoan community leader named John Nauer. At the end of the year, KMEL announced that beginning in January 1992, *Street Soldiers* would be moving permanently to Monday nights, and I would be its co-host alongside Kevin Nash.

By that time, the format had been established. Kevin kicked off each show with what he called "The Interlude," a half hour of pertinent music and audio clips from urban movies such as *American Me* and *South Central*. Then he would put on some jazz, lower the volume to background level, and announce, "It's time to save some lives."

John Nauer, the Samoan leader, continued to work with me through the early months of *Street Soldiers,* and often I brought along Preston Worthy and one of the Omega kids such as Macio or Joe Collins, a group-home teenager and sometime drug dealer who hung around me so much that the guys called him Little Joe. It was John and Little Joe who were in the studio on the memorable February night when, in the course of one of our first shows, a Samoan patriarch known as Papa Smurf phoned in vowing revenge against the Filipinos for his son's murder.

Prior to that point, we had taken numerous calls from gang members and urban warriors caught in the strangleholds of street violence. Never before, though, had we found ourselves positioned in the line of fire; never before had our show been the turf on which the gauntlet was dropped. But there was no mistaking Chris Faataui. His words were intended for both the Samoan community and the Filipino, and they were crystal clear. "Somebody," declared Papa Smurf, "is going to die."

Faataui's son, Shawn (Papa Smurf called him Shawny-Moe), who at fourteen was a talented musician and already a father, had been gunned down that afternoon, allegedly by a carload of Filipino boys, while waiting for a bus on a quiet street corner in Daly City. When he called *Street Soldiers,* Papa Smurf and his brothers had just returned from the coroner's office and were washing down their grief—and fueling their anger—with a few beers. They were a close, proud family, and the men defended the Faataui name with a guerrilla vigilance.

Between Papa Smurf's threats of retaliation toward the Filipinos, the listeners could easily pick up the anguish in his voice—even when he lapsed into native dialect. John Nauer, who was a cousin of Faataui, attempted to talk down Papa Smurf in his Samoan tongue, and while the words were unfamiliar to the rest of us, we understood implicitly what was being said. After the Samoan sidebars, Papa Smurf returned to English to communicate his intentions to the Filipinos and other Samoans. "They took out one of ours," he said with a frightening firmness, "and we're gonna take one of theirs. You know how I play this game, John. You know how I live my life. Somebody's going down, my man. Somebody's gonna die. I want them to feel this pain that I have."

"How is that going to solve anything?" I asked.

"Let me put it this-a-way," Papa Smurf explained. "It would make them feel what we feel. How's that? The only one I'm going to cause harm to is the son of a bitch who took my son out. I don't know if anybody else wants to retaliate, but I got too much fuckin' heart. My son went down, but I'm not gonna let him go down again."

"I know what it's like to lose somebody," said Joe Collins, who had witnessed more death than any teenager should, "but you—"

"No, you don't know," Faataui interrupted. "You lost a friend. I lost a son. Nobody knows how I feel unless they've lost a son, had a son shot down in cold blood."

Using the same sort of impassioned reason that I had laid on Corey Monroe and Omar Butler when they were on the gurney bleeding from bullet wounds, I tried to appeal to Papa Smurf's sense of logic and to his powerful sense of family, arguing that neither would be served by a turf war. I felt that my words were winning the moment, but it was a hollow triumph, because they didn't seem to be winning over the Faatauis. Papa Smurf and his many brothers remained bent on retaliation.

As we went back and forth in this manner, Margaret Norris

called in on another line to read a poem she had been moved to write while listening to the agony and anger of the Faataui men. The poem paid tribute to Shawny-Moe, and with it Ms. Norris hoped to show the family that he could best be memorialized in ways that had nothing to do with revenge. By showing that she cared deeply about their pain, she hoped, as all of us in the studio hoped, that Papa Smurf would grab one of the many hands held out to lead him off the path of violent self-destructive retaliation. But he wasn't having it. When he finally hung up, Papa Smurf was still vowing to even the score with the Filipinos.

I fully expected Filipinos and Samoans to start going down in the days ahead. As determined as the Faatauis were to kill some Filipinos, however, Doc was just as determined to stop the madness. She lived and taught in Daly City, and on her way to school the next day, she stopped at the home of Papa Smurf, whose address she had finagled from county authorities. There was no answer at the door, but as she returned home from school that afternoon, she tried again. Approaching the house, she carried with her a plant and a copy of her poem. Papa Smurf was not there, but two of his brothers were. They greeted Doc warily and let her in only when she convinced them that she was the woman who had called *Street Soldiers* the night before to read the poem. Later, after she had become good friends with the Faatauis, she learned that the brothers, suspecting at first that she might be an intruding reporter or perhaps an intelligence officer for the other side, had kept their hands on their guns, fully prepared to use them, until Doc proved herself to their satisfaction.

The crisis had not been averted, however. The Faatauis were still looking for the bad guys. They thought they had a lead, in fact, when Ms. Norris asked her ninth-grade class at Westmoor High to write letters to the family, and some of them wrote that they knew who the shooters were. Papa Smurf and a couple of his brothers came to see Doc at the school, perhaps thinking that they could pull out further information on the Filipinos. Standing in the hall outside her classroom, they asked her what she thought they should do. "The police might catch these guys, and they might not," she answered. "If they do, it might take a very long time. But you've got to trust them. You've got to focus on your family and how you all are going to pull through this thing and stay whole without any further damage. The rest of it you should leave to the authorities."

"Well, then," Papa Smurf replied slowly, "I guess that's what we're going to do. We're going to leave it alone and let the law handle it. I'll tell my brothers."

He did more than that. The next Monday, Papa Smurf phoned *Street Soldiers* again and called off the operation. "You Samoans out there," he announced. "I know you're listening to me right now. This is Papa Smurf. I met with the Filipino community last week, and I gave them my word that nothing was gonna go down. *Usos,* brothers and sisters, we are not like that. We can't judge a whole group of people by one man's mistake. If anybody wants to do some shooting, it should be me. That was my son. But it's not like that. By going out there to shoot up everybody else, we'll just make it worse against us. We've got to let the law handle this. You've got to stay out of it. So I'd like to take this opportunity to say for my son and all the *usos* out there: Let it go. Let it be a lesson to you. Do something positive." With that, Papa Smurf slipped into his native language and passed along patriarchal wisdom in more intimate tones. As an elder among the Samoan families of the Bay Area, he had the authority to start a war or end one, and in this case he was ending one before it started. Many Samoans, including some of Papa Smurf's brothers, disagreed with his decision, but because of his stature they honored it nonetheless.

It was a monumental development—not just for the Samoan and Filipino communities but for *Street Soldiers* as well. The program had played a conspicuous role in saving lives, but more than that, it had proven the universality of its message by intervening successfully in a situation that did not involve black people. The Papa Smurf episode established our credibility and broadened our audience in the same stroke. Chris Faataui himself saw to this, calling back a third week to thank all those who had not only helped but had inspired and changed him.

In fourteen remarkable days, Papa Smurf had been transformed from an avenger to a minister of peace. "I want all you kids out there to really listen to what your parents have to say and start paying attention to them," he advised the KMEL audience. "Because when my son left home that morning, I didn't know I would never see him again. You have to understand that your parents love you. And if you love them, listen to them. You shouldn't let your parents go through this, like I am going through it. Time is too precious to be wasted that way. Spend time with your people. I don't know any other pain that hurts worse than this kind of pain. Like that song they play, it's hard to say good-bye. It's real hard to say good-bye."

Soon thereafter, Papa Smurf began joining us on counseling visits to Juvenile Hall and area prisons. He also reconnected with Shawny-Moe's daughter and her mother. In his first call, Faataui had put out a plea for the mother to let him see his granddaughter. "My son's got a daughter out there," he said, "and I hope this lady is listening to me. I want you to bring my granddaughter to let me see her, because as long as I know my son has a daughter out there, my son lives. So don't cut me out, you hear me? I'm waiting for you to come home, baby." The girl's mother, recognizing the unimportance of their differences in light of his love and pain, had complied.

Things remained calm between the Samoans and Filipinos after Papa Smurf plugged up the gathering violence, but his was just one meaty finger in a dike full of gaping holes; it seemed as though new holes were breaking through so often that we might soon run out of fingers. Several months before, a black student named Eddie Braden from Westmoor High—Doc's school—had been fatally shot by Filipinos on his way home from basketball practice. The shooting was in response to a dispute the previous day over an outdoor basketball court, which, in the climate of a turf war, is the sort of silly thing that invariably results in dead teenagers. Unlike the Filipinos and Samoans, the Filipinos and blacks waged an ongoing rivalry around the Daly City area, which meant that murder, as a rule, did not go unrequited. It was a scenario that threatened to blow open at the high school.

The drive-by happened on a Friday, and kids from school called me all weekend telling me that the retaliation would come at school on Monday. A lot of kids had already hidden their guns at school. It was on.

I went to school Monday prepared to spend the day dealing with the problem. The first thing I did was open up my classroom and get as many of the black students in there as I could. Other teachers were holding sessions in the auditorium and in the hallways. A lot of the Filipino parents had kept their kids home, and it was probably a good thing they did, because the situation was tense. One boy decided he was going to go off on somebody, and I had to physically grab him to hold him back.

Around ten o'clock, I could tell that we needed help, so I called Marshall over at McAteer High (where he had been reassigned after leaving James Lick) and told him to get over here as fast as he could. I also called Coach, who had been coming to Westmoor to assist me with a violence-prevention counseling program I had been conducting I called it The Knowledge in my classroom at lunchtime. I told Marshall and Coach that the only people who could handle this thing were us. The administrators were aware of Omega's reputation for stemming violence, and they were receptive to the support the club would provide. Occasionally a staff member would ask me, "Margaret, what do you think we should do?" I said, "Don't worry. We'll handle it."

It was really basic Omega stuff that got us through the day. Because of our knowledge sessions at the school, the kids were in the right frame of mind for what we were telling them. There's no way of knowing how many lives Omega saved that day.

Margaret Norris

By the spring, Doc had joined me as a regular on *Street Soldiers*. She was the perfect complement for the show, a strong serene female voice of reason and knowledge. To me, her capacity for reason and knowledge was the key thing because it meant we could maintain an ongoing dialogue about the issues to which we both devoted so much thought. Our objective in those discussions— sometimes on the air but mostly off—was to keep coming up with more and better answers.

We already knew the questions. "How do I get out the gang?" "How can I survive without my money?" "Who's gonna watch my back if I don't hang with my potnas?" "How do I keep my brother away from the gang?" "How is it my fault if she wants to smoke the crack I sell her?" "What good is school to me?" "What can I do?" "What do you know about it, anyway?"

The kids calling the show or visiting the club didn't always *ask* those questions, but invariably those were the questions we had to answer for them nonetheless. Doc and I knew that every gangbanger, every pusher, every dropout, every mean-mugging homie we dealt with had to somehow cope with the anger, fear, and pain of his experience, and we also knew what the obvious everyday manifestions of those things were—guns and drugs and death and making babies—but we longed for and talked our brains out to come up with a more scientific list, the full comprehensive catalog of symptoms for the at-risk city kid. If we were going to be a hardware store of answers for the street brothers and sisters, it was important that we stock every nut and bolt that they might some-day need.

In the meantime, not having all the perfect and specific answers—and realizing that we never would—we did a lot of listen-ing to the young people who called *Street Soldiers*. We often found that it wasn't even necessary for us to answer or respond with advice; it was enough just to let the caller hang himself with brutal ignorance and twisted self-defeating logic.

One of the most flagrant examples from the first year of the show was a nineteen-year-old gangbanger from Vallejo who belonged to a set known as Romper Room. He telephoned late into a Monday night on which we had read letters sent to us from prison and taken calls from several reformed criminals, all of them testifying poignantly to the senselessness of the game. There had also been some braggadocio coming over the air from the south side of Vallejo, the audacity of which our Romper Room brother could simply not bear.

"Man," he started off, "I can't help laughin' at those fools from the south side that keep callin'. Them guys from the south side are straight simps [simpletons]. They're scared of us."

"Us? What are you talking about—us?" replied Kevin Nash, who routinely established contact with the callers before turning them over to me and the other guests.

"Us. The Crest. Romper Room. See, we run Vallejo. If they come up in our 'hood, they'll get shot. They ain't even a gang, man."

"And what are you guys?" I asked.

"We run Vallejo."

"You run it?"

"Yeah. We run it. They a bunch of simps."

"What do you mean you run it?"

"We did so much shit, we sittin' on so much money right now. I'm probably sittin' on a million."

"A million?"

"Yeah, from so much shit we do."

"So you're runnin' the city of Vallejo. You run the mayor's office, the government . . ."

"Nah. We run the underground shit."

"Oh, I see, you run the underground stuff," I said.

"Yeah. Them simps from the south side shouldn't even be callin'. They ain't even a gang."

"You sayin' they shouldn't even be callin' on the telephone?"

"Yeah. They suckers."

"Why not? They got freedom."

"They shouldn't even be a gang. They should just quit. They a bunch of simps. They simpin'."

"And you're not."

"No, we ain't simpin', we up. We up."

"Who is?"

"Romper Room."

"What is that?"

"You don't know what Romper Room is, fool?"

"I'll tell you," I said, "I have no idea."

"Well, you should be readin' the newspapers, 'cause we up."

"That doesn't mean anything to me."

"I'm makin' more money than you right now."

"That doesn't mean anything to me, either."

"How much you make?"

"It doesn't matter."

"I been in and out of jail. All of us been in and out. It ain't nothin', man. I'm livin' high."

"So what?"

"What do you mean, so what?"

"Just what I said."

"You wouldn't come down to the Crest and say that."

"So you're livin' high. I'm sayin', so what?"

"What do you mean, so what?" he repeated incredulously, assuming that wealth spoke for itself and unable to fathom the concept that I wasn't impressed with his.

"You heard me very clearly. So you're livin' high—so what? So you got a lot of money—so what?"

"I'm just sayin' those guys from the south side better stop sayin' they a gang and shit, callin' in like they hard. Their gang ain't shit. They come to Gateway, they get shot up. I don't want to hear from the south side."

"Now he doesn't have the ability to talk."

"No, he doesn't have the ability to talk."

"Why is that?"

" 'Cause I'm tellin' him to get out of Vallejo."

"So you're his master."

"I'm his master, that's right."

"I thought only God was the master."

"Well, I'm the master."

"So you're God."

"Yes."

"Check this out," Kevin murmured into the microphone.

"I got hoes, I got everything," the kid went on. "I don't need nothin', man."

"Keep goin'," I urged him, relishing every misguided word that he delivered to the listening audience. "I want everybody to hear this. Now you don't need anything."

"I been shot up; I'm still livin', you know."

"And you're not gonna die?"

"Nah, I ain't gonna die. When I die, I die. I don't live my life worryin' about dyin'. Nobody messes with us in Vallejo, you know what I'm sayin'?"

"Nobody messes with you. I understand. You got parents?"

"Yeah. I moved out."

"Do you love 'em? Are they happy with the way you live?"

"Yeah, I love 'em."

"And they're happy with the way you live?"

"They don't know my business."

"Well, why don't you share your business with the parents that you love so much?"

"It ain't none of their business."

"If you're so happy with your life, why don't you share your happiness with your parents?"

"I don't know."

"You got any kids?" I said, banking on the fact that this brother would only get himself in deeper.

"No. I got some bastards out there, you know what I'm sayin'?"

"You want them to grow up like you?"

"Nah."

"Wait a minute. You want it for yourself, but you don't want them to grow up like you."

"Just do me a favor, all right? Next time a south side simp calls, you tell him—"

"No, I'm not gonna do that. I want you to answer my question. You said you have some bastards; I really think they're young children. But do you want them to grow up like you?"

"I don't know. I don't know who they are."

"You got anybody you love at all?"

"I got a girlfriend."

"And you are willing for this girl you love to live in your lifestyle with you?"

"Livin' in the fast lane, you know. She likes it, man, you know what I'm sayin'?"

"You're livin' in the fast lane, you got it all. So all the stories we heard from the people on the phone tonight, the guys from prison, they're just chumps, right?"

"No, they're just like me, you know?"

"They're not just like you, because if they were just like you, they wouldn't be writin' in and callin' in sayin' that you're a fool."

"I ain't a fool to them because they servin' long terms. If they got out in three years, I don't think they'd be sayin' that. They weren't true to the game to begin with if they're gonna cry like that."

"Are they cryin', or are they giving advice because they know more than you?"

" 'Cause they got caught. They don't know what they're talkin' about."

"You're better than them, right?"

"Yeah, I am. I make more money."

"Why do you keep talkin' about money?"

"All my life is money and bitches. That's all I live for. I'm down for money and bitches."

"What's a bitch now?"

"You know what a bitch is."

"Now, wait a minute. Is your mom a woman?"

"My mom's got nothin' to do with this."

"So what is a bitch?"

"A bitch? You know what a bitch is. Don't even be sayin' my mom."

"What is a bitch?"

"It's a female."

"Now, wait a minute. I'm not gonna keep goin' now because by your definition, a bitch is a female. And you know what females are. All women are females."

"It ain't my mom, so I don't give a damn what you say."

"All right," I said finally. "We wanted everybody to hear the whole thing. We wanted everybody to hear you and how you talk. I wanted everybody to hear the logic and the line. And please, I'm gonna tell you, man, we don't want to read about you in the papers."

"You probably have, potna. I can't be stopped. That's how I choose to live. I got another job, too. I take the money I make from my job, and I make more money off of it. I take my paycheck, buy o-z's [ounces], quarter-pounds, and I lock it up, sell it, and make more money."

"What about all the pain you're dealin' to the people?"

"That's not my problem. You see, I don't care about anybody else."

I'd been waiting for him to say that. "That's it," I answered. "You said it. But you know what? We care about you, anyway."

"I don't know what the other life would be like. I can't go that way, you know."

"We're just trying to extend that hand, that lifeline, to keep you alive. No mortal being is above God. Listen to Him."

"All right."

I embrace callers like that because they condense the preposterous logic of the 'hood and lay it bare for all to hear. Underlying my fondness for those dialogues is a fundamental trust that the folks out there listening are able to recognize the fallacies inherent in any defense of bangin' and slangin'; a faith that, given ample opportunity, ignorance will ultimately expose itself and be recognized as the serpent that it is.

One of the street brothers listening among the fifty thousand that particular night was a former all-city football player from Oakland Tech High School named Otis Mims, a big teddy-bear kind of kid whose addiction to crack cocaine had cost him a full ride to the University of Washington. He never even made it to the campus. Despite his success as an athlete, it seemed—as I would later come to know very well—that Otis was somehow fearful of too much success, which accounted in part for his self-destructive behavior. His failures, in turn, would induce long periods of depression that reinforced his dependence on crack.

When he heard the Romper Room call, it had been four years since Otis blew his scholarship. He had been listening to *Street Soldiers* for a few months and had thought about checking in, but for him, picking up the telephone required a lot more courage than leaping off-balance to catch a touchdown pass between a couple of head-hunting defensive backs.

I had this security job, and me and this janitor lady that worked there started listening to *Street Soldiers* on Monday nights. The first time or two I heard the show, I thought it was funny to hear all these guys arguing with Mr. Marshall, actually trying to convince him that selling drugs was the right thing. I had been clean for a few months at that time. My mental capacity was there, but I still couldn't see the light at the end of the tunnel. I'd say I was on the verge of going back to the streets. Listening to those people call made me see how desperately I needed some guidance. Things weren't right, and I knew it. It was like a light went on inside me.

I told the janitor lady the story about my football career. I told her I'd had it all. I told her that right now I should be sitting here with three Rose Bowl rings on my fingers and a college education. That lady was like, "Man, you really messed your life up. I'll tell that story to my kid early in his life. I'll say, 'This will tell you what the street can do for you and do to you.'" She said, "Why don't you call up to that show and talk to them?"

What made me finally call was realizing that Mr. Marshall and Ms. Norris were just trying to talk some sense into those guys, and they were telling the truth. I had no support at the time. My father had been in eight penitentiaries, and my mother was mentally ill. I was raised by my grandparents and the streets, and at that time my grandparents had kicked me out of their house. When I realized what Mr. Marshall and Ms. Norris were doing, I thought, "Damn, I'd give my right arm to have somebody care for me like that."

I was practically in tears the first time I talked to Mr. Marshall on *Street Soldiers*. Even though I had stopped smoking crack, I was still selling it. I told Mr. Marshall I don't want to sell drugs, but I got to do something. I got to make some profit. I guess part of the reason I felt the tears in my eyes was that somebody was actually listening to me, trying to help me. I'd never known anybody to really help inner-city kids before, especially me. I guess Mr. Marshall could tell how much I really needed some help, because he told me to come into his office at the Omega Boys Club the next day and see him.

When I got there, I sat down and told him the whole story. I broke down and cried in front of him at least twice that day. I was hurting. It took me a long time to get to the point where I could talk to somebody about my life, and Mr. Marshall has told me that once I started talking, he couldn't get me to shut up.

I told him about the first time I smoked crack. It was after I had three touchdowns and 187 yards receiving in one game. I did the crack to celebrate. I never thought about it harming me; it was like I was invincible. After a while, I was getting high every day. At first it was mostly marijuana, but I was doing crack at the same time. Sometimes I was so high on the football field that my head would be spinning and my helmet would be buzzing in my ears.

Up until eleventh grade, I was doing some gangbanging, like everybody else. When crack hit the scene, everybody split. After that, it was all about money. It got so that your friends would beat you up or shoot you for a hundred-dollar bill. I saw two guys— potnas, best friends who grew up next to each other— get into a fight over fifty dollars and one of them shot the other in the head in front of everybody.

Crack screwed me all the way up. I practically stopped going to school. I didn't do an ounce of homework my senior year and was pushed through school because of my athletic ability. I hung around with the rough types, and just about every dime I got went to crack. I bought most of it from my cousin. I sold it, too, and was a runner for my cousin, but I smoked my profits. My cousin is in the penitentiary now for attempted murder over some drug nonsense.

After I stopped going to class and my grades went to hell, one of the coaches from Washington told me that he couldn't get me in school. I was amazed. It was like every touchdown I had ever made didn't matter anymore. I thought my life was over. A junior college offered me some scholarship money, but I went to one practice and said no, this isn't for me. For me, junior college seemed like failure.

It was funny—when I was a big football star, the drug dealers used to give me a little extra because they knew I was going to play college ball somewhere. Then, when they realized I wasn't going anywhere, they started to laugh at me. That made me use more.

The summer after I lost my scholarship, my buddy and I started smoking crack every night from about ten to two-thirty in the morning. One time I sent my potna into this rock house because he knew the guy, and he came out with something real small. So I took the crack and walked back into this rock house, and they're sitting there with rifles and machine guns. But I was so high, I wasn't trippin' over that. I complained about what they gave us, and the guy said, "There's nothing I can do for you." I recognized one of the guys in there holding a machine gun, and he said to me, "Otis, why don't you run me down to West Oakland to pick up something?" I figured I could talk to this dude and he would give me some more stuff, so I said okay. We went to this other crack house in West Oakland, one of the most dangerous places in the city, and he said, "You keep the car running. I'm gonna go in here and rob these dudes." I said, "Man, as soon as you're outta this car, I'm gone." He took out a gun and stuck it to the back of my head. I was sitting there frozen, tears coming out of my eyes. I was thinking, damn, he's about to kill me, but I'm not giving up this car. This is my grandfather's car. The dude clicked the gun back. My potna said to me, "Stop bein' a punk, man." I said, "I'm not gonna sit here for no robbery. They gonna recognize this car pulling away from the scene." And here was my potna who I rode with all day telling me I'm a punk. The other dude clicked his gun again, looked at my potna, looked back at me, and said, "Otis, don't ever kick with this guy again, man. He'd let you sell your life, and he doesn't even know me. Now, I'm gonna go in here and just buy these drugs. I'm not gonna do no robbery. I just wanted to see where your heart was." When he got the rock, he gave me what he owed me and told me not to give any to my potna.

Another time I was visiting a girl in East Oakland, the deepest part. I had a knife with me, and at the bus stop two guys approached me. They walked up to me and said, "What's up, man?" So I reached into my pocket and said, "What's up?" There was no doubt they wanted to fight me because one was standing on the left side of me and the other on the right. I told them I was just trying to get home after visiting this girl, and they asked me the girl's name. I lied and said Kim. They said, "There ain't no Kim in this neighborhood." Then they walked across the street. I'm looking for the bus, and when I look back across the street, I see a gun pointing straight at me from about thirty yards. I turned and broke running, and all I heard was *Boom! Boom! Boom!* I was just runnin' and zigzaggin', runnin' and zigzaggin', just like I used to do on the football field. It had been a long time since I ran like that. Finally I saw a guy in his car and said, "Save me! Save me!" He pointed me to his backyard, and I stayed there until he rode me out of the neighborhood. I sat under the seat, and there was a guy in the front with a gun and a guy in the back with a gun. There was only one way out, and on the way out they saw about twenty-five or thirty guys standing around just waiting. The guy who saved me said, "Oh, yeah. Boy, you would have been in trouble." They dropped me off at another bus stop, and I didn't catch my breath until maybe an hour later.

After that, I got kicked out of my grandmother's house and really hit bottom. I stayed with friends and girlfriends and uncles. In actuality, I was homeless. Crack made me steal money from everybody I stayed with. I'd go to see uncles I hadn't seen in ten years and lie to them, say my wallet had been stolen, just to get some money to buy crack.

I ended up moving to San Bernardino with another cousin and runnin' with him. That's when I sold drugs heavy. Our reputation being from Oakland was so strong that nobody would try us. One night I was walking through an alley when this little dude, not more than thirteen or fourteen years old, pulled a chrome .357 Magnum on me and said, "Man, I think you the police." Then he said to his buddy, "Do you think we ought to kill this fool?" His buddy saw the fear in my eyes and said, "Naw, man, don't kill him." I found out they were little Crips.

I got involved with some Crips myself when I was there. We started robbing stores. They'd be going for the cash register, and I'd be going for food. I was going for the necessities. One day all I ate was a package of macaroni, uncooked. At the same time, I smoked maybe two hundred dollars worth of crack every week. I got to bed at four or five in the morning because that stuff wires you and you can't go to sleep. I'd lie there looking at the ceiling. That stuff is crazy. It makes you so you can't talk. You're speechless. I've seen guys sit in a room for an hour, and nobody says a word because the drug is so overwhelming. All you want is more and more and more. If you can't get more, you get depressed.

I'll tell you when I realized how devastating crack can be. My potna knew a guy who was a manager at a Payless store, and he told me the guy was a crack head. He said, "We'll go over here to this guy's place, get high, and get our money back." So we went over there and smoked a base pipe. While we were there, my potna whispered to me, "Watch this. We're gonna get all his money." So my potna said we smoked his last rock. The other guy told my potna that he was out of money, but if my potna would go get some more rock, he'd have something for him when he got back. So my potna went out to his car and said, "Watch this. I'm gonna take that man's gold watch." I went back in the house to wait, and this guy is walking around the room a hundred miles an hour, looking under tables and stuff. All of a sudden he looks at me and says, "Don't mind me." Then he gets down on his hands and knees and starts picking it out of the carpet. With a total stranger in the house. It was scary. He was looking for anything that resembled white. When my potna got back, he had a piece so small you could barely see it. But the guy took off his watch and gave it to my potna. That man was on a mission. And the whole time, he's missing work. It was the first time I actually saw somebody transformed by crack.

I could have easily become like that, the way I was going. I decided I needed to get back to Oakland where I knew people. When I got back, I said to myself that I'm never using that drug again. I laid in my grandmother's house for two weeks to get myself together. I ate well, got my strength up, and then went out looking for a job. I took that security job, and when I was waiting for the bus to go to work, the drug dealers would drive by in their Mustangs and laugh at me because they could remember when I was a crack head. So I got a rent-a-wreck and spent all my money on that. I worked for this car. I was constantly seeing other guys ridin' up in Benzes and Mustangs. So a guy made me an offer. He said he'd pay me $350 to be his dropoff man. All you got to do is drop the dope off at the house. I wasn't making that in two weeks with my security job. Something told me no, don't fool with that, and I didn't, but there were temptations. I felt like I had to somehow make more money.

I was pretty depressed. One time I thought I might as well just end my life. One buddy that I grew up with, who never used drugs in school, was sitting with me in the house, and he said, "You know, Otis, you're one of the stupidest people I've ever known. Man, in high school you had it all. And you let it all go for that drug, man." He said, "You might as well just shoot yourself." I knew it was the truth. I was a fool. I knew people who would give anything they had to go to Washington on a football scholarship. When people heard I was going to Washington, they straightened up. And now they were laughing at me. I was thinking I might as well rot away and die.

This was about the time I called *Street Soldiers* and went in to see Mr. Marshall. I just felt the time had come. I felt the opportunity had come. When I started going to Tuesday night meetings at the boys club, I felt deep down in my heart that these were the people I wanted to be with. There was something spiritual about being there, something uplifting. It was like my body would just elevate. When I'm at the club, I feel like I'm among family.

Everybody in the Omega family has their own special qualities. Mr. Marshall, he's like the father, the business type. Ms. Norris, she's real powerful, a strong black woman who helps you with your studies, like a mother would. Coach is like the grandfather—constant wisdom, sayings that stick with you. Then there's Jack, who is sort of like the family minister, the spiritual presence. You have to respect Jack because he deals with the kids that nobody else wanted to deal with.

I had only gone to one or two meetings before Mr. Marshall called me one day and said, "Do you still wanna play football?" I said, "I know I still got it." I said that even though my weight was up to 255. I was 185 in high school. Mr. Marshall said he could hook me up with the coach at Contra Costa Community College, who figured maybe I could make it as a tight end. They couldn't give me a scholarship, but Omega took care of my tuition and books.

I'm twenty-four now, and a lot of Division I colleges don't want to give you a scholarship when you're that old. But I'd still like to take it to the top in football. If I don't make it in the NFL, I might like to try the Canadian League or maybe Arena football. Football is fun for me. When I'm playing ball, I don't feel the pressure that I used to because I've been through so much. Down by two with five seconds to play? That's okay. Watch this.

If I don't make it anywhere in professional football, that's all right. It won't ruin me this time. My grades are up there, and Omega has prepared me to do other things. Every time I leave an Omega meeting, I feel good, like I've been to church. It's like, okay, I'm ready now.

Otis Mims

One of the things that separated Otis from some of the young people in our radio audience who haven't been able to escape the game or leave crack behind—even though they might desperately want to—was that he followed through immediately after calling *Street Soldiers*. It was significant that he not only came to the club but came *the next day*. I suspect that if Otis hadn't come the next day, he wouldn't have come at all. That's usually the way it works. Every Monday night, we give the club's telephone number to any number of callers and urge them to get in touch with us the next day. They all say they will. Few do. If we don't hear from them the next day, it's a good bet we're not ever going to hear from them again.

For the most part, that's all right. We regard the follow-up as a bonus. We don't expect it and generally don't consider it essential to our mission on *Street Soldiers*. We rely instead on the fact that by the time the brothers and sisters have hung up their telephones on Monday night, they've gotten the message; they've heard the other side of the story; they've spoken to somebody who cares about them and is there to help them. Often, that's enough to make the difference. Other times, however, it isn't. In Otis's case, it most likely would not have been enough because Otis, by his own admission, was crying out for a personal support system, someone to mother-father him. Even after he resumed his education and football career at Tennessee State University two years later (when Otis arrived there, the coach immediately took such a liking to him that he gave him a scholarship without seeing a single minute of film), he still telephoned us practically every day.

It's deeply gratifying, of course, that Otis and others have joined the ranks of Omega through *Street Soldiers*, but at the same time I have ample reason to believe that many callers—there's no telling *how* many—take the knowledge we give them over the airwaves and use it to turn their lives around without our ongoing assistance. For instance, there was the twenty-three-year-old sister whom we all knew as Grambling. She never told us her name. She did tell us, at great length and very sincerely, that she wanted to stop selling drugs but felt she had to sell to support her two children, who were six months and two years old.

"I was listening to what y'all were saying to that other girl about we don't care and stuff," she began in an emotional tone, "and you don't know us enough to be saying that kind of stuff. I do care. But I have to think about myself first. I got kids, and you asking me to come up off the streets. You don't even know me. I'm making in a week what most people working hard every day make in a year. I'm making forty dollars in a half hour, maybe fifteen minutes. And I'm trying to do right with the money. My kids is looking nice. I'm dressing good, I'm putting up money so they can go to a better school and I'm putting up money so I can go to college and own my own business. When I do that, I'm gonna be out of all this, and my kids ain't gonna know it ever existed."

"Those kids don't want money," I told her. "They want their mama."

"I'm gonna be there."

"Oh, I see. You gonna be there. Nothing ever gonna happen to you 'cause you got some kind of magic system. Do you know how many brothers are behind bars for doin' what you're doin'?"

"Of course I know. A couple of them are my cousins."

"Then why do you put yourself in that position with two little babies who need you?"

"What else can I *do*?"

"You can go out like everybody else and get a job."

"I've tried that. I would like to get a job, but all I have is a high school diploma. The only place I can work is McDonald's, and I'm not gonna settle for no minimum wage job. Minimum wage is just like welfare. Those are my only alternatives—McDonald's or welfare, and one's no better than the other. I've been on welfare. Those people will give me $663 a month. That ain't but enough chump change to keep me from being homeless on the street. Then they gonna treat me like a second-, a fourth-, a fifth-rate citizen."

It soon become evident that this was a sister who was doing the wrong thing for the right reasons; that she was trying like hell to provide her children with a better life than the one she knew, but her methods were misdirected by what she perceived as the hopelessness of her situation. Given her intelligence and her good intentions, I felt I could reach her by addressing her conscience.

"Would you rather be on welfare or kill your own people?" I asked. "Does it feel any better to bury someone killed on dope than it does to bury someone killed by the Klan?"

"Look," she replied, obviously firm in the conviction that she was doing the best and only thing she could, "my mother and father were in the game, and it tore our family up. It hurts me to be the same as them. I swear to God it does. But what am I gonna do? I got two children by two different daddies, and neither one of them sorry niggers is taking care of his kid. I'm the one that's got to do for them. Where's the money gonna come from if I don't do this? Here's a perfect example of what I'm talking about. I took my daughter to the hospital because her head was real hot. I sat in that waiting room for I don't know how long, and while I was sitting there, with my daughter's head still on fire, I saw this little white girl come in and go straight upstairs and out the door. I asked the officer, 'Why am I still sitting here?' He said, 'What kind of medical coverage do you have?' 'I don't have any.' He said, 'Then that's why you're sitting.'"

I felt for her predicament but didn't fall for her logic. "Is selling drugs gonna get you medical coverage?"

"No," she answered. "But it's gonna give me the money I

need to get my children the things they need. I'm not gonna get that kind of money at McDonald's, and I'm not gonna get it on welfare. Almost everybody I know, which is almost everybody in Oakland, feels like this. We got women out here getting homeless checks three, four, five times a year. We got women with two or three different Social Security numbers so they can get two or three checks. That's what we got. None of us wants to be living this way. I'm only gonna be doing what I'm doing long enough to make enough money to send myself to college and get my own business so I can take my kids out of here. And they'll never know how it happened."

It was time to get to the bottom line. "What is it exactly that you would do if you had the money?"

"I want to go to Grambling."

"Will you stop selling dope to go to Grambling?"

"Yeah. I would if I had enough money."

"All right," I said. "You're gonna put up or shut up, okay? See, I can't afford to let you keep killing. I'm very emotional about this because it's about my race, my blackness. It's about Malcolm and Martin and Harriet and Sojourner and all the people that have died—died—died just to get us here. So if you want to go to Grambling that bad and if you're willing to give this up, you call me and we'll talk about you going to Grambling."

"All right."

"You call the Omega Boys Club, and we'll see if you're serious. Your children need their mother."

"But I'm there for them."

"Oh, honey. You got to call me so we can get you out of this and you can be their mother for life. Call me tomorrow after four o'clock. Call me, sister. Call me."

She never called. For about two months, nearly everyone connected with *Street Soldiers* was on edge waiting for this young woman to call—including the audience. Listeners would phone the show and ask, "Have you heard from Grambling?" The special aspect of her case was that this was a sister who claimed to know precisely what she wanted and was being handed the opportunity to get it. As the months continued to pass, however, it appeared that the opportunity had gone unclaimed and probably unconsidered.

Nearly a year after we first heard from Grambling, we were conducting an anniversary show and played a tape of her conversation on the air. Minutes later, we received a call from a woman who said she was listening to the show and was taken aback by the tape we had just played. "I said to myself, 'My goodness, what's wrong with this girl? She needs help,' the caller said. "Then all of a sudden, I realized that it was me talking on that tape." She told us that upon hanging up the telephone after calling us the first time, she had immediately dialed her grandmother in Louisiana, who invited her to live with her and go to school down there. She packed her bags and her children and a few months later was a freshman at Grambling (which is located in Louisiana). She was on Christmas vacation visiting family when she recognized herself on the radio and called back.

Living with a grandmother is not a cure-all in every instance, but it's something we frequently recommend for young people—especially young women and girls—who are trapped in their environment. Among others, we recommended it to a seventeen-year-old caller from Stockton who was so deep into the gang life that she didn't see a way out.

"How do I get out?" she pleaded one Monday night on *Street Soldiers*. "I been in the gang three years. I saw my homie shoot my other homie. My own homie was killed right in front of my face . . . I really wanna get out, but I'm scared. They popped my car. After they popped my car, I had to go out and do 'em . . . I've popped quite a few people. I really don't know how many I've killed. I've been in a lot of drive-by shootings where you don't know how many got hurt. I'm a killer; I know it—I just want my baby to be brought up the right way, not the way I was. My mom and dad are both in the pen. They're in for drugs and for killing. When they went to the pen, they left behind eight boys and seven girls.

"How can I get out of it?" she asked again, and then again. "I really want to get out, but if I try to get out, I'm scared of what they might do to me. If they do something to me, who's gonna take care of my baby?" Margaret asked Stockton if there was a grandmother she could live with, and she replied that she had one in Vallejo. So Doc urged her to take the baby and go live with her grandmother and also to call the club the next day so that they could talk privately.

Less than an hour after the girl from Stockton hung up, a call came to the show from an eighteen-year-old former gangster in Oakland who started off by saying that he wanted to respond to Stockton. "I got out of the gang after six and a half years," he said. Hearing that, I assumed he had called to encourage the Stockton sister by testifying firsthand that it is possible to safely extricate oneself from the life. Then, after chatting dispassionately for several minutes about the perils of the game, he dropped the other shoe.

"My baby daughter was shot and killed out on the street corner with my girlfriend," he said softly. "Guys just got out of cars and shot her."

I was stunned. "When did this happen?"

"Today."

"You say your baby was shot today?"

"Yeah. She was a year and a half. I seen a lot of people die before, but it had to happen to her. . . ."

By this time it was obvious that he was choking back tears. "Is your girlfriend all right?" I asked.

"They took her to the hospital."

"Which hospital?"

"I don't know. I just been wanderin' around all day. . . ."

"Is there somebody there with you now?"

"Nah. People keep coming to the door, but I'm not letting 'em in. I'm just sitting here on the floor listening to Street Soldiers."

There are times when we don't have all the answers; nobody does. We didn't need to tell that brother not to go out after revenge, because it was apparent that he was beyond that. We didn't need to tell him that we loved and cared for him (although we said so anyway), because he obviously knew that. We could only tell him that he now had two new members of his family, and we were there for him if he wanted to come by the club and be with somebody who was in his corner. He didn't come. I can only hope that he didn't need to because he found strength within himself and his family.

Stockton never came, either, although in her case we eventually found out why. Four weeks after her first call, she phoned the show again to tell us that she had intended to contact the club the following day, but that morning she was in a shoe store when a girl walked up and shot her four times. She had been in the hospital for the past month. When she got out, she grabbed her baby and, taking Doc's advice, moved into her grandmother's house in Vallejo, where, to my immense satisfaction, she had hooked up with Philmore Graham and the Continentals of Omega.

9

Risk Factors

We've never recruited anybody for the boys club. *Street Soldiers* does that for us now, to some extent, as does our annual Knowledge Conference, a huge event featuring socially conscious rap stars (such as MC Lyte, KRS-One, and Chuck D. of Public Enemy) and other public figures, which we initiated in 1992. Then there is the publicity that comes our way in increasing volume and scope.

On the national scale, the media attention started with a *New Yorker* article in which *Street Soldiers* was featured. To our astonishment, that spawned an almost berserk outbreak of television coverage on the club, including reports by all three major networks, CNN, *MacNeil/Lehrer,* MTV, and even Swedish TV. The good press, in turn, led to awards and appearances that further enhanced our profile. Washington even got into the act. I was honored at the Bush White House for our work fighting drugs and crime in the community and a couple of years later returned to the capital along with Ron Foxx—the sullen high school student and former drug dealer whom Ms. Norris had turned on to the written word through *Native Son*—to speak before Senator Christopher

Dodd's Subcommittee on Children, Youth, and Families. Subsequently there came a long article in the *Los Angeles Times,* appearances on the Oprah Winfrey and Ricki Lake shows, a story in *The New York Times Sunday Magazine,* and plenty more.

I wouldn't indulge the media to such a degree—and in fact, I've turned down more overtures than I've accepted—if I didn't believe it would help kids; not so much *our* kids, who already know what we're about, and not so much San Francisco's, but minority, ghetto, disadvantaged, throwaway kids in cities and towns across the country. Every time I do an interview or allow a television camera into our meetings, it is with the hope that somebody somewhere will get the message. In that regard, my target audience is not only the kids but the adults everywhere who have the power—that is, the *willingness*—to get off their behinds and save the children.

While *Street Soldiers* and the remarkable media exposure in general has brought countless young brothers and sisters into our midst, and that alone is enough to make those things worthwhile, some of the most effective recruiting is done incidentally by the kids themselves. We don't put them up to it; they just do it as their privilege and duty and their way of being true to what they have been taught: The more you know, the more you owe.

A couple of our fellows, for instance, were playing basketball one day with a big-time drug dealer named Reuben Terry when, knowing what they had come to know, they became annoyed by Terry's constant use of the word *nigga.* Terry, in turn, was annoyed by their critique of his language. "Reuben," they asked, "could you just do us a favor and quit saying that word?" He gave them a look that said, "Who the hell are you young punks to tell me what I can and cannot say?" But our guys stuck to their convictions and patiently explained to Reuben what the Omega Boys Club had taught them about the connotations of the word *nigga.* Reuben was unimpressed, but the Omegas said, "Hey, man, we'll make you a deal. If we win the game, you have to come with us and sit in on one of our meetings." It so happened that our guys could shoot it up, and as a consequence we gained an opportunity to enlighten a brother who had handled a million dollars in drug money during the course of an infamous career.

As worldly wise as he was, we were able to teach Reuben things he had never known. He didn't say much at first but sat quietly in the back of the room taking it all in, apparently silenced by the foreignness of the surroundings.

I felt like a hypocrite when I first started coming to the meetings, even though I wasn't talking. No one ever knew this, but I was sitting there with six or seven ounces of dope in my pocket. At the same time, though, my reaction was, wow, I can't believe all this is going on. The word *family* stuck in my mind. That's what it was that really got to me. I had a family, but I never had a family like that. When you walk into that room, you get hit by love from all angles. What you look like doesn't matter. Where you're from doesn't matter. Where you've been and what you've done doesn't matter. You're not judged on all that. I didn't feel like part of the family at first, sitting there with dope in my pocket, but Coach helped me, and I talked a lot to Mr. Marshall. One day I finally opened up.

I grew up in the ghetto, but my parents saved me for a lot of years, up to the time I left home after high school. After that I was getting up every morning and going to work until one day I watched my cousin go outside and come back in the house a couple hours later with more money than I would make busting my butt for two weeks. I asked him how can I be down. We went to Palo Alto together, bought some drugs, and it took off from there.

Before long we moved on to selling weight, working in large quantities. Then we expanded our San Francisco dealings to Oakland, Richmond, Vallejo, all around the Bay Area. We made trips to Arizona and New York, buying and selling. There were five of us. One night in

Oakland, on an exchange on a dead-end street, we were set up by a girl I knew and got robbed of close to a hundred thousand street value in dope. We didn't have any weapons because I'd had some dealings with the girl, but they came with handguns and shotguns. There were two of us there. While my counterpart was up the street looking at the money with one of their guys, another one put a sawed-off shotgun to my head and made me get down on my knees. Then he took the drugs out of the trunk and ran. As they drove past us, he opened fire and put some bullet holes in the car.

Our guys wanted to kill the girl and kill her mother. I was the only one who knew where to find her, but I didn't believe in killing no one's mom. They said they were going to burn her complex down, and they didn't care who was in it. I told them, look, it was my bad, and I'll get your money back. I didn't know what I was going to do. I definitely wanted to find them, and yeah, I wanted to kill them, but I had to find them first and see what happened. It wasn't easy because they were hiding, and after a while my counterparts started getting suspicious. It looked to them like I was involved. I got leery of them. Some things went down that told me I had to keep a closer eye on what was going on. Finally we decided we should all go solo so that we wouldn't end up killing each other.

It worked out pretty good. Every day from six in the morning until three, I had an ordinary construction job. I kept everyone off-guard like that. People would page me throughout the day, and that way I knew what I would have to do at night. My cousin and I developed a twenty-one-man turf consisting of teenagers. We called ourselves NAW, Niggas At Work. All I did was provide them money for firepower. I bought them clothes, shoes, turf shirts, and hats. We had our own colors. We had some rappers in our posse, and they made up some rap songs about us. I bought them some equipment. Nobody ever saw me hanging around on the corner with them, though. I was never with them when they went to other sets shooting and acting up. You might see me riding by, waving, that's all.

Niggas At Work sold dope for about four years. I tell people I was close to being a millionaire. I would say, "Do you know what it feels like to yawn and have a hundred thousand dollars put in your face? Do you know what it feels like to do nothing and have money fall in your lap?" I used to sleep with thousands of dollars lying in the bed with me. I'd just lie there, sleeping in money. Money had to be around me. I couldn't go out of the house without at least a thousand dollars in my pocket.

After a while I started getting sloppy, making bad deals, buying bad drugs, splurging, squandering my money. When I got caught, I had half a kilo and $185,000 in the car with me. I was set up. I was in a K-mart parking lot, and all of a sudden a police van came down the aisle and cut me off, then a bunch of black and whites pulled in front of me and detectives started jumping out of the van. I couldn't believe I got rolled up. I did two years in San Quentin. When I went to jail, all I had left was memories and a Rolex watch.

If it wasn't for these people at Omega, I'm pretty sure I'd be dead now. The company I kept was pimps, pushers, hustlers, and murderers. Of the five of us who started out working together, the other four are dead. They all died by drug violence except for one. I really believe the police killed him, but I can't prove it. Every bone in his body was broken. The police stopped him and one other guy. They handcuffed the other guy and knocked him out. The next thing he knew, he was waking up in a jail cell. To this day, everyone in Richmond believes the police killed my potna.

Another one of the guys in our clique—the real millionaire of the group—was missing for a couple of days, and when we called his cellular phone, somebody else answered. After five days he was found in the trunk of his car handcuffed, with one side of his head beat in, one of his eyes missing, and bullet holes from head to toe. He was like a brother to me.

Reuben Terry

After he stopped thinking of himself as a nigga and understood that there are legal ways to survive—that was a major breakthrough in his case—Reuben wanted very much to attend one of the black Southern colleges. He had the talent to make it on an athletic scholarship, but his age worked against him, so he enrolled and played ball locally at a junior college, making all-conference both of the years he was there. He's still setting his sights on one of the black colleges, this time as a law student.

Reuben learned a hell of a lot from us, and we learned as much from him. He was an imposing figure physically and presented a calm straightforward demeanor, a combination that brought him plenty of respect at the club and in other circles. But as much as he had going for him, Reuben had even more going against him. He seemed to be a classic example of the brother at risk, a young man who blatantly disrespected his race and, as a result, himself; who had broken ties with both home and family; who idolized money and material things above all else; who fell under the ruinous influence of bad company; and who, by the nature of his trade, was colluding brutally in the degradation and destruction of his own community.

By observing brothers like Reuben, Ms. Norris and I had engaged in a protracted attempt to develop a list of what we called risk factors, which we defined as behavioral traits that put the life, safety, and citizenship of young black men in serious jeopardy—put them at risk of falling prey to the violence so prevalent in their lives. Our reasoning was that if we could give the homies a tangible checklist of behaviors they had the power to control, we could lessen their chances of committing or being a victim of violence. Such a list would also help us identify the kids who were most at risk and the specific areas in which their rehabilitations should be concentrated.

We learned a lot from books like *Monster,* by Sanyika Shakur, and urban movies like John Singleton's *Boyz 'n the Hood,* which put familiar characters before us on the screen and condensed their complicated profiles in a way that magnified the defining traits. Doc and I sometimes opened *Street Soldiers* by discussing the latest Spike Lee or Singleton movie, which gave us and the audience a common frame of reference. We all knew all the characters; only the names changed according to the circles we ran in.

Certain that the latest urban genre film would give us a lot to talk about, Doc and I decided to turn over the *Street Soldiers* program to Jack and Preston Worthy one Monday night in 1993 while we went to Daly City to see *Menace II Society,* a story about an essentially good kid named Kane caught up in the spiral of street life. Before we were fifteen minutes into the film, I was already angry—not at the film but at the silly girls behind us laughing at things they shouldn't have been laughing at, things like, "Get that nigga!" "Get that bitch!" The girls were back there saying the same damn things, echoing behavior that was obviously destructive. It was all I could do to restrain myself from turning around and telling them to shut up.

Beyond that, the movie made us numb. When it was over, Margaret and I sat in my car in the parking lot and tried to break down what we had seen. "Damn," I said, "how did all that happen? How did Kane die? What did him in?" We turned on the light, pulled out a pencil and a piece of paper, and started listing the things that we felt had produced the tragic ending. In a way, the outcome was predictable, but why? What, specifically, made it that way?

For starters, it wasn't hard to pick out the type of brother who was doomed to Kane's fate. We had seen the same patterns in

Boyz 'n the Hood and recognized the same danger signs in kids we knew from the club and school and the streets—drugs, alcohol, attitude, all of it. Like the guys in the movies, for example, the homies in our circles were always drinking those goddamned forty-ounces (malt liquor bottles); realistically, the movies couldn't be made without the forty-ounce. More significantly, the attitude portrayed by the character O-Dog in *Menace II Society* was just as common to us as the forty-ounce: "Fuck it," he had said. "I'll kill babies, old people, I just don't give a damn." We knew way too many O-Dogs.

Those were the obvious things that jumped out from the screen, but just as important were the subtler characteristics, such as the negative view of women. In the tradition of the ghetto, all the girls in the movie were bitches and hoes to the homies, and the more we reflected on it, the more convinced Doc and I became that the words themselves were just as damning as the attitude they reflected. The words those characters chose—the words our brothers and sisters in the neighborhoods throw around so thoughtlessly—serve no purpose other than to demean and destroy a brother or a sister. *Punk, sucka, bitch, hoe, motherfucker, mark*—it's a language based upon putdowns, upon disrespect, upon self-hate. And of course there's the most common and vicious word of all: *nigga.* It's no coincidence that "nigga!" goes before so many murders. Prior to shooting someone—in the movies or in the streets, it's all the same—does the killer ever shout, "Break yourself, black man!"? Or, "What's up, African-American brother?" It's always, "Break yourself, nigga!" "Get ready to die, nigga!" I believe there's a profound relationship between the murder rate in our neighborhoods and the use of that damn evil word.

Another important revelation that night was the concept of what the homies call friendship but what we have come to regard as fearship. Our use of the term *fearship* goes along with our rule for living regarding friendship, which identifies a friend as someone who will never lead a friend to danger. When the boys in the 'hood say that they stick together and watch each other's backs and slang and bang and steal and murder for friendship, we maintain that they do it not for friendship but for fearship; that is, out of fear of what their so-called friends are going to think of them or do to them if they don't go along. Fearship is peer pressure at its most destructive.

One of the most vivid cases of fearship I've come across involved an Oakland woman who called *Street Soldiers* to tell us that she had returned home from work one night to find her four-teen-year-old daughter pointing a shotgun at her. After she wrestled the shotgun away and called the police, she learned that the daughter was trying to join a local Crip set and had been told that to become a member, she would have to kill her mother. The girl was sent to juvenile jail but remained so desperate to join the gang that she wrote her mother requesting that she send a photograph of herself. The mother knew damn well that the girl wanted the picture so that she could show it to her potnas and have *them* kill her. She was forced to go into hiding to escape her own daughter.

While the Oakland girl was uncommonly eager to comply with a shockingly heartless demand, it's not uncommon at all for less zealous homies to be driven by fearship to commit murder and mayhem. *Menace II Society* demonstrated how it happens. Kane didn't want to kill anybody, but O-Dog insisted, shamed him into it: "No, we gonna do this, man. Are you a little bitch or what?" To the kids of the street, the greatest fear is being called a punk and not being respected or accepted within the clique; then, they worry, they would have nothing and nobody.

After the movie put it all in big pictures for Doc and me to analyze, we were able to focus in on the behaviors that were destroying a generation of black men. By the time we finally turned out the dome light that night, we had listed nine risk factors:

1. destructive language
2. alcohol
3. drugs
4. guns
5. fearship
6. a negative view of women

7. attitude ("I don't give a fuck")
8. material values
9. environment (family/neighborhood)

Some of the factors—the environment, for instance—are often out of the individual's control, but the risk they impose can be regulated by minimizing other factors. A kid from a dysfunctional family is not necessarily doomed, nor is one who places an inappropriate premium on cars and jewelry, any more than a smoker is absolutely destined to have a heart attack. As a model for reducing the risk of a violent outcome, we often refer to the medical profession's preventive recommendations for heart disease. Even though an individual may be predisposed to heart problems by heredity or whatever reason, the emphasis is on controlling the other factors that might lead to heart failure: alcohol intake, high cholesterol, obesity, nicotine, drugs, and stress. By the same token, even though the homie comes from a dysfunctional family or lives in a violent neighborhood—things over which he may not have control—he can decrease the risk of violence in his life and the lives of others by not engaging in certain behaviors: by not packing a gun, by not using destructive language, by steering clear of drugs, and the like. The greater the number of risk factors that remain in his experience, the greater the chance of violence. It's that simple. Our task, meanwhile, is to convince the street kid that he can and must control these behaviors.

When our list of risk factors was complete, Doc and I knew that we had at last come up with a prescription to combat the anger, fear, and pain that we recognized in all of the troubled brothers and sisters. We had boiled it down to specifics—things to look for and treat—and we were so enthused by this that we wanted to call the show immediately and talk about our discovery. But it was already past two o'clock. We hit the risk factors hard the next week, though, and have been referring to the same list ever since. When a gangster calls in, or a kid at the club reaches out for help, I can just run down the litany of risky behaviors. Are you drinking Eight-Ball (Old English 800 malt liquor)? Are you packing? Who are you hanging with? If you can eliminate this or that characteristic, I tell them, you can control your behavior.

This breakthrough came on the heels of my grudging realization that I alluded to earlier—that knowledge itself was not enough to save the kind of young people we were dealing with. Don't misunderstand me: I still trusted fervently in the power of knowledge and remained dedicated to the sharing of it. To this end, Ms. Norris and I compiled a recommended reading list that we pushed hard on *Street Soldiers*. (At the top of the list are *Malcolm X on Afro-American History*; *The Autobiography of Malcolm X*; and *Monster*, Sanyika Skakur's riveting autobiography of a big-time Crip.) I held doggedly to the conviction that knowledge could change one's life in a dramatic way, based on my own experience, but gradually I had come to recognize that my experience was not entirely applicable to that of the inner-city boys and girls of the 1990s. For me as a college student, knowledge had been sufficient because I wasn't caught up in risky behavior: my family life was very strong, my values were solid, I didn't run with a posse, and because of my respect for my mother and grandmother, I had a high healthy regard for women. I didn't have much mess to clean up; but these guys do. They live on landfills of risk factors.

As a way of underscoring the danger that the risk factors place them in, Ms. Norris and I now inform the homies that their lifestyles have exposed them to a very deadly social disease—HIV. That never fails to get their attention. Then we explain that HIV stands for Hood Infectious Virus, which is spread through the inner city by unprotected social contact. One becomes infected by HIV through the transmission of bad information, bad examples, or bad instruction. If left untreated, the virus can develop into full-blown AIDS—Addiction to Incarceration and Death Syndrome. But unlike the traditional form of AIDS, this disease isn't necessarily terminal. The more we know about it, the better equipped we are to beat it with constructive, healing information. The insidiousness of the social version of AIDS lies in the deceitful fact that it doesn't *appear* to be fatal. The risk factors that contaminate the neighborhoods are passed along under the clever guise of rules for survival, which in actuality are rules for incarceration and death. In an atmosphere through which the brothers and sisters are exposed to HIV from the time they're toddlers, survival becomes a matter of identifying and overcoming the risk factors.

Once we had isolated the risk factors at large, our job was to do the same on an individual basis—to help each young person clean up his own mess. With Reuben Terry, as with so many of the brothers, the major factor in his decline was the pursuit of material values. With Otis Mims, it was easy to home in on his dependence on crack and his decaying environment. Guys like Jermaine King and Andre Aikins were motivated by fearship. Lamerle Johnson's downfall was the "I don't give a fuck" syndrome.

Probably the riskiest of the behaviors we listed is carrying a gun, and not for just the obvious reasons. In addition to the evident danger in which a gun places everyone in its vicinity, the possession of it also assaults the character of the one packing. When you place a gun in the hand of a homie, it plays on his attitude. He becomes harder, more challenging, less respectful. He takes on that mad-dog, don't-fuck-with-me stare. Even his language changes; suddenly, everybody he talks to is a nigga.

Not long after Margaret and I saw *Menace II Society*, *Street Soldiers* received a call from a Richmond teenager who was a textbook example of a kid whose lifestyle was defined by a gun. His name was Nate Pique, but he called himself Nuke, which spoke for itself. Nuke worshiped guns.

"I'm nineteen years old," he said by way of an introduction, "and I got a gun. If a brother approaches me the wrong way, I won't hesitate to smoke him."

"Why would you smoke him?" I asked.

"It would depend on what side of the bed I woke up on."

Nuke carried a chrome .380 automatic with a rubber handle that he kept in his pocket at all times. The gun was his best friend. It soon became apparent that Nuke, in a sense, thought of the .380 as his *only* friend. As for his father, Nuke said that he considered him to be scum, "the lowest thing on earth." Nuke ran with a clique, but it was the gun that he trusted. He loved that damn gun so much that he couldn't see what it was doing to him and was capable of doing to anybody who crossed his path. We talked on the program that night about a little girl in Richmond who had been shot while jumping rope on her back porch. I explained that a gun did that. "The little girl is irrelevant," Nuke said. "Bullets ain't got no name. It's not like they were aiming at her."

It has never ceased to amaze me how the game warps the logic of its players; how the flash of the gun blinds the street brothers to the simple truths that seem so clear to the rest of us: Guns kill, and not only that, sometimes—often—they kill people they weren't supposed to. We hear it all the time on *Street Soldiers*. One of the people killed by a gun in the Bay Area around that time was a two-year-old girl who was sitting in the backseat of her mother's boyfriend's car at three in the morning when a bullet meant for the boyfriend hit her between the eyes. Ms. Norris and I talked about it at the top of one of the radio shows, using harsh words to condemn the violence fostered by "slangin', packin', and brothers playin' Wild Wild West."

All of the callers agreed with us that night until a female friend of the shooters phoned in to say, "You can't blame that shit on my brothers and my man. They wouldn'ta shot if they knew that baby was in the car. Anyone got anything to say, they can say it to me." The rest of the crew was in the background, and they passed around the phone so that all of them could get a word in. It was the same old bullshit. "What was that man doin' out at three in the morning with that baby?" one of the young men asked. "He risked that baby's life." Ultimately the telephone made its way to the most reasonable brother in the clique, whose purpose was to clear his potna's name. "He's the kind of guy who woulda stood there and took bullets if he knew that baby was there," the brother said. "How was he supposed to know there was a baby in that car?"

"When they shot that gun," Ms. Norris replied, "they knew someone was going to get it."

"That's the streets. It's survival."

"Are you surviving?"

There was a pause. "He's not no baby killer, that's all."

"We're not blaming nobody," I said. "If I check myself, and brotherman checks himself, we won't have babies dead. That's all."

It's difficult to understand the thought process by which one can blame the death of a baby girl on the fact that she was in the backseat of a car at three in the morning. Certainly, she shouldn't have been there, but the offense wasn't hers and it should not have been punishable by death. It's a tragic commentary on our cities that its residents can attribute a baby's death to the simple fact that she is in a car at three in the morning.

That was the way Nuke thought, too. By dismissing the death of the girl on the back porch—by saying that bullets don't have names—he was saying that, hey, you step outside, you take your chances. He was placing the responsibility for death not on the gun but on the very fact that one lives in the city. What a chilling notion that is.

Nuke, though, despite his trigger-happy veneer, was reaching out. He may not have *sounded* like it on the phone, but after his call he visited the boys club and without too much resistance was persuaded to put down his gun. Two weeks later, a guy rolled up on him, stuck a gat through the window of Nuke's car, and robbed him. That was more than he could take. The next night, Nuke called the club and left a message. "I got to handle my business," he explained. Then he rounded up some potnas and went looking for the guy who jacked him.

Before she went to bed that night, Ms. Norris checked the messages at the club, as she always does. When she heard Nuke's, she immediately called his pager. Nuke noted the number, knew it was Doc's, and turned the pager off. A while later, he turned it back on and saw that Doc had called him again. Finally he told his buddies to pull over and let him return the call.

Doc picked up the phone by her bed on the first ring. "I'm not gonna be your mother," she said. "You know that what you're doing is wrong. But I will tell you two things that will happen if you find that person. You're gonna go to jail, or you're gonna die. Now, I'm going back to sleep because it's late and I'm tired. Good night."

Nuke rolled those words around in his head a few times—

"you're gonna go to jail, or you're gonna die"—and when he got back to the car, he told his potnas, "Take me home." That was the night he broke up with his gun for good.

Before long, Nate—the nickname no longer fit—was working as a volunteer in the Omega office, answering letters written to us from brothers in prison, and sitting in on *Street Soldiers* now and then as an advocate for disarmament. Behind the microphone, he was able to call on his experiences in a way that Doc and I couldn't. One Monday a misguided brother phoned the show to say, "You got to carry a gat. You got to carry a gat to watch your back. 'Cause you never know what's on the next man's mind." I replied, as I often do, that I've never seen a gun protect anybody; I've only seen them kill people and send people to jail. Nate took over from there.

"Man, listen to what happened to me," he said. "I'm in my car. I don't have no gun no more. A guy came up to me and stuck his gun through my window to my head. If I woulda made one false move to reach for something, my brains would have been on the window. Now how you gonna tell me that's for protection? Carrying a gun don't do nothing but put a target on you." It was hard to believe this was the same young man who, just a few months before, had been on the line telling me that getting up on the wrong side of the bed was reason enough to smoke somebody.

Nate's eagerness to help other brothers was not surprising or coincidental; it was something he felt strongly about. A significant aspect of his own awakening was his realization that there were actually people in his corner. Since his father had never shown that he particularly cared about him, Nate had armed himself against the vicious notion that nobody did. He became Nuke, regarding the guys in his clique not as friends but as potnas in anger, hostile allies in his war against the world. The potna he trusted most, the .380 automatic, was the one he considered his friend.

Although his buddy happened to have a rubber handle, Nate's relationship with his gun was essentially the same as the one shared by so many unloved homies in the 'hood. It was fearship. Nate carried his gun out of fear that nobody or nothing else was looking after him. The problem was that the gun wasn't, either.

When guys, as they often do, call *Street Soldiers* or babble on at the Nabe about doing such and such for their friends—going after this guy because the guy dissed his homie, or riding with so and so because he's a potna—I find myself borrowing from our rules for living and saying one thing over and over. "A friend will never lead you to danger," I tell them. "That's the definition of a friend. A friend is someone who will never lead you to danger." When the guy rolled up on Nate and Nate realized that he would have been dead if his gun-friend had been along, he began to understand. When he realized that there were people who cared about him—the Omega family—he was able to chuck the gun for good.

The nature of friendship—and by extension, the larger issue of how to actively, truly care about somebody—is a matter that we take up virtually every Monday night on *Street Soldiers*. Countless young people have called the show in a quandary over what to do about a friend or relative who has joined a neighborhood set. It started with the first call ever made to the program, on the original show that Hammer hosted, and it has continued week after week with the likes of the twenty-three-year-old woman who said she had been "caught in a triangle of drugs. Since 1982," she told us, "I've seen sixteen of my blood brothers killed—thirteen cousins and three uncles. It seems like everywhere I turn, I run into somebody trafficking in drugs. My ex-boyfriend is in jail now for murdering a dealer from the next set. My current boyfriend has been robbed, stabbed, shot, and held at gunpoint. I want him to stop, but I don't know how to get through to him. I've got people shooting at me because I'm his girlfriend. And I'm pregnant with twins."

A thirteen-year-old sister from Pittsburg—the suburb where I live—called to say that her brother and cousin were "into that Bloods and Crips thing. It scares me to think that one of these days I'm not gonna see them again. My cousin got dropped into X-I-V [a Mexican-American gang] last year, and he got torn up. He's like bruised everywhere still. My brother got out of it, but then he went back in. It's like that all the time."

"People," I replied on that occasion, sympathizing with the

girl through an appeal to the audience at large, "listen to the pain those boys are putting that little girl through. Listen to her voice. When you're out there bangin', carryin' that gun, drivin' by, putting yourself in constant danger, look at what you're putting your family through. Please. This is not just a thirteen-year-old girl in Pittsburg, folks. This is a thirteen-year-old girl all over."

Often, when friends or sisters (girls phone in worried about their loved ones considerably more often than boys do) seek advice about what to do for someone they're worried about, we urge them to report the information to the other person's parents or grandparents or, if those are not available, to school authorities. The common reply is that if they do, their friend or brother will be mad and might even break off the relationship. "Friendship," Doc and I have answered many times, and the same applies to being a family member, "is letting a friend get mad at you in order to save their life." The opposite—putting a friend in danger or allowing him to remain there for the sake of preserving the relationship—is a very deadly sort of fearship.

Nate's variety of fearship was the deadliest possible because it connected him intimately to the vehicle by which African-American genocide has been perpetrated. The rate of gun mortality is so frighteningly high in many American ghettos that a boy has a longer life expectancy in Bangladesh. The leading cause of death for black males between fifteen and twenty-four in this country is homicide. In 1992 there were thirty-three handgun deaths in Great Britain, 13,220 in the United States. And handguns aren't the whole of it, by any stretch. When drive-bys became the fashion, kids used .22s until they noticed that the victims kept getting up. They upgraded to .357s, but those ran out of bullets too fast. So they upgraded again to weapons with two clips, then extension clips, then AR-15s and MAK-90s, an automatic with a clip that holds five hundred bullets. The latest rage is the hollow-point bullet that will ricochet around a person's insides, breaking bones and piercing organs along the way. Of course, there is always a place for the M.A.C.-10, the Uzi, and the Glock, not to mention the ever-popular AK-47 assault rifle, which of course is used only for *protection*.

In my estimation, the proliferation of guns—more importantly, the *worship* of guns—represents one of three major differences between growing up in the inner city today and when I was a kid in South Central. Guns bushwhack a community in at least two ways: They not only rub out lives but transform people, turning Nates into Nukes. When guns became status symbols, it ensured that most of the homies would be carrying one. I once asked some of our members, "If you passed ten guys walking down the street in one of the neighborhoods, how many of them would be packing?" The answers ranged from five to ten.

Another deep-seated contemporary change in the inner city is the evacuation of jobs. This is a complicated topic that involves the decentralization of the cities, white flight, and urban renewal, all of which have broken down the old-style, self-contained inner-city neighborhood. One of the effects is fewer drugstores and shops and corner markets where young people can find work. And one of the effects of fewer jobs in the community is more violence. Research shows that the level of violent behavior in this country is nearly identical for employed black males and employed white males. The far higher incidence of violence among black men overall can be matched up neatly with the higher incidence of unemployment among black men.

Of course, some would argue that the unemployment rate among young blacks these days is actually quite low if you count the drug dealers as working people. I choose not to count them, instead defining work as an activity that is productive for self and society. As a source of income alone, dope slangin' does a colossal disservice to its practitioners, deluding them with the notion that big fast money is the only kind that amounts to anything. With the predominance of crack cocaine over the last six or eight years, the money is not quite as big for each transaction, but it comes faster to more. I regard the flood of crack cocaine into the urban neighborhood as the third major difference in today's inner city. What crack did was lure the entire black community into its snare.

Jack and Ms. Norris have often likened the drug dealer to the slavemaster, mindlessly destroying the lives of others for the love of money. If the dealer is the slavemaster, crack itself is the slavery system, and this time there is no North, there is no Frederick Douglass, there are no abolitionists to take it on. It is up to us— you, me, the cities, the states, the federal government, and private organizations—to fight the war on crack. I don't purport to have a national strategy in my head except for the deeply held conviction that everybody has to be involved. I do my part through education —by showing kids the deadly effect that crack has on them as well as their communities—and the governments and organizations have to be creative in finding ways to do theirs.

Crack cocaine is the most insidious enemy that the black community has faced in its perilous history. It's a different kind of beast. Like five-hundred-pound termites, crack gnaws away at the superstructure of a community, destroying values, people, and families. So powerful are the jaws of crack cocaine that they have chewed through the steel cords binding black mothers and their children. Crack is the only thing in our history, chemical or whatever, that has been able to come between black women and the mothering process. The KKK couldn't do that. Jim Crow couldn't do that. The Old South couldn't even do that.

On one of his frequent mentoring visits to the California Youth Authority, Coach came across a young man who was a product of a crack-mother household. Michael Gibson is the second oldest of five children, two of whom have become intimate with the California juvenile justice system. A close relative recently recovered from being raped, strangled, and left for dead on an Oakland street. Michael's several brushes with death have usually revolved around his mother's cocaine habit. A dealer once placed a gun in Michael's mouth to make him pay for the crack his mother had bought. He has seen people overdose in his home and others get stabbed in crack-crazed knife fights. Violence and sex were as familiar to his youthful eyes as television. Starting when he was nine or ten years old, he watched his mother's friends perform oral favors to pay for drugs. As a teenager, his potnas would tell him that his mother had been buying crack by turning tricks for dealers. Often, she would straggle home at night looking "like a truck had run over her," which meant that she had been beaten for money or sex or both. In a rage over seeing her that way, Michael, who by then was a dealer himself, would shoot up crack houses and do drive-bys on other dealers.

At Coach's urging, Michael started coming to Omega meetings after two and a half years in YA for strong-arm robbery and attempted murder of a police officer. It was obvious that he had very profound feelings about his childhood, and he spoke about them on Tuesday nights with arresting candor. He recalled happier times, before crack hit the house, when his mother would walk him to school and tenderly answer his questions about the homeless people they passed along the way. Michael would take an apple or a cookie out of his lunchbox to give to them, and his mother would be proud of his kindness. She was good to her children.

But once she became entangled with crack, "my mother didn't have time for us," Michael said. "She only looked for the pipe." He argued with her about her habit, telling her that he loved her but crack was tearing apart the family. "Get the fuck out of my face," she would say. "You don't love me. I gotta calm my nerves, and if you won't give me the twenty dollars I need, you can just get the fuck out of here."

One Tuesday night before Mother's Day, Doc asked the kids in her Omega class to write letters to their mothers saying things they couldn't say in person. Michael's was memorable.

Dear Mama,

For years I carried around with me the painful memories, the painful scars from my childhood. I have suffered a long time, and I continue to suffer. I know you won't understand, or show any signs of affection, or even show some kind of emotions. Crack cocaine has got a hold on you. You don't know the pain you caused me as a little boy. I'm still hurting. The difference between me now and me yesterday is that I choose to deal with it. Seeing you strung out on crack, leaving me alone raising three boys is hard. I've been a drug dealer, a jacker, a drive-by

*shooter, all because of the stress and pain you cause me all my life.
Because of you, I shot at other people who look like me.*

*I'm writing this letter to you because I can't talk to you face to
face. I can't even tell you I love you without you cussing me out. We are
supposed to love one another, but I can admit I hate what you allowed
me to become. I hate what you became. I ain't forgot and I won't forget.*

Michael's twenty now, and he works at the Mentoring Center in Oakland, learning how to counsel young people. He's very
good at it and speaks all over the Bay Area for the boys club. When
Doc took him to Detroit to address a youth conference, his testimony was so powerful that two women—former crack mothers—
stood up and said that this was the first time they had been able to
express their sorrow for what they had done to their families.

Because he does good work in the daytime and immerses
himself in Omega at night, Michael has gone a long way toward
beating his risk factors. He has also come a long way since writing
that bitter letter to his mother. It was important for him to grasp
the fact that, while he had every common excuse to sell drugs and
lead an angry violent life, there is no such thing as a *good* excuse for
what he was doing. He turned his life around when he realized that
the enemy was not his mother—he tries to think of her as a black
queen—but that bastard crack.

Now that he understands what and what not to hate, Michael can also understand it when I say that I have no patience
with the predators who sell crack in our communities. If they call
the show or, like Michael, come to the club for help, I will help
them in any way I can; if they need a father figure, I'll be it; but I
will never ever condone, justify, or tolerate what they do. Omega's
position will always be to love the sinner and hate the sin.

Sometimes this takes the form of a harsh diatribe. Coach
minced no words when he first counseled Michael Gibson at YA,
and similarly, drug dealers—even those who profess they want to
change their ways—can't expect to receive tender encouragement
from Doc and me when they call *Street Soldiers*. As a group, they
don't much like it when we attack their lifestyle, but we don't give a

damn about that. In fact, their mouthy defense of themselves and their industry usually leads to enlightening dialogue.

"I've been listening the last few weeks," one dealer said, referring to ongoing, unforgiving radio conversations we'd had with another player, "and you gettin' on his grind. Y'all was puttin' the brother down. He's working, and you see something wrong."

While purporting to sympathize with the previous caller—this is a common tack—the dealer made it obvious that he was actually speaking up for himself. He attributed his occupational choice to the fact that he never knew his father, who was an addict, and justified it by reasoning, "When I'm out there, I don't ask them to come get it."

"Don't you see the problem it causes for the community?" I asked him. "Crack babies, mothers on crack, brothers on crack. You're killing a whole lot of people."

"Look," he replied, "I got to survive, too. My fuckin' job don't pay the rent, PG&E, the cable. Don't look at me as a bad person. I'm just the middleman. I don't own the poppy field. I don't own the plane that brings it over here. I'm just the middleman. I give it up to the little man. All I do is take advantage of what I got. That's the American way."

"That's not the reason you sell drugs," Margaret said. "You don't want to deal with the truth. You're killing people. We're trying to wake you up. You're living in a dream world. You're running away from reality."

"You are contributing to all the pain, the madness, the funerals, the people getting shot up," I added. "You are doing it. I know you know where the dope goes—to our people. Don't play ignorant. You know it."

We were double-teaming him, swarming him before he could get off a shot. "You're nothing but a killer," Doc said.

"You're no better than the Ku Klux Klan, no better than a skinhead," I chimed in. "What's the difference between what you're doing and what they're doing?"

On that, the guy hung up.

"He was all the way lost," I said.

What set that brother apart from the ones we had saved—what made him different from Nate, from Grambling, from Otis—was that he didn't want to hear the truth. We can't save a homie who doesn't want to be saved. On the other hand, we don't always succeed with the ones who reach out, either. Sometimes their fingers slip out of our grip, and they're gone—from view, at least. We frequently don't know what happens to a young person when we lose track of him or her, and the worst-case scenario is not always the one that applies, but we understand the odds. Nobody goes undefeated against the streets.

Among the callers we still worry about is a girl whose tears moistened our own faces through the telephone. She said that she came home from work to find the police carrying away her parents and brother in body bags. It looked to her as though her ex-boyfriend had arranged the murders through his set. "He called and said he didn't have nothing to do with it, but I know he did," she sobbed. "How could he do this to me? I'm all alone now. How could he take their lives?"

I told her to stay on the phone so that Doc and I could speak to her privately on another line. Kevin put on some hip-hop music, and I explained to the audience, "This ain't theater."

When we picked up the other line, the girl began whispering, obviously afraid to be heard by someone nearby. "I'll call you back," she said. I asked if there was a number where we could reach her. "No, no," she answered frantically. "I'll have to call you back. I gotta go." Click. That was the last we heard from her.

There was a younger kid named Jasper with whom we and the listeners became very familiar through *Street Soldiers*. He used to call in just kickin' knowledge. It amazed me that he was only twelve years old; that little brother had it together. Then all of a sudden, his calls stopped. A few weeks later, a woman phoned in to tell us that Jasper had been in the hospital. He had taken a bullet in the head on Easter Sunday. The same eighteen-year-old had also shot Jasper's father in the face.

We talked about that tragedy on the air and tried to deal with it, just as we do at the club. We could only hope that, by getting to know Jasper, the homies out there might begin to comprehend the magnitude of the cruel horrible havoc that is caused by guns; that they might begin to appreciate the breathtaking injustice inflicted by even a single bullet.

As the case had been originally with the boys club, it was the realness of *Street Soldiers* that made it so compelling to the young people in the neighborhoods. We had a professional survey taken at one of our Knowledge Conferences, and 71 percent of those questioned, when asked why they listen to *Street Soldiers*, said the reason was that "it's real." Even more—74 percent—said that the program had affected the way they thought, and more than half the respondents said that it had affected the way they acted.

When acquaintances or news people tell me they're impressed or surprised that so many people listen to and call *Street Soldiers* at one o'clock in the morning, my response is that I'm surprised more people *don't* listen and call. I ask them, "Wouldn't you pay attention if you thought someone sincerely wanted to help your situation and had the wherewithal to do it?"

At the risk of overstating our role for the sake of an analogy, I've often thought of Omega—and *Street Soldiers*—in the context of Harriet Tubman. The brothers and sisters we try to save are like the ones who were sitting on the plantation when Harriet came by and said, "I'm here to lead you to freedom. Let's go." Some of them were ready to leave as soon as she got there, and off they went on the arduous trek to a place where they were safe from the oppression and hardships of their enslavement. Others were afraid to go, or perhaps there was something on the plantation itself that kept them there. But they would get another chance. Harriet always came back for those she left behind the first time.

We're like Harriet: we'll be back. If you're not ready for the knowledge now; if you're not ready to be saved; if you're not ready to leave the gang; if you're not ready to lay down your gun; if you're not ready to flush those rocks down the toilet, maybe you will be next time. All we can do is keep coming back with maps and lanterns to show you the way to freedom.

10

Uncut Diamonds

I f, in the excitement over *Street Soldiers* or grant money or media coverage, I should ever lose sight of what has made the Omega Boys Club what it is, all I have to do is spend a day with Jack at Juvenile Hall. Or better yet, a Monday night at the San Francisco Youth Guidance Center.

I used to join Jack at the YGC until other activities—mainly the radio program—called me away. Meanwhile, Jack hasn't missed a beat. Every Monday night, he and a few of his guests are led through locked doors and down long hallways to a meeting room deep in the center's security section, where the juveniles, dressed in their pale blue pajamas and slippers, listen impassively in desks and chairs lined against the walls as Jack gives them all he's got, pacing and gesturing and laying it on the line as only he can do. Because they're smart, the kids know that Jack is their best chance of getting out of there and staying out. He is also their best chance against the streets. There's no way to estimate the number of lives Jack has saved in the seven years or so since Dennis Sweeney first allowed him through the iron door of YGC. What Jack did then was gain entree into the institution. Seven years later, he *is* an institution.

On this particular summer Monday, most of the inmates in the room wear their hair in braids or dreadlocks, and some of the faces under the braids are incredibly young, such as that of the small, long-haired thirteen-year-old who has been dealing drugs since he was eight. The street life has overdeveloped the boy's survival senses, and as he walks into the meeting, he searches for strangers, constantly glancing, constantly moving, constantly worrying. In a few days, he will be sent to a youth camp in Arizona.

The thirteen-year-old finally settles uneasily into a desk next to a large older boy with twenty-two counts against him. The room is full of kids with long rap sheets, kids with stories, and Jack knows them all. There is the star football player ("I'm not easily impressed by talent," Jack tells the crowd, "but I saw this brother carry the ball, and believe me, he's got it.") who was talked into robbing a bank by his uncle, who had just gotten out of jail. There is the aspiring rap star—hell, they're *all* aspiring rap stars—who, when Jack calls his name, performs a long, tough song he has written about AIDS. There is the unsmiling, inarticulate, tightly bundled teenager who has never reported anything positive to the group until tonight, when he says that he can't promise, but for the sake of the baby on the way, he will try not to sell dope anymore. "I should have died by now," he mumbles, working very hard at his words and staring at his slippers. "God must want something from me, you know what I'm sayin'? I love you all."

The kids speak about their potnas, and they speak about friends who have died, concluding invariably with "Peace." A half-dozen volunteers speak their piece, and before Jack closes the session with his signature prayer, he calls attention to one more brother, a tall slumping young man named Bing who has a big day tomorrow. Bing will go before the judge in the afternoon, and the judge will decide where the teenager will spend the next phase of his life—here, at the California Youth Authority, or at home, wherever that may be. Jack will be with him in the courtroom. Bing is counting on Jack. Jack is also counting on Bing, who is blatantly bright and talented. He, too, is a rapper.

"I don't care anymore about impressing people," Bing says, his head lowered in the tradition of the room. "I've got to do what I've got to do. I'll try to do my rap thing, you know what I'm sayin'? If that doesn't work, I'll have to get a regular job, you know what I'm sayin'? I don't care what my homies or anybody thinks anymore."

The next afternoon, Bing sits uncomfortably in juvenile court. Also there, on his behalf, are his Samoan mother from San Francisco, his black father from Los Angeles, and his very distinguished black grandfather from Louisiana. If the judge chooses to place Bing on probation, it might be in the custody of any one of the three. The fourth and final person in Bing's corner is my Omega Boys Club co-founder.

Jack has two court cases on the day. The other one was actually scheduled earlier but was delayed and then was delayed again when Bing's case convened. The second delay was imposed so that the court could wait for Jack.

While the juvenile judges obviously value Jack's opinions, the public defenders, like many of the kids they represent, have a more vested interest in Jack's courtroom presence. They have come to realize that he might be their best chance of keeping their clients out of detention. Consequently, they confer with Jack in the morning, before the docket starts, and all day long, pulling him over for private consultations by the Coke machine across the hall from the wooden benches engraved with dozens of names, where city kids wait sullenly—or nervously; sometimes it's hard to tell the two apart—with hoods and sweater caps pulled over their heads. The defenders know that a good word from Jack, and Jack's promise that he and Omega will keep tabs on a kid, can sometimes persuade a judge that incarceration may not be the best option.

Jack's role in sentencing is a counseling function, not a legal function. It never supersedes probation. A juvenile still requires a probation officer, and the ultimate responsibility rests with that officer. But it's not infrequent that if Jack is in the court, the judge or commissioner will make the condition that if the kid will stay in touch with Jack or participate in Omega, he will suspend the sentencing or place the juvenile on probation instead of sending him to one of the detention centers.

When a kid is involved with Omega, you can relax a little bit because Omega will keep you abreast of his progress. If the kid's not doing well and sliding back, Jack has a way of communicating that without divulging a lot of confidence. He has a way of letting the system know that you need to get out there because this or that kid is backsliding. He's supportive of the children but doesn't sell himself out when it comes to a kid who's really not making it. Jack never deceives the people in the system. And I don't know of a single judge in our system who isn't aware of that.

Jack has saved any number of kids from being sent to the Youth Authority, given them a second reprieve. If there is a candidate for one of our out-of-home placement facilities, Jack will tell me about him. He knows how to work within the system. Even though he might disagree with the system and he feels there might be institutional racism working within it, Jack has adapted his ways, which makes it easier for him to gain access to the system.

Some of the kids take advantage of all of this. I've backed off because a lot of the kids have used Jack and used me. A lot of them burn their bridges. But even those kids who haven't turned it around 180 degrees, they're still kids whom Jack has affected. He's made them more introspective. They've broadened their views of themselves. You've got to realize that ninety percent of the kids that Jack works with, there is no male in the family, no father figure. Often there's a mother who is dysfunctional herself. These are kids for whom there is not much visible hope. These kids have gotten into the cycle of criminality. When you see what goes on in some of the families where crime and delinquency go hand in hand with family values, you can see that it's not so much that they're throwaway kids, but it's something they're born into. These kids come from public housing situations and whatever the ghetto entails.

You can look at it this way: We're spending three thousand dollars a month on the average to place one of these kids in a juvenile facility, thirty-six thousand a year. When you think about investing thirty-six to two hundred thousand dollars on a kid, then dropping him back on the street with no support, that's like pissing away a two-hundred-thousand-dollar investment. And that's where Jack will take on the system. Or at least argue it.

Dennis Sweeney
Supervising Probation Officer

Bing's case involves a gun, and as a result his probation officer, a red-faced man with whom Jack has had occasional run-ins, pushes hard to have him sent to the Youth Authority. Aside from Bing, the only people to speak up to the contrary are Bing's public defender and Jack, who do so privately in the judge's chambers. After the closed-door session, the judge needs to hear from the probation officer and also from Bing, who addresses the bench in a voice entirely unlike the one that his fellow inmates heard the night before. There are no "you know what I'm sayin's" in his speech this time. There is no staring at the floor. Looking directly into the judge's eyes and speaking distinctly, Bing says that he has been working with Jack Jacqua and learning that the way of life he previously practiced is a dead-end street. "My family here," he says, acknowledging them with his eyes, "I'm letting them and everybody down." When all is said and done, the judge suspends Bing's sentence and remands him to the custody of his mother, with Jack very much in the wings. As the decision comes down, the grandfather, dressed nattily in a beige suit and hat, sobs privately in the back of the courtroom. He then calls Bing over, places his hands on his grandson's shoulders, and speaks to him very closely, very softly, very sternly. As this occurs, there is a clear impression that if the grandfather had been able to place his hands on Bing's shoulders more frequently, neither one of them would be here now. Bing listens, nods, and hugs.

It is Jack's hope that the grandfather will become involved in Bing's daily routine, although that much is out of his hands. On the whole, Jack puts great store in grandparents. Sometimes, because they seem to care more and try harder, he does what he does in deference to them as much as to the kids.

There was a young man who went to court yesterday, and his grandmother was there. I've spent a lot of time with this kid over the years. I really loved this kid, had a beautiful relationship with him. But he listened to the wrong people. He listened to his cousin and got involved in a drug deal over the weekend. I've been so fucking mad at him I haven't decided what I'm gonna do with him yet. He's been crying to me ever since he got arrested. I haven't given him a nickel's worth of time, and I don't intend to for a while. I went to court with him yesterday, though, with Grandma. I had to be there with Grandma. Eventually, I'll get around to him and tell him what a jerk he is. I could easily say with this kid that enough is enough, I'm sick of this, but no, I can't do that to him or to Grandma.

There are gonna be failures. I understand that. Most adults don't understand that, and they take this stuff much too personally. I know it's not my problem; it's empowerment. Teachers say things like, "Well, I'm never gonna loan that kid any money again—he didn't pay it back," but you can't take any of this personally. I understand what's going on out there. There was a kid killed two weeks ago, a kid I helped bring up. Sure, it bothered me, but hey, I'm amazed I don't have fifty funerals a week. One's not bad. I'm just a realist about this stuff.

There's a girl I've worked with over the years, I've had a real love affair with this girl. I helped bring her up. She got paralyzed five months ago when a cop shot her. She's lost sixty pounds, she's in a wheelchair, and she'll never be able to walk again. The girl's just seventeen. I could get in a funk about that, but you learn to take it as it comes. This is the way it is. This is the way it is.

Jack Jacqua

Jack has developed a hard shell to protect himself against the horrors of the lifestyle he deals with every day. His defense against caring too much is to stay so busy in the practice of caring that he doesn't have time for the feeling part. While I've been expanding Omega geographically and through the radio, Jack has been widening our sphere of kid-saving with hard, hands-on labor.

To that end, he sent Coach to check out the Glen Mills reform school in Pennsylvania and on Coach's recommendation worked it out with Dennis Sweeney and Juvenile Judge Donald Mitchell to have some San Francisco teenagers sent there instead of to YA. A ninth-grade dropout named Johnny Releford was the first to go. When his time at Glen Mills was up, Johnny passed his GED and enrolled immediately at Alabama State University. "I think somehow God was watching over us on that one," Jack said, "or else our luck was enormous. We got the right kid to send to Glen Mills."

In truth, Jack got the right kid, and usually does, because he *knows* the right kid. He knows virtually all the juvenile system kids, right and wrong. He makes it his business to know them, and it's a growing business. In addition to his Monday night peer-counseling sessions at the YGC, he and Coach also meet Tuesdays at Juvenile Hall with Omega kids who are on probation. Often those are the ones most at risk, young people whose citizenship is so fragile that it can come apart with a single indiscretion.

Jack makes a lot of headway with his kids when they're locked up, but it's when they're out that they really have to prove themselves. It's when they're out that they have to be saved. Some of them, of course, are not ready for that, and if the issue comes up in court, Jack will let the truth be known. That's why the judges trust him. That's why he has more influence in sentencing than anyone in the Bay Area outside the justice system.

And that was why, after Bing's sentence was suspended and the grandfather laid his wisdom on the boy, the case down the hall could finally begin after waiting on Jack for an hour and a half. The boy whose fate was in the balance, a small, playful fifteen-year-old, had passed the time slap-boxing with his cousin while the public defender paced the corridor and the grandmother fidgeted on the wooden bench, both of them watching for Jack.

There have been many milestones in the eight years the Omega Boys Club has been in existence, but perhaps none so gratifying as what occurred on May 22, 1994. That was the day Joe Thomas graduated from Morris Brown College with a degree in communications.

Technically, Joe was not our first student to bring home a degree. That distinction belonged to Cassandra Brown, who received hers from San Francisco State College in December 1992. But Cassandra was already a sophomore when she earned her Omega scholarship, and although we were extremely proud of her accomplishment, it in no way diminished Joe's remarkable odyssey, which took him from dope pusher, jailbird, and cop beater—the quintessential "throwaway kid"—to college graduate and role model.

It required six years for Joe to make it through Morris Brown. At that, he won the derby—the first and, to date, the only one of our original class of eight to finish what he started in the fall of 1988. Shervon Hunter was on her way to graduating from Delaware State, but her baby arrived before her diploma and she returned home to take care of it. By then, the other six Omegas had given up their studies, at least temporarily. Most of them intended to return to college, but the longer they stayed out, the harder it became.

Meanwhile, we made sure to keep the club members up to date on Joe's progress. The word was that he wanted to stay around Atlanta after he graduated and eventually start his own branch of the Omega Boys Club, but it wasn't quite that simple. His daughter and her mother were still in San Francisco, and Joe knew what that meant. So out of respect to them and to his obligation as a father, he put aside his personal desires and went job-hunting close to home. Naturally, he paid frequent visits to the boys club to share his knowledge with his successors. "Omega taught me how important the black family is," Joe told them, saying things he had never contemplated when he was dodging bullets and hiding under cars. "It taught me to stand up for myself and be a father, be a man. As much as I liked Atlanta and wanted to try to make a go of it there, the boys club taught me better than that."

For his senior project at Morris Brown, Joe had filmed a video on race relations in Forsyth County, Georgia, borrowing his title from the famous plea of Rodney King, *Can't We All Get Along?* He made an A on it, and he also used it on job interviews with television and radio stations around San Francisco. It was hard not to be impressed by the things Joe had accomplished. Ultimately, and to my delight, he accepted an offer to work in the production department at KMEL.

After Joe broke the ice, our graduation rate picked up considerably. Much of that, of course, had to do with Ms. Norris's academic preparation program. By 1995, we had twenty-one graduates among the hundred-plus we had sent to college since our scholarship program began with those underprepared, overwhelmed eight.

There were also many more Omegas who by then had graduated from junior college and enrolled in four-year schools, each of whom had his own special story. Among them was a football player and former fist-fighting drug dealer named Terrence Hanserd who completed Laney College in the spring of 1995 and accepted a scholarship to New Mexico State. Joe Thomas first peer-counseled Terrence when T-Top, as we all came to know him, was serving time at Log Cabin Ranch after one of his twenty or so juvenile arrests. Coach took over from there, becoming the father that T-Top hadn't known since he was five. When Terrence returned to Galileo High School to become Player of the Year in San Francisco as a running back, Coach was at all of his games. T-Top paid back the favor by attending all of our Omega meetings. "I used to get on the bus by myself and go to Omega every Tuesday night," he says. "That's when turf was real strong and it was considered slippin' to be caught by yourself out of your turf. It had to be something real serious to get me on that bus. But the power of Omega used to bring me up there and keep me safe."

Given T-Top's dedication to going straight, I have no doubt that he will join our ranks of college graduates, which by then ought to include my buddies Jermaine King and Andre Aikins. After starting at Morris Brown, Andre transferred to Grambling to pursue a degree in math. Jermaine moved on to Atlanta Metropolitan College, where he majored in criminal psychology—something he already knew a hell of a lot about—with the intention of eventually working in a police department or a prison counseling program.

By no coincidence, the career aspirations of many of our guys have to do with law enforcement or counseling, which basically represent the two phases of their young lives—before Omega and after Omega. The only field that rivals those in the hearts of the Omega kids is music. Jermaine, like so many others, has dreams of making it as a big-time rapper. He and his partners have recorded about half a dozen songs. One of them got some air time on the radio, but after all the expenses and shares were figured, Jermaine only saw about five hundred dollars from it. After that, the group formed its own production company. Jermaine writes, composes, produces, the whole bit. He has talent, and he works faithfully at it, but I could be more encouraging toward his music ambitions—and those of all our guys—if they weren't so damn common these days. In our circles, rap has supplanted basketball as the career in which seemingly every brother thinks he can be a superstar and get rich.

Andre is an exception in that regard, as he is in most regards. For a guy who was so bent on proving his manhood—his badness—for so many years, Andre's strength of character is inspiring. He has an instinctive sense of merit to which he commits himself wholeheartedly, and as a result he remains the most level-headed, down-to-earth young brother in the club, one whom I can trust implicitly to do the right thing. Andre says he wants six kids, and I hope he has them because I'm pretty sure that those are six we won't have to worry about.

Before he went off to college, Andre made a vow to himself that the mother of his first child would be his wife. He also made one concerning his career, which he shared with a couple thousand people in a memorable speech at our first Knowledge Conference:

"My whole goal now is to teach ninth-grade math at the junior high I was at when I turned away from school," he confided to the large crowd that day. "In ninth grade, a kid can go either way. I think in that position I'll be able to nudge a boy one way or the other.

"We have to impress a different vision upon young people, show them that there's more to the world and we have a lot to offer, and that the world has a lot to offer us. 'Cause we only see as far as they let us see, the powers that be. The TV will only show us so much. Some teachers will only show us so much. Our neighborhoods will only show us so much. Especially the neighborhoods. See, I'm twenty-one years old and already an OG. I think that's kind of a shame. The OG's is getting a little bit younger, and I helped contribute to that because the younger ones were looking up to me just as I was looking up to older people. All I saw for a long time was people trying to get over and hustle, just hustle, hustle. I never seen no doctor get up at three in the morning, wash off his car, take his briefcase and his stethoscope, and go straight to the hospital. I didn't see no lawyers, no rocket scientists. All I seen was just somebody trying to get over."

Andre is well aware that he is not the most gifted speaker to emerge from the boys club. When he addresses a big audience or even a single stranger, he nearly always makes a point to apologize for the state of his language, which he describes as midway between 'hood and bachelor's degree. Those very elements, however —the down-home combination of vocabulary and humility—give Andre a disarming charm that lends power to his words. If he is not our most polished speaker, he is perhaps our most believable.

"I feel the biggest impact any single person in our community can make," he continued, "is if you get a job, any type of nine-to-five. You got to put yourself out in a place where other people can see you doing your nine-to-five, because so many of us don't see it anymore and don't believe it even exists. We don't see what goes on in everybody *else's* life. All we used to seeing is one picture.

"The information is out there, and that's the tricky thing about information and education: When it's held from us, we want it, but when it's given to us, we don't want to take it. That's something that's hard to understand. Why is it you got fifty people telling you what exactly is gonna happen if you do this particular thing, and you don't believe they know what they're talking about? Why would anybody lie to you about telling you you gonna go to jail? I had the attitude that I could always do it one way slicker and get through. That's what hustling is, if you wanna come down to it and break it down. That's all I was—a hustler. It seemed like life was free, everything came easy. School was a place to make hook-ups and get at girls. But I paid a price for not finishing school. I never went to my own prom. I never got a diploma that says I graduated from this high school.

"That's why people who haven't seen me around expect me to say I've been in jail. When I tell 'em, nah, I been at school, it's like, 'School . . . *yeah.*' Like it's something they've never even thought about before. Most people out there seem to have a vision of not being out of the neighborhood. The only thing they see is the candy [paint job] on the top, you know. Well, if somebody wants to spend two G's on a paint job, that's on them. I need it for my tuition.

"I understand why they never think about college. It's because of what they see every day. I never thought about it either until Mr. Marshall told me I could go if I really wanted to. Even after I got there, it still felt like I didn't belong. It seemed like I had to work three times as hard as the other students. It seemed like everybody else was a model student in high school, probably came from a college family, and they all knew their whole lives that they were going to college. It made me feel really alone.

"I also had a lot of worries that the other students never had. To this day, I still worry about my past catching up with me. I guess I'll always worry about that. But that's all right. I'm gonna punish myself, anyway. I've always been ready to pay the price for what I've done. The fact is, I'm probably lucky I haven't done time already. One potna was giving up a lot of information to cut a deal with the police, and I'm sure he could have given them some information pertaining to me. But the dude was snitching on the wrong people, and it started to get back to him. Finally he decided he would just take the time. Luckily, he decided that before he got around to talking about me. It probably saved me.

"One thing I don't worry about anymore is what my old potnas think. My true potnas accept me now, even if they're still on the streets. Most of my friends are dead now or in jail. I'd say no more than five or six of them are still around, and that's out of a hundred or maybe two hundred. There's no doubt in my mind that if I hadn't joined the Omega Boys Club, I would have been one of three things—dead, in jail, or a rich dope dealer.

"Sooner or later," Andre said, drawing credibly on his own experience, "you gotta find your own niche in life. Like my niche is mathematics. I maybe can't spell, but I can add like hell. So I'm gonna use that and become a math teacher. I'm gonna live on Seventy-first Ave. I've already picked out the house. It got a fence. That's all I want. My personal thing is that a lot of people are gonna have to let go of the materialistic values and how important money is in our lives. I set myself some realistic goals that I know I can reach with a lot of hard work. That way, whatever I do will affect my goal. Then and only then can you be master of your own destiny. When you set an unrealistic goal way out there and fall, it's hard as hell to get up. Basically in the black community, we good for tearing one another down instead of supporting one another. But we can make ourselves one more good person to combat that one bad person that may be in our community.

"I personally don't think nobody should move out of the neighborhood. I stress that because a lot of *other* people have the jobs *we* need to have because we know what's goin' on and we know how to educate our own. I think it's up to us to construct, educate, and rebuild. At college I see people going into law, that's good; business administration, that's good. But we need people at the grassroots level, somebody that's willing to take the job that seems to pay too little and you work too hard. 'Cause we gotta have a foundation before we can build. I don't see no reason to be no millionaire. Chill all that. I just want me one house, a dog, a family, and a nice car, you know. The way I look at it, I came from Oakland and I ain't going nowhere. Because I know that after I would have left, there would be little kids coming up that need somebody to look up to, that need somebody that's gonna get up for that nine-to-five and show that with a lot of hard work you can be anything you want to be. Because we don't see that enough. We don't.

"Mr. Marshall is always saying, 'The more you know, the more you owe,' and that's the way I feel. That's why I want to teach at my old junior high. And while I'm doing that, I'll go to grad school at night.

"The other thing I want to do is start a boys club in Oakland. We really need one in Oakland."

I wish I could say that Andre is the prototypical club member in terms of personal metamorphosis, from alpha to Omega. More typical, however, is the evolutionary pattern represented by the triumvirate in which he ran. In this business, I figure, two out of three is enough to keep our chins up. We can save a lot of lives at that rate.

The third musketeer in the posse with Andre and Jermaine, the second-generation gangster Lamerle Johnson, has taken an entirely different road. That much was predictable. Even when he was riding around in my car, even when he was giving over a night or two a week to the Omega Boys Club and (ostensibly) all that it stood for, Lamerle was a vocal apologist for his criminal side. My challenge with Lamerle was not only to rehabilitate his mindset but to keep him from infecting Jermaine's. When I ultimately heard that Lamerle had been arrested again, my first question was whether Jermaine was with him.

My skepticism concerning Lamerle was based upon the pathology of his disorder. While the chemical addictions of drugs and alcohol have been widely chronicled, not enough has been said about the addiction of *selling* drugs. That's the habit some of our guys have been unable to kick—the addiction to the action and, more to the point, to the money. Although anyone who watched Lamerle's drug series on Channel 7 might be startled by the news that Lamerle himself was still caught up in the game, it wasn't at all surprising to me. The lifestyle of the street is similar to alcoholism in the sense that one is never immune from its temptations. They can be staved off with knowledge and conviction, but while Lamerle chugged down plenty of knowledge and appeared to act under its influence, he never really let it into his bloodstream. Returning to the streets, he was convicted as an adult for kidnaping another drug dealer, a little stunt that earned him a twenty-year sentence.

A worse fate befell one of our charter members, Emanuel Powell. As sweet a kid as Emanuel was, he was never able to overcome his risk factors. In his case, the temptations of the street —money and prestige—were stronger than his commitment to beat them, and he eventually stopped coming to the club. At one point, when it was evident that Emanuel had been away too long, Jack and I paid a visit to his house. He wasn't there, but we spoke with his mom and made clear our purpose—to bring him back into the fold. Unfortunately, Emanuel was more interested in doing his thing. It eventually got him killed.

When I heard about Emanuel's shooting, I couldn't help but think back to when he first started coming to Omega meetings with his homie from Potrero Hill Middle School, Marcel Evans. They were comrades in Omega, the difference being that Marcel remained involved with the club after his potna went his own way. With help from an Omega scholarship, Marcel attended Tuskegee Institute for a couple of years before returning home to take care of his daughter. He now works full time at a boys and girls home, with intentions of going back to school for a degree in social work. At every turn, Marcel's first priority is his family. He even brings his daughter to Omega meetings. "I never had a father figure in my home," he says. "I always told myself I'd be there for my children."

In that context, what sets Marcel apart is not his promise but his commitment toward upholding it. I've found that many of the city kids who grow up without fathers swear to do better for their own children, but swearing to do better doesn't put meat on the table or presents under the Christmas tree; swearing to do better doesn't teach a young son to keep his eye on the ball, or to always tell the truth, or to be responsible for his actions, or to stay the hell away from the homies on the corner. Being there does that. And being there is a matter of the first priority. For the brother from the 'hood, being there is a matter of identifying the temptations, the risk factors, the obstructions—all the things that would get in the way and prevent him from raising his kids. "I think I'm out of the woods now," Marcel says. "But there are so many traps out there you can get caught up in. You've got to get away from the material aspect of things and stay focused."

If we could get our guys to understand that—to recognize that their pursuit of material things underlies so many of their problems—then we would have more Marcels and Andres on our hands and fewer Emanuels and Lamerles. To that end, Omega deemphasizes the material by emphasizing the spiritual in a nondenominational sense. It's been said that our holy trinity consists of Malcolm X, Martin Luther King, and Jesus Christ. However, while those three certainly get good publicity inside our walls, the generalization is not entirely accurate. Jack's prayers give equal time to

Allah and any other entity that would encourage a kid to exchange objects for ideas. What he tries to promote by closing every meeting with one of his eclectic wandering prayers is an individual spirituality that may or may not be related to religion.

Some of our members have made personal decisions to exercise that spirituality through organized religion. Macio Dickerson is foremost among them. This would seem peculiar to those who were exposed to Macio's hard edge and his very evident fondness for material possessions even after he joined the boys club. Macio was always a determined young man, and I had faith from the beginning that he would beat his addiction to drug money and all that it could buy, but I hadn't imagined that his turnabout would be so extreme—that he would become a devoted Bible student, minister, and missionary. He had demonstrated a striking gift for oratory when speaking to his peers at the Neighborhood House, but it never occurred to me that he would carry that talent to the pulpit.

The transformation began to occur when Macio's eventual wife, Luwanda, took him to the Christian Life Church. Bible college followed, along with outreach work in area prisons and the attending desire of both Macio and Luwanda to deliver their religion to central Africa. Previously, Macio had taken a semester of college work at Tuskegee Institute, but he wasn't ready for it. For him, Bible college—the study of theology—was a different matter entirely. It contained a spiritual relevance that he'd obviously been searching for.

Even when I was going to college, I was going for the wrong reasons. My values were messed up. I was going to college to make a lot of money. In America, everybody wants the finer things. But if getting things is first in your life, you're messed up, man. Because we have a fallen nature, we feel that material things make up substance. The material thing can't be who you are. It can't be your substance. You have to make God your substance. The answer is changing your values, and the only one who can really change your values is God.

I felt good when I read Malcolm X and learned about black history, but there was something still missing. I felt good when I got up and spoke at the club and people got excited and gathered around me, but there was something still missing. I was somebody who always said, "I'm never gonna be a Christian. That's the white man's religion. They ain't doin' nothin' for the black man." But when I walked into my church, the presence of God was there and that void within me was suddenly full. God showed me that unless man's inner self is changed, he's not really changed. I'm not talking about going to church or making confession or praying five times a day to Allah; that's duty. I'm talking about who you are. When your inner substance changes, everything on the outside will change along with it.

Everybody's focus is always on the outside: We need more programs; we need more structure. No. Society needs to be changed from within. People need to change from within. You have to understand who you are. You don't do right because it's the right thing to do; you do it because that's who you are. God loves because he *is* love; that's his very nature. And when a person's nature is pure, they're not going to do anything but what's right. That's who they are.

When I met Jesus Christ, I walked by the cold beer in the store and I didn't want it. They pass the joint to me at a party now, and I don't want it. How come? Something's different inside me. You remove sin by not wanting to sin anymore. I don't want to cheat on my wife. I don't want to smoke weed. When I gave my life to the Lord, I began to learn discipline.

The problem in the black community is sin. But the values of the black community only reflect the values of America. Money is the heartbeat of America.

America portrays that in order to be somebody, you have to have money, power, and fame. We're getting all the wrong information. Black kids are seeing the same thing on TV as they're seeing on the streets. Violence is a way of life on TV. Most of the shows for teenagers are based on sex. Most of what you see on TV is sex, sex, sex.

We can't try to change that from the outside; we have to change it from within. There are a lot of guys running around saying we need to save the black family, but they're not committed to their wives, to their families. They're not committed to taking care of the kids, to being on time for work every day. That's what we need. We need to teach kids commitment.

Macio Dickerson

Macio's experience has essentially formed him anew, and for the better, but it is not one that we can reasonably expect many other brothers to share. The bottom line is to change if you're not doing right, or if you *are* doing right, stay that way. We are more than satisfied if, like Corey Monroe, who carries no discernible baggage from his hazardous Hunters Point adolescence other than the bullet in his hand, a homie can step out of his environment into solid citizenship; or if, in the manner of former "crazy niggas" like Little Disease and Frank Newcombe, he can surmount the behavior that previously put him at serious risk. Little Disease, who once flaunted a classic "I don't give a fuck" attitude, now cares. While working two jobs and going to San Francisco City College at night for computer classes, he has managed to stay out of jail for more than two years—his longest stretch of free time since he was fourteen. Frank Newcombe has kept himself off the streets long enough to take care of his baby and, at the same time, job-hunt (for a while there, he was calling me every day about his various possibilities) while his wife works.

A few of our erstwhile bad-asses have found employment at a local food company called Mother Dear's, whose owner, Bill

Washington, came to me saying that he would like to hire some Omegas. There were no strings attached, which is the only way I would have cooperated. The club members, a couple of whom report to work in suits and ties, have turned out to be some of his best employees.

While calling attention to these temporary outcomes, I should point out, however, that the gainful steady employment of our members—or even the contrary—by no means concludes their stories. I'm certain that there are chapters yet to be played out in the sagas of young men like Joe Thomas, Jermaine King, Andre Aikins, Lamerle Johnson, Macio Dickerson, and Little Disease. And even as those brothers move on to the next stages of their lives, younger homies—our numbers are now in the range of six hundred kids—take their places on our priority list, authoring tales of their own that are just beginning to unfold. The new kids are actually the ones who keep me apprised of how far we've come. By looking at them, I'm reminded of what Joe and Jermaine and Andre and the others used to be like: raw uncut diamonds waiting to be mined, refined, and polished. All it takes for them to become gems is work—lots and lots of hard work.

One of those new kids—a work in progress—is an angry young man named Enoch Hawkins whom I met under adverse circumstances at McAteer High School. Enoch had been kicked out of the Oakland school district and wasn't crazy about being at McAteer in the first place. I discovered this as I stepped in front of him one day in the lunch line—a practice common among teachers who have duties to fulfill during the lunch period. Enoch was unsympathetic with the custom, however, and expressed it by cursing me. "I don't care who you are, nigga," he said. When I faced him and asked for his name, he refused to give it, made a few menacing remarks, and stormed off. I followed him down the hall and through the school, trying to find out his name. I finally caught up with him on the second floor and got right in his face. He didn't back off a bit, saying, "Fuck you, man, I'm not tellin' you nothin'." Enoch made it clear that he would rather fight than talk, but I didn't care. I had determined by that time that I wanted this kid bad. He kept mad-dogging me, then storming off, and I kept hounding him like a shadow, driving him crazy. "Back off me, dude!" he screamed.

The commotion ultimately attracted the dean, Mr. Levels, and when he arrived, I explained the situation. Mr. Levels said, "Enoch, why didn't you tell Mr. Marshall your name?"

"I don't know this motherfucker, man," Enoch replied.

I found out that Enoch was a nineteen-year-old with a history, having played on one of the best high school basketball teams in northern California before blowing his chance at a scholarship with a series of stupid actions. After being run out of Oakland, he had come to the San Francisco district on a trial basis to see if he could finish his last semester and graduate. He was on the threshold of blowing that, too. "If you don't tell this man your name," the dean said, realizing that by this time I knew Enoch's name but Enoch hadn't *told me* his name, "you're kicked out of school as of right now." Finally, Mr. Levels persuaded Enoch that it was in his best interest to report to the office. I said that I'd be in my classroom when they needed me.

A while later I rejoined Enoch and Mr. Levels in the office, at which point Enoch mumbled some sort of half-ass apology. "You ain't sorry," I shot back. "You're sayin' that because he told you to say that. I'm not concerned about your apology. I'm concerned about your behavior."

"Yeah, well, fuck that, man," he said. "I don't give a damn about no San Francisco schools." The dean asked me if I wanted Enoch suspended. I said no; I wanted him back the next night with his mother at our open house. That really set the kid off. There was nothing more for me to do there, and as I walked out of the office, Enoch was right on my heels. He went straight to the fire extinguisher case and, bam, with a vicious blow shattered glass all over the hall.

It was more than twenty-four hours later when Enoch and his mother showed up at the open house, and Enoch was still in his mad-dog mode. As soon as he spotted me, he said, "I been lookin' for you."

"Who you talkin' to?" I asked him.

"You, motherfucker. You dragged my mother down here; now let's get this over with."

With that, I greeted Enoch's mother, whose first reaction was one that I had seen countless times from mothers in her situation. "Why are you picking on my son?" she asked.

"He was out of line," I said.

"Were there other kids doing that?" She was obviously tired of dealing with her son and the school system and was taking out her frustration on me. So I laid the whole thing out for her and then went into my Omega thing.

Turning to Enoch, I said, "I'm gonna tell you what your problem is, son. You're a walking time bomb. You exploded yesterday over nothing. Let me ask you something. Where is your father?"

As soon as I said those words, the entire room changed colors. Suddenly, all of Enoch's profane pent-up anger faded into a profound silence. He just shut up. Then, as if a tap had been turned on, he began pouring out everything he could think of about himself and his life. He told me about stealing cars, about robbing dope dealers, about putting on a ski mask and mugging people on the street. He told me about the time he jacked a white man who was loading groceries into his car at the supermarket. Enoch put his gun to the man's head, made the guy drive him around the city, and shouted in his ear the whole time, saying things like, "How does this feel, motherfucker?" He had a whole litany of crazy acts like that.

Enoch's spontaneous outburst of unsolicited, highly personal information marked the most immediate transformation I had ever witnessed. After that, I couldn't get rid of the kid. Every day at lunchtime, he came into my class and sat down so that I could talk to him about black history and culture or show him tapes and films. "Marshall," he said at one point, "no one ever came at me like that before." I felt like Enoch's dad, which is what he obviously needed.

Enoch was by no means out of danger at that point, however. He had begun the process by coming to me for help, but he still had not handled his risk factors—the company he kept, the things he indulged in, his attitude toward women, and so on. A few months after our episode, he got kicked out of McAteer for smoking and drinking in the bathroom. Then he got his girlfriend pregnant and lost his composure for a while. Enoch was like a lot of guys I've seen at that stage of rehabilitation: when they have a setback, they go into a funk and do nothing for months at a time—totally unproductive behavior. They get up in the morning, strap on their beepers, gather up their gear, and go out and stand around all day. Joe Thomas had been no different than Enoch. Jermaine had been no different. They were just as bad as he was, if not worse, before they navigated their way through the three crucial steps to freedom:

1. acknowledging the problem, which is a matter of identifying the behavior that has placed them at risk;
2. coming to grips with the anger, fear, and pain that's behind their behavior; and
3. adopting a new way of doing things, that is, new rules for living.

Enoch is still negotiating the same course right now, halfway to becoming Jermaine or Joe or Nate or Corey. He has pulled himself together for the time being, studying for his GED while planning to go to a junior college and play basketball. Like those who have gone before him—some of whom stayed the course until it led them out of the game, some of whom turned off prematurely—Enoch has reached the point at which he has to adopt a new way of doing things or else face up to the alternative, which, as we have explained to him and so many others, is basically jail and death. It's up to him now.

As he steers through that perilous passage, however, he has something on his side that the older Omegas didn't: He has them to help him.

11

Letters

Periodically we focus the radio show on a particular theme, the theme generally involving one of the nine risk factors Ms. Norris and I have enumerated for young brothers and sisters. We've done several programs, for instance, on the black man's negative view of women and the women's negative view of themselves. On one of those occasions, Margaret opened the show by reading the disturbing passage from Nathan McCall's book *Makes Me Wanna Holler,* in which McCall and his so-called friends "pull a train" (a gang rape) on an unsuspecting, overwhelmed teenage girl. Another time we played the audio from a scene in *What's Love Got to Do with It?* in which Ike beats the hell out of Tina Turner.

We also frequently use letters to make a point—to share the perspective or the experience of someone who has been moved to write to us at *Street Soldiers* or at the boys club. We receive a lot of letters. A good many of them are testimonials from people whose lives have been changed by listening to the program. Others are pleas. Others, some of which we single out for our theme shows, are specifically topical, pertaining to a subject we might be discussing on a Monday night—such as the black man's treatment of black women.

KMEL *Street Soldiers*

I've been watching Black men for a long time. Particularly the young ones who don't seem to have a clue as to what being a real man means. I am the mother of a seven-year-old son. When he's asleep at night, I look at him long and hard. At how innocent he is. How smart. How beautiful. How vital. But sometimes I look at him so long that it makes me cry. I squeeze my eyes, and behind them I see this kaleidoscope of hundreds of young brothers I've seen hanging out on street corners in San Francisco, Oakland, L.A., Chicago, and New York, to name a few. I look at these young men very hard, too. I watch them drink from swollen paper bags. I've watched them packing their stuff. I've watched them rap to young girls and disappear inside pissy project doors because their rhetoric worked. I've watched them bop, boast about how much pussy they're getting and still "she can't claim me as her man." I watch the teenage mothers of their children watch the fathers of their children from the windows of small hot cramped apartments. They chain-smoke, feed the baby, while the young fathers do everything and anything they so desire except be fathers. Because they don't know how. Don't want to. And I watch young brothers wear blue or red and give themselves a name and terrorize the very neighborhoods we used to feel so safe in. I watch how they rob, kill, hurt people whose skin is the very same color as their own, and I watch how there is no remorse, there is no guilt. The boys who wear colors and brag about how many casualties fill their lists. I watch these young boys pretend they are men. They are so proud of their big dicks that they boast about its power.

I sit on the edge of my son's bed and look at how much he's grown already and realize one day I'll blink and he'll be twenty years old. When I pull the covers up and kiss his small forehead, I know that no matter how much I love him, no matter how much I try to teach him self-respect and respect for others, when he goes out into the world, he's going to be the kind of man he wants to be. I just pray that he won't be one of those young men in red or on the corner or hitting the pipe or making babies without bearing the responsibility. And I think of KMEL Street Soldiers. I pray that when he grows up that he carries on the insight and wisdom of Street Soldiers. Or better yet that he grows up and has one-tenth of Malcolm X's courage, insight, and wisdom. That what I am able to teach him and expose him to will deter him from the bullshit in the streets because he'll be more interested in being a real man by making something out of himself and adding something to our community instead of being a burglar of Black life in all its shapes and forms. I hope that he will make me proud. I hope he'll grow up to be a role model for somebody. I hope he never grows up wanting to kill or hurt anybody. I hope he grows up knowing that being a Black man in America is going to be hard, but he will know from history that men are made, not born. I hope he will be strong enough to say no to anything that will strip him of his power. I hope he will worry about the moral fiber of our community. I hope he will grow up knowing that if he is not an asset to anyone other than himself, then he will be a liability. I hope he knows how hard moral debts are to pay back. I hope that in the morning when he wakes up, he has dreamed once again about solving the world's problems. I want to continue to hug him for being brave even in his dreams. So that one day when he walks out my front door and waves and gets in his car, I hope that all the young men whose mothers are worrying about them right now, who cannot sleep, who ache inside because they are afraid, I hope that one day when I walk down the street I will see those young Black princes helping old ladies across the street, protecting our neighborhoods, doing their homework, writing letters home from college, and realizing that manhood is not measured by anything that's visible with the naked eye. It's the work you do inside yourself that makes you on the outside a man.

Mrs. LPF

Hi my name is B.H. I'm a Black woman living in the projects of west Oakland. I see a lot of Despair, Drugs, poverty and hopelessness. It's hard to try to cling on to hope, when all you see is your black people around you who have no respect for Black women, who use drugs to the point of total oblivion, who steal from you. I've been mugged in my own neighborhood 4 times. I've been kidnapped and I've been called Bitch so much I almost thought it was my name. It's really hard. I work very hard. I have tried to educate my people, and I've tried to form groups to better our living situation. Some of our people just have no awareness of a real life. My neighbors are crack smokers and I have 14 year olds outside my door who sell all kinds of Drugs.

Black men are hard to come by. All of the black men around me sell drugs, or either do drugs or whore, where they feel a woman should take care of them. I'm so tired of my black men just losing sight of what's real. I see black women whose fathers they never knew, and who deal with the most despicable behavior from their men. They get beat, treated like shit, man never has a job, waits on the woman's AFDC check, gets the money and goes and gets high. I'm tired of dealing with men who come from prison with no new insight except how they can get back into the game. I don't have a man because I haven't found one who's out for the same thing meaning job, family, and morals. I have had some men around here get offended at me for talking to different women about low life men. Where they wanted to fight me. Because I'm telling a black woman she doesn't have to be abused and mistreated by her man.

I really don't know any woman around who has a man who's really happy. It's a shame because every woman wants a man, and when you look around where are they? Even the ones who get out of prison half of them stay in the streets, don't come around except when they're hungry or tired but when they get caught and go back they want you as a woman to go thru those years with them. So many Brothers think you owe them something. All they have to do is throw some dick around and we as women have to deal with them. I'm tired of being a bitch a tramp a hoe and having a brother trying to take over when he ain't got and ain't trying to have shit. Selling crack doesn't pay into a pension fund. Going back and forth to prison does not look good on a resume. Black men need to wake up stop throwing your dick and throw your brain, and stop putting your women down cause right now it's us upholding our race. Cause right now our Black men are proving to be stupid and weak and Black women are getting fed up. I love myself and

I'm going to have something and I'm going to the top. I just hope I can have a Black man with me.

> Sincerely
> B.H.
> Stop the Violence.
> Stop the drugs.
> Peace out.

A problem I've had with reading letters over the air or at the Nabe is that so many of them come from guys in prison, which isn't surprising because they're the ones with the most time available for writing. I'm glad to hear from those who are incarcerated, and I'm glad that the show is reaching them; I appreciate that some of Omega's best work is going on behind prison walls; I think it's important that the guys from the club continue to share their knowledge with the brothers in prison; and I think that Jack is a hero of major proportions for what he does within the juvenile justice system in general. But notwithstanding all of that, I'm not comfortable reading letters publicly from guys locked up.

Jailhouse letters and jailhouse poets mean little to me because there's almost no connection between what a guy writes on the inside and what he does on the outside. I've seen too many guys write all the right stuff from jail and then flop once they hit the streets. There are no temptations in jail—no homies from the neighborhood, no drugs, no fast money to speak of. We've had a couple of Omega kids who were wonderful writers from jail, brilliant kids, but a week after they got out, they were hangin' with the set, and we never heard from them again. So I don't like emphasizing the guys locked up. I don't like glorifying them. I just want them to get out and stay out.

Unfortunately, the prison system itself doesn't seem to give a damn about the homies getting out and staying out. Rehabilitation is the last thing on its agenda. Prison, as we know it in this country, is little more than warehousing. For the most part, guys don't learn a thing when they're in—certainly not about the forces that led them to prison in the first place—and they don't become any better prepared to fend off those same forces when they confront them all over again on the outside. Prison is operated as merely a money-making economy for both the state and private citizens. If brothers want to put the prison industry out of business, they should stop feeding it.

The inmates who *do* learn something while incarcerated are those who teach themselves. They are those who, like Malcolm X and Nathan McCall and Sanyika Shakur, use their prison time to study history and culture and philosophy and ideology. Those brothers sometimes send insightful provocative letters that I can't resist sharing. The fact is, guys in prison know things. They've done things. They have stories and, within those stories, things to say that maybe can help somebody.

Revolutionary Greetings:

My name is A.X. I am a 27 year old Afrikan male, presently held kaptive at (a Kalifornia) koncentration kamp (i.e. "prison"). I was listening to your "Peace Rap" program, and I commend you all for your efforts. I would like for you to share this letter with your listening audience, especially with the young Brothas & Sistas out there; for they are the ones who are subjected to the vast majority of the madness out there.

As I was listening to you all on Street Soldiers *and after hearing the young brother/"gangsta" with the one year old manchild, I had to immediately get up and write to you as I couldn't call. I really hate to hear how foul that young brotha came. He sounded angry, hurt, disgusted, and very ignorant. But also, he sounded like he was under some influences (as Mr. Marshall said)—not just an intoxicant, but the influence of his "potnas" in the background. I heard some laughing and rooting on. Maybe he was trying to impress his so-called "peers." Afterall, he did say that this was his new family. Mr. Marshall asked him was he happy, and he said hell yeah; that he had an AK, Mac-11, and a "nine," so "hell yeah, you know I'm happy!" That brotha had to be high on something. That young "boy" has yet to be a man, and he didn't even sound like a hell of a gangsta! He's like so many other kids out* there who think they're "hard" because they got a gun. But in reality, those kids really ain't nothin but a bunch of young punks without a gun. They are nothing but a bunch of young, wild, cowards with guns, who incidentally, can't even shoot straight, as most of their victims are usually innocent bystanders.

Nonetheless, this doesn't make them any less deadly. In fact, this makes them all the more deadly because they become so damned reckless with guns in their hands. But if you were to take those guns away, they'd be like little naked babies in the wilderness. And this has never been more evident than in places like level 4, maximum security prisons. Prisons like Pelican Bay, Tehachapi Max., and new Folsom will either make or break a man. Those yards stay pop-pin & onlock-down. The inmates & "cons" don't have guns, only those racist ass gunmen. I've seen so many so-called "gangstas," "tough guys," and "riders" get straight punked when some funk jumped off on the yard, especially when those Southern Mexicans go on a warpath and take off on everything Black!! Brothers who were just a minute ago walking around with swollen chests & bold talk, be just-a-runnin' and a hollerin'; leaving their shoes behind trying to get away. Not to say that all brothas are this way, because there are some true Warriors left, I'm one of them. I have much love for all my Warrior-like brothas, inside & out, and for that matter, I have much love for all my Warrior-like sistas, inside & out, like you, Miss Norris and Mr. Marshall. Warriors, or Soldiers are not just physical, but they are mental & spiritual as well. I see a lot of "false bravado" in prison, and sometimes, I have to laugh. Not that by no means seeing another Black man getting stuck or shot on the yard is funny, but it's just a big trip to see a dude go from hella hard to hella soft in a matter of seconds. It seems like so many youngsters, male and female nowadays want to be a gangsta, hard or tough, but then usually buckle under some foreal "funk."

My young brothers, incarceration delivers the death of your physical freedom, at least until you get out, if you do get out, and even then, one will have to contend with parole, which is just about like being incarcerated in the streets. Incarceration delivers the death of your free choice; for then you are told what to do, as opposed to doing what you want, when you want. It delivers the death of your sex life. Prison is not "co-ed;" your cellmate will not be a woman. And there is never a guarantee that such a living arrangement will be "harmonious" or "compatible," which often it isn't. You may be living in a cell with another man whom you don't like, don't trust, and don't appreciate, as is often the case. And to complicate this situation; you'd have to put up with smelling another man's fart, or put up with the stench of another guy's defecating, or the disturbing sound of him urinating in the morning . . . when you're trying to sleep!

This and more is what entails being in a small grab box . . . or cell, with another dude! One could not possibly be all the man he needs to be while incarcerated. And my young brothers, I would never want you to experience such an emasculating existence!! A lot of you may think you're tough or macho because you can pull a trigger. Hell, a little child can do that!! The only ones who have guns in prison are the guards, and they won't hesitate to shoot & kill, or maim you for life! I have seen guys shot with the high powered, indiscriminate rifles they have here, and it is far from a pretty sight! If you are not killed, you'd wish you were when you see your leg literally shot off, separated from your body, jumping, twitching, and bleeding profusely. It should be noted that most of these shootings I witnessed were allegedly "accidental." It should also be noted that the ethnicity of the victims of the "accidental shootings" were Black! Coincidence? I DON'T THINK SO!!!

So when I hear young brothas talking that tough "yeng-yang," I can't help but wonder how they would hold up under some real "funk." Also, on the streets, brothas be gang-bangin', and don't truly realize the full extent of the funk that they'd be facing. Kickin' it with the homies, getting high, slinging "D," trippin' with the girls, and having love for each other, may seem to be "all good," but how do they feel when the so-called "enemy" catch them, their mamas, grandmamas, or any loved one of theirs slippin', and smoke them . . . then is it "all good?" You see, in that gang life, you and everybody you kick it with is open season to the so-called enemy! Dudes are out there kicking in the doors of everybodies mama or loved one, killing them and whomever else is around. A lot of youngsters who think that it's cool to wade through the waters of that gang life, not taking it all that serious, don't realize that it can get real deep, and they can easily drown, and take some loved ones with them. Back in the O.G. days, couldn't just anyone be a gangsta or a dope dealer; they not only had to be "down," but they had to have respectablity and some degree of self-control. But these days, you got all these overnight, initiation-free, wannabe gangstas, who are straight perpetratin'!! I only hope that that young brotha gets his act together . . . before it's too late.

Peep, there is no doubt that violence has increased considerably in the past several years. And the iciest part of the bloody & tear stained scenario is that the Black Communities are the greatest recipients of the physical, psychological, emotional, and even spiritual carnage caused by violence. My brothers and sisters, I will challenge you to be responsible, true to yourselves, and to exercise discipline & self-control. This is the key to a less violent society. You young brothers & sisters out there are the future generation, you can be great warriors of positivity who will take us into the 21st century with our hearts swelled with pride & admiration. In this mad, mad, but also beautiful world in which we live young brothers & sisters, you must be true Revolutionaries. I am talking about you launching a full scale mental revolution. Revolt against violent mentality; revolt against stupidity; revolt against illiteracy; revolt against drugs & alcohol; revolt against any & every negative influence in your lives . . . and become "Real Men," and "Real Women," and true lights of society!

And just for the record, it doesn't make you any less of a person to give some knuckle-head a pass. As long as you know where you stand as a person, no one can ever push your button for something petty & wack, and make you do something that you might regret later on in the game. When facing that often times troublesome bull of life, just remember to always take him by the horns, and ride that chump til his neck snaps. Stay smart, safe, and sucka free. See ya in 94.

All That I Am,
A. X.

Greetings Miss Norris,

Miss Norris my relationship with my mother isn't good it's just a hi and bye sort of thing to me. I come from a disfunctional family and *my mother and my father departed when I was 4 yrs old and when I was about 9 yrs old my mother started smoking cocaine (crack) and that's when my life became a straight nightmare or I became a threat to society at age 9. I went out into the streets and started hustling so that my siblings could have something to eat as well as myself because my mother stopped working and it was rough in the home so I went out my way to keep a meal on the table for us.*

My mom is or was a cool mother until she started messing with that stuff and ever since she started on that I became involved with the streets because I felt loved by the streets. I moved with my father at 9 yrs when my mother wasn't taking care of us right and when I moved with him I caused a lot of trouble because I started assaulting teachers at school and became a bully taking people money and so forth. Then I became involved with the law and my father stated to me I was going to be nothing in life so that hit my heart and I really started expanding my criminal behavior. While I stayed there with him his wife stayed with us and it was like I was neglected the only attention I got was when I got locked up. So I kept doing my thing and when I turned 11 yrs I went out into the streets to stay with my older associates that was in the game and when I got locked up my father would come get me and then I would leave because I was hooked on getting my money on and buying all type of material things on my own without my father or anybodys help at an early age. I never felt loved so I wasn't caring about myself or anybody else that came along I could make a victim. I was an impulsive, hostile young brother with alot of animosity towards anybody and everybody specifically at my family. I was just in the game and told myself get what I can because I'm going to die sooner or later. So I did alot of dirt to people with no remorse. My attitude was "I don't give a f———." So it was like get what I got coming and make it for what its worth. Thats how I thought about my life. I got locked up more, got out and on and on until I ran away twice from the boys ranch and I went back to the streets to get my money on both times and when I was on the run I committed the crime I'm in here for now. Miss Norris the crime I'm in here for is ugly I mean scandalous. I'm ashamed of talking about it but I have to if I want to change so here it goes.

Me and 3 of my older associates when I was 15 yrs old we went to a club for adults only before we went there we smoked dank all day (meaning weed) and drunk gin liquor and we was all messed up we were assaulting people for fun and then we went to the club and me and my one associate went in and got kicked out so we got in the car and started smoking more weed and this prostitute was walking pass the curb and my other associate came out and grabbed her and I got out the car and he said let's get her so she can hoe for us and I was like I'm cool and then he started. I was going out like a punk so I got pumped up because I had to keep my reputation of being crazy or down out there so I went along with it and we was grabbing her we kidnaped her and took her to our place and my older associate took her in the room of our apartment and talked to her then he came out and said I could go back in the room and have sex with her so I did and she wasn't fighting me off or anything because she was drunk too but I'm not trying to justify my actions because I was guilty for the whole thing but I had to keep my rep and my respect so I did it and the rest had sex with her too. The next morning my homie went to go buy her some clothes and she was washing dishes. I went back to sleep then my homie came back and we smoked some weed then in a few minutes later we got our door kicked in and we all got arrested.

Miss Norris I am truly sorry for my actions on participating in that act. I was pumped up to get my money on and I had this other female in her 20's approach me wanting to prostitute for me and I was all pumped up thinking if I had 2 I'll be rich. Its all crazy and I wish I could help that woman and show her how sorry I am for taking part in it.

Please don't look at me as a crazy person or whatever because that was my yesterdays and I'm a totally different young man now in searching for support and wisdom to fully change my bad ways and become the real me because all my life I've been someone I'm really not and now I'm ready to take all steps necessary to become a productive member of society. I'm 18 and I've been incarcerated for 3 years in the California Youth Authority and have 3 more years to go all because of me wanting to impersonate something or somebody I wasn't. I was putting on that facade of portraying a gangster, mack, pimp whatever you want to call it I'm not. Brother it ain't no gangsters out there, all the *gangsters are dead or in the pen doing time and what your doing out there is living your life for the city not for you! Your so called partners ain't your partners because when you end up in a casket they ain't going to do nothing but go to your funeral and cry and you need to look at why they are crying, when they are the ones who got you where your at helping you dig your own grave doing all that dirt with you. But to top it off after your gone you ain't nothing no more you just R.I.P. and that will be the end of you.*

I started listening to Street Soldiers in 91 and it has been inspiring me to do right plus I got an auntie who supports me. She came into my life in 91 too and now I'm looking for success. When I first stepped in here I was in all type of stuff riots, fights, all that jail house game stuff. Now I have my goals set and I'm using my time to get educated like my Brotha Malcolm X. For a change of life I reclaimed my inner self. I be preaching to young brothas in here with the little knowledge I have to help them turn themselves into positive people and it's working and I'm going to keep it up because it gives me something positive to do in here instead of being pessimistic.

Much love
T.

P.S. I got a letter from Jack today. Tell him I'll be responding soon. I put my last stamp on this letter.

I'm often amazed at how the letters from jail reveal their authors as virtual textbook examples of the behavioral patterns we talk about at the club and on *Street Soldiers*. The brother who wrote the letter above provides a classic model for no fewer than six of the risk factors we list among our nine: fearship (reflected by the fact that, for the sake of preserving his reputation and not being labeled as a punk, he committed deeds he knew were patently wrong); alcohol; drugs; a negative view of women; attitude (he stated plainly that he didn't "give a fuck"); and family/environment, which is the area to which he attributed most of his problems. The three risk factors that were not alluded to in the letter—destructive language, guns, and material values probably would have been if he had kept writing.

While not putting a lot of stock in letters written behind bars, I acknowledge that they do represent excellent therapy for their authors. By laying out their stories on paper, the inmates, perhaps unwittingly, come to identify and recognize their risk factors on their own. First-person writing is inherently an introspective process, and through it the prisoners—much as the Omegas do when they bare their souls at our Tuesday night meetings—put themselves in touch with the anger, fear, and pain that they must subdue before they can truly change their lives.

No matter how candid and thoughtful a jailhouse letter comes across, however, it is all but impossible to divine whether the brother who wrote it is truly free and clear of his problems. It's hard to read how angry he is, or scared, or hurt, and it is even harder to know if he can resist the temptations of his old ways once he gets out of prison and hits the 'hood. The authors of the following two letters, for example, describe themselves respectively as "a changed man" and one who is completely sincere about doing what he can to avoid becoming "just another casualty of the street." These brothers have written the right things, and by all appearances they are well on their way to recovery. But there's no definitive way to know if they'll make it. What we *do* know is this: They have obvious risk factors to deal with; they have histories of weakness in the face of those factors; and they should hook up with Omega when they get out.

Greetings Jack and Omega family,

Well Jack if you don't remember who I am, let me try to refreshen your memory. Back in 1989 when I got in Y.G.C. you and the Omega family came to my aid. You stood by me in every court date when I was facing four years in C.Y.A. I turned eighteen in Y.G.C. and you and Omega helped get me only ninety days in the county jail. You also set it up for when I got to the county jail, I could get my G.E.D. I got it! I told you that when I got out, I was coming to join the

Omega family and change my life. Did I? No! I got out Dec. 22nd 1989 and on Jan 15th 1990 I was standing on the corner and was shot in the back. When I came out of the recovery room and was put in my private room, guess who was there? You and the Omega family. You told me everything would be fine and I always had a family at Omega. Once again I told you that I was coming to Omega and change my life. But did I? No! I recovered pretty quick and some of my so-called "Homies" turned me on to what some might call "A new twist to the game," and before I knew it, I was back out there in the street life. I had a couple of jobs here and there but all the time I was still making money on the side from the street.

Yeah Jack I thought that I was slick but what I came to find out is that you can't mix right with wrong. Me and the "Homies" played our slick game for about two years until instead of picking up the "Homies" to go riding or out to a night club, I found myself picking up the "Homies" in caskets, carrying them to an awaiting hearse to take to the burial site. I told myself that it was time to get out of this game because it was only a matter of time before I would be the one in the casket, but before I got out, I decided to make one more move. Well Jack I made that one more move and it got me an 8 year sentence to state prison!!

I stayed in the county jail almost two years fighting my cause and many times I wanted to pick up the phone and call you or pick up a pen and write but I didn't because in a way, I felt stupid. I had my chance to come to the Omega famly for guidance but I didn't and I didn't want me being in a bad situation again to be the only reason for me to get in contact. Before I go on with this letter, I want to thank you and the entire Omega family for being there for me when I needed you. Thank you!

I have been incarcerated for two years and four months now and I have had plenty of time to think. I finally decided in my heart to change my life around and when I say this, I say it from my heart. I have been building my mind on a daily basis so when I come out of here in the next year and a half I will be a changed man with positive goals in life. Jack I'm hoping you read this letter to the rest of the Omega family so let me say this to everyone:

Brothers and Sisters of the Omega family, in this day and age, we *are living in a society where disease, drugs, and killings are getting to be an everyday routine within our communities. We have sons, daughters, nephews, nieces, etc., growing up seeing these things go on and we all know the young mind is sometimes easily influenced but we can help change the foul things that our younger generation is experiencing but first we must help ourselves so we can build the path for us and our future generation. Nothing is easy but we must try! So preach one and teach one! Preach one, teach one!*

We must continue to push for knowledge, pull for strength, and stride for our goals. Push, Pull, Stride! Push, Pull, Stride! Education and determination "is" the key to succeed but you have to want it and keep wanting it!

Brothers and Sisters, I write to you at this time a changed man, not the man I once was and I hope you feel me in your hearts. Don't be like me and wait until you are in a situation such as mine before you decide to make a change. Do it now!! Omega can and will help you build that positive path.

Peace Out
M.J.M.

Dear Street Soldiers
(Mrs. Norris Mr. Marshall),

Your show Street Soldiers *has instilled alot of courage in me. It took alot of courage for me to write this letter. I never expressed my feelings to anybody else about how I felt about the show. I was afraid of what the guys would think about me.*

Well my name is [F.M.C.] I'm 21 years old and I'm a black male. I am presently incarcerated at one of the California Youth Authority institutions. This is my third time. All my crimes have evolved around drugs. I don't use drugs but I do consider myself to be an addict. I'm addicted to the monetary gain associated with the money that comes from the sells of drugs.

I write to you tonight because I need help as well as advice. I am eligible for parole once again in four months. I don't want to sell drugs or participate in any illegal activities anymore. What I'm about to tell you I haven't told or spoke with anybody else about. I figure it's time for me to stop hiding and come out. This is the first step to a successful recovery for me.

My mom is an addict (crack). My mother used to be a very successful computer programmer. We were a very happy family. Just her and myself. I'd say the year was 1985. My father left my mother when I was 2 years old. My mother married twice. Both marriages didn't work out. The last marriage the guy was abusive towards my mother. He even once forced her into having sex with him in front of me. Well right after this my mother's only brother got killed. It was a very violent death. At the time I wasn't doing too good in school which didn't help matters any. So with all this pressure she turned to drugs. I can't remember the very first time I seen her because I've blocked it out of my mind. I do know that I started selling drugs soon after. I didn't start selling drugs for the money at first. I started selling drugs out of anger. I wanted to get back at all those who destroyed what my mother and me once had. I now realize that I was wrong and that it only made things worse. I want to change.

My mother is out there in Berkeley somewhere. I really don't have anybody but myself. My mother's parents are really well off financially and are really good grandparents. They've dis-owned me because of my involvement with the streets and drugs. I've been living with my father's mother off and on. She's all that I have. I can't go to her house this time when I get out because she lives around the corner from where I've sold drugs and established this notorious drug dealing character named "Dancer." I've hid behind Dancer too long. I want to be [F.M.C.] again. I just don't know how or where to even begin. I'm seeking help now because I don't want to end up just another casualty to the Oakland streets.

I give great thanks to Street Soldiers because if it weren't for you I know I wouldn't of had the courage to write this letter.

Thanks,
F.M.C.

I feel the same way about testimonials that I do about prison mail. When it comes to publicizing congratulatory letters, there's a fine line to consider between positive reinforcement and self-aggrandizement. I would prefer to weigh in on the side of modesty unless that preference is superseded by the purpose of the Omega Boys Club and the purpose of *Street Soldiers*, which is to light the path to a better way. Keeping my sights on the North Star, I'm more than happy, in those cases, to let somebody else carry the lantern for a while. Some of the brothers and sisters who write us know the way as well as I do; they've walked it before.

Street Soldiers,

My name is [F.] and I'm a addict. Well about nine months ago while I was getting high on crack, I was listening to the show and I heard Mr. Marshall say "There is nothing you can't do, that you really want to do." And for about 10 mins I could see myself not getting high on crack anymore. But naturally I kept on getting high. Then two weeks later I was listening and I heard just what I needed to hear and that was that "Street Soldiers is about saving lives." And believe me my life needed to be saved.

See I thought that Street Soldiers was for the younger brothers and sistas of the world. I'm 31 years old. And I had no clue that I'm important to you guys too. [smiley face]

Thank you for my new life.

F.

Oh yeah I'll have nine months clean on the 28 of March. [smiley face]

Midnight, and once again I'm up listening to Street Soldiers. I just heard Ali, Raymond and Preston talking to a 12-year-old and his mama and I got tears in my eyes. God bless all of the Street Soldiers everywhere.

I've been listening for about a year. I put my kids to bed, turn on the radio around 11:00, listen, think, talk to the radio and myself—but

I never call. I went through the drugs, booze, sex scenes, mental hospitals, you name it, when I was young. But, I'm now 34, and living in suburbia, with the requisite two kids, dog, cat—everything but the picket fence. So I wonder sometimes about how I'd be received if I called.

But, after a year, I have a few things to say.

I work, I play, I stay involved with my kids, their schooling, my community . . . but I listen every Monday night and it hardly compares to what you are putting out there. I am inspired every time I tune in. I learn so much from all the Street Soldiers and I learn from those still in darkness and pain. I'm not in a gang, I'm not black, I'm not in a whole lot of misery right now, but I still learn a lot about me, and you, from listening and hearing. I am moved to tears yet filled with joy when I hear what is going on in the world beyond my little piece. From Street Soldiers I get the real news, what's really going on in the hearts and minds of those fighting in and against the war going on in our country. It's late and I'm rambling but I needed to let you know that I'm out here, I'm listening, I'm caring a lot, I'm pursuing a teaching degree for secondary school and headed for the inner-city to do what I can.

God Bless. Peace. Thanks for being there.

J.
Petaluma, Calif.

Dear Sister Norris and Brother Marshall,

It's 2:45 a.m., and I am up, studying and finishing a paper for tomorrow's class. As a college student, the program has meant more to me than you know, as something that continues to keep me inspired, as well as keeping me focused and determined to graduate so that I can contribute to my community in the way that I think I am best suited for. It is my goal to become a college professor and researcher of issues that relate to the upliftment of the black community.

The name I go by is Makai. It is not my real name, it's my pen name. Unfortunately, I cannot give my real name since my academic environment is very conservative and I do not sense that my professors here would understand my need to listen to Street Soldiers, write music, and give back to my community instead of concentrating 100% of my time on doing more "relevant" activities.

Shalom
Makai

Dear Mr. Marshall and Miss Norris

You guys have been there for me since day one. Both of you guys have been more of a friend than a homie or a "patna" could ever be. I can't put into words the trust, respect, and head strong feeling you have placed upon me. From day one you never down me for the way I use to be or the road I had chose to travel, but instead you took me under your wing and showed me a better way. You never tried to force anything on me but let me know there's a better way and you guys could show it to me if I was willing to listen.

So now thanks to you I no longer feel the need to have a gun by my side, or a crew that will walk behind me. I can walk alone and can do bad by myself. Thanks to you I have decided to get my GED and become what I have always wanted to be, a police officer. Thanks to you guys I am somewhere I never thought I would step a foot on unless it was to cause trouble or problems for someone else—a college. Thanks to you guys I have my head on straight and not backwards and it not filled with dank smoke. Thanks to you guys I no longer feel the need to have a yo or 2 to make me feel good, because just knowing I'm a street soldier gives me the highest high that no drug or drink could ever give me. Any time I want to do something that I'm not sure is right or wrong I think "what would Mr. Marshall or Miss Norris think or say about that," and then I can move on. You guys will never know what you have done to my life. It's so many things that I don't do anymore, I don't hang-out, I don't mug people anymore.

All I can say is thanks, thanks a lot, you have help me more than you will ever believe. If there is anyone out there that feel they can't do it, I was once in their shoes. And, if I can do it, I know they can.

I would like to thank you guys and gals one more time, and tell you this:

I am damn sure proud to be a Street Soldier for life.

Nate "Nuke" Pique

Although I can state unequivocally that the Omega Boys Club has made a profound difference in hundreds, possibly thousands of young lives within our reach—and it's important to make that point for the sake of hope, encouragement, and proof positive concerning the model we've established in California—I don't mean to give the false impression that what we do is magic, above human frailty. I don't intend to suggest, by any means, that every letter in our post office box contains a glowing testimonial from a brother or sister who has been delivered from the chokehold of the streets. Some of the homies out there still argue that drugs and guns can do more to improve their situations than we can. Some maintain that we're out of touch because they've tried to change— or at least they *think* they've tried to change—and it hasn't worked.

We also hear quite often from sincere folks who feel the cold steel of urban life pressed against their temples. Some of them are struggling to wrestle the weapon away from the life that has placed them in such peril; others are actually groping for the trigger. Those people write letters, too, and those letters serve a purpose, too. They let us know in no uncertain terms what we're up against. In a very real way, they define our task, even as they're breaking our hearts.

Dear Mr. Marshall and Miss Norris:

Several weeks ago, on Valentine's Day, I wrote your program a letter asking for your help in locating my son Jacques so that he wouldn't die on the street like his dad. Thank you so much for your help for it brought the result I was hoping for. Jacques did get the message from someone off the street and did in fact call me two days later. We met for about a half of an hour but he refused to live in Vallejo. He said he was doing fine, working and not selling any drugs. For some reason I didn't believe him because he looked tired and worn, had the same clothes on he had when I saw him for Christmas. Things just didn't feel right.

A friend of my daughter had also heard your program the night you all read my letter and told her exactly where Jacques hangs out. Mr. Marshall I went one night to find my son and I did. I saw for myself the life he really lives. He is a drug dealer. It hurts me to see my son so satisfied with destroying lives in the black communities of Oakland.

I can't reach him, Mr. Marshall and Miss Norris. He's so entrenched into this lifestyle. It will take near destruction to bring him back. He made me promise not to come back looking for him because it's too dangerous. I can't do that. I won't do that. Somewhere folks our society of grown-ups failed our youth. I failed to provide the man figure in my son's life as an example of how a man should be. Will you help me KMEL Street Soldiers and your listening audience? Help me save my son. I can't handle a trip to the cemetery. His son, my grandson, needs him. We need him to stop drinking and smoking so much weed, just for a while, perhaps for a year to turn his life around.

Mr. Marshall and Miss Norris, bring Jacques into your KMEL Street Soldier family and help me find out what I can do to help him get himself together. He needs to hear from a man like you Mr. Marshall. A man who serves the community rather than destroy it; a man whose grammar base consists of phrases other than "It's all good Mom;" a man who didn't blame everything on the white man but chose to shape a clear-cut destiny for himself. I failed as a mother in that respect, but I myself, as a single black mother, had an uphill climb and I succeeded. Anyone can be a success. No one can succeed if they're drunk forever, sleeping all day—up all night, living on GA and loving it. You know folks, I never thought this could happen to my son. I'm mad as hell that a whole generation of black men will and is dying, and it took the destruction of my family to see that.

Therefore, I'm volunteering to go into the schools. I want to organize my friends and others to help mentor our young black men. Oh, let's not forget the girls. (When I was on the street looking for Jacques, it was a girl I saw distributing the drugs. Somehow the drug dealers are

encouraging their women to sell so they won't get a case I was later told.
The courts are more lenient with the women especially if they have kids.
So now we're dragging our women into this system of black genocide.) If
I can't save my own son maybe I can take my love for our children
where it can be effective.

S.W.

The following letter is directed to your radio program, Street
Soldiers. *It was constructed with the intent to convey a message to your*
many listeners. In no way do I intend for this letter to justify my new
found choice in "career decision." Morally, I realize that it is the wrong
thing to do. Personally, I see no other choice.
    Let me start with my definition of what I consider a "real nigga"
to be. "Any male individual, be it black, latino, Asian, and even Cau-
casian who positively believes himself to be expendable, be it consciously
or unconsciously, and can justify his attitudes at any point in time, in
any arena." Do y'all see where I'm coming from? Aint no glory in the
word nigga, aint no good that comes from it. However, please don't
think you got all of this from someone who is against individuals who are
real niggas because I happen to consider myself as a 100% "real nigga."
I drafted this letter in an effort (a twisted effort I guess) to help bring
clarification as to what this word really brings about in the lives of those
who feel they have been forced to wear it.
    I felt compelled at this point in time to make this statement due to
what has occurred, and is occurring, and what is soon to occur in my
personal life. I am a 24 year old African American male who could be
viewed as blessed and fortunate. But it is quite hard at this point for me
to view it as such. My story is no harder than the next man's, I make no
excuses, but it is "my story" nonetheless.
    I lost my mother on Dec. 31st, 1981, 19 days after my 13th
birthday. I have a father who has never once verbally conveyed to me he
loves me, and has alienated me since the day of my mothers death. He
told me the day after she died "Your moma's death was the best thing
that happened to me!" He was referring to the fact that had she lived,
she had plans on divorcing him, subsequently splitting all of their marital

assets down the middle and leaving him broke. I understood his position, but that was still my moma! However, I kept cool, respecting his position and didn't make waves.

To make a long story short, I graduated from high school and in an attempt to appease my elders (father, grandparents, aunts, uncles) I entered college in the fall of 1988 at a California State University. I was only an average student in high school and was just lucky enough to get in. I worked very hard to keep up with the other students, but by the summer of 1990, I was stressed out, the pace had me beat, add on the fact my GPA was 2.2 (and steady dropping) and my father was looking at me and my report card straight up saying "You aint trying! You waisting time and all my money!" I took a bottle of pills in June of that year and attempted suicide.

Much transpired during that summer, but in the interest of time I'll only say I showed back at school 3 months later and over the next three years I managed to raise my grade point to over 3.00, make the National Deans list and earn my Bachelors of Science degree. Not to mention I was the first grandchild on my father's side of the family (out of 7) to complete college. I, after much (I repeat much) pounding of the pavement in search of a job opportunity, constructed a resume, and landed a job. My struggle, one might think, was over, my mission complete. Not so:

I returned back to my fathers house (due to financial incapability to fully support myself) to be told by my father that the job I had landed was "a waste of time and energy," even though it's in my major. My grandfather, shortly after I was released from school told me "You should have chose something else, that mess you got your degree in aint nothin'." Yet and still, out of respect for my elders, I said nothing. I bowed my head in frustrated and futile silence, or as a real nigga would say, "like a punk!" But after all that has transpired in my 24 years, I simply refuse to go out like that! I have done numerous and extreme "self checks," "gut checks" if you will, and have come to the honest conclusion that there is not a motherfucka on the face of the planet that ever once cared about or for me. The messages I've received from my elders, people I ONCE respected, are plain as day.

- My mother liked alcohol better than me!
- My father only likes me if I make money in six figures and my grandfather, the same! (And I don't come close to that.)
- Grandmother doesn't care, just stay good and out of trouble!

At this writing, I am single, no children, educated, and living at home. I am also black, employed but barely making enough to pay a cheap car note, broke, and a torn and shattered young man. I harbor nothing but hate for my fellow man in this society (except for my niggas and the almighty dollar) and truly feel cheated by my "elders" and the system in general. However, like Patti LaBelle, "I got a new attitude." I once had a plan, to go to school and complete it, get a job, and live positive. And I did it!

All that has changed!

By the time you read this letter I will have joined the ranks of countless African American men in every major city in this country who sell drugs for a living. I personally see no other alternative. I have never been convicted of a felony, and have never owned a gun of any sort. This I am happy to say (I repeat) happy to say will soon change. I've got me a pistol on the way. I realize as you read this paragraph you are ashamed of my personal decision, and condemn my negative attitude. I value your opinion. Due to the fact I listen to your show objectively and truly believe change can come about, it just has to come about now without me, for I am beyond rehabilitation.

My final plea goes out to all parents and other family members in general who hold a genuine concern to this issue. We are not losing a generation, we have lost a generation! But all hope is not lost, not all of us (your children) are hopelessly lost. Please, if you got the strength and love in your heart, go and reclaim your son from this madness. Most of us want out of this shit, we just feel that unwanted, that we can risk our lives for a numbered piece of paper. If the people that bring you into this world show no effort to guide you through it, you must guide yourself. As a collective, us niggas out here are really messing up. Let my life (if it must) be the telltale story: The white man's dream, another black boy turned hood only this time it's sweeter, this one finished school.

Mr. Marshall and Miss Norris always speak of the old African legacy of the elders guiding the tribe, giving wisdom and knowledge to its young. So far, they are the only two elders I know with both feet in the game trying to pull us fools out! I may sound inexperienced by the way I presented myself in this letter but let me say this, I grew up in the streets. I however chose to be a leader and stand on the curb and be an example. I ain't tryin' to lead no more. I'm following, and it ain't on the sidelines no more either. . . .

Signed:
A Wayward Black Man

There was no return address on the letter. I never had a chance to write the brother back.

12

L.A.

Even as the club was making its mark in San Francisco, Los Angeles stayed on my mind. It was inevitable, considering that I had grown up in the heart of the most notorious gang turf in the country. What's more, I felt it was incumbent upon me, in my role with the boys club and *Street Soldiers*, to keep abreast of the most pertinent contemporary works about urban violence, and invariably those were set in South Central. The most relevant books (*Monster* and *Do or Die*) and the most relevant movies (*Colors, American Me, South Central, Boyz 'n the Hood,* and *Menace II Society*) all were about Los Angeles. It was as if the boys club had discovered an antidote for a deadly virus that had originated in Los Angeles and spread to cities like San Francisco; no matter how effective we were in treating the disease locally, L.A. was going to keep screaming at us anyway.

The screams reverberated in my ears and Margaret's on the same day late in 1991. Monster's brother, Kershaun Scott, himself a notorious Eight Tray Gangsta known as Li'l Monster, and an Athens Park Blood called Bone (whose real name is Cle Sloan) happened to be in San Francisco that morning promoting *Do or*

Die, Leon Bing's book about South Central gang life. Doc and I heard them being interviewed on radio station KNBR and were so captivated that I called the show to tell them about the Omega Boys Club. I was too late, though, and was still miffed at missing the chance to speak to Li'l Monster and Bone when someone flipped on the TV, and there they were again with John Singleton, the movie director, on a Channel 5 show called *People Are Talking.* I said, "Doc, we got to meet these guys."

With no further delay, we raced out to my car and within a matter of minutes were in front of the KPIX studios, where we waited for the group to come out. Singleton emerged first. We introduced ourselves and chatted a little, then he handed us his card and climbed into the limousine. (Later, I would run into Singleton again and again—we were together on a *New York Times Sunday Magazine* panel, among other things—and he has commented that he sees me wherever he goes.) Li'l Monster and Bone emerged a few minutes later, and when we greeted them, they were conspicuously wary. Kershaun, whose powerful build and grim demeanor create a forbidding presence, was especially impassive, but Bone loosened up after several exchanges. "Yeah," he said at one point, "you guys really do understand. Y'all are for real." He gave us his phone number. Li'l Monster gave us nothing, including the time of day.

We kept in touch with Bone, who in turn relayed our discussions to Kershaun. The next spring, when we hosted our first Knowledge Conference, we invited the two of them to conduct a panel on the riots that followed the Rodney King verdict, entitled "Los Angeles: The Real Story." Even Kershaun, despite his apparent indifference toward us, was keenly interested in getting out the truth about gang members. His agenda was to counteract the image of the gangster as some sort of savage without a heart, soul, or conscience. And he was good at it. He and Bone were so strong, in fact, that we took the tape of their panel and played it on *Street Soldiers.*

More significantly, the success of their appearance gave us a starting point from which we hoped to build a relationship with the

Crips and Bloods. "This is great," I told Bone afterward, "but what we really want to do is talk with some of the homies." We kept having that conversation for more than a year—until after our second Knowledge Conference, when Bone and Li'l Monster did their thing again. "All right," I said. "You've done two conferences now. We're coming to L.A." One Friday a few weeks later, Doc and I rented a car and took off down I-5 along with Corey Monroe and two other Omegas.

The plan was that Bone would gather a bunch of his homeboys—Athens Park Bloods, of course—and we would just kick it. Then we would go see Kershaun and his Eight Tray potnas. We really had no idea what to expect; we knew only that we were headed into the heart of the nation's most infamous battle zone to talk peace to brothers who no doubt would be highly suspicious and heavily strapped. As we drove through South Central on the way to the first get-together, Corey gawked at the low houses, the fences, the palm trees, the drawn curtains, the gangstas lurking on the corners—all the scenes he had seen in so many movies. "Man, this is no movie," he said. "This is real."

When we came to Bone's house in the middle of the afternoon, there were Bloods hanging around outside keeping watch over the place. The patches on the house indicated that it had been riddled by bullets, and the piano inside was so damaged by gunfire that it didn't play. Instead of staying there, Bone led us through Athens Park, where clusters of brothers and sisters were barbecuing. I wondered how we were going to do any serious talking with all the barbecuing and partying going on. But Bone kept walking out the other side of the park to his mother's house a couple of blocks away, and one by one guys I recognized from the barbecue began filing into the living room. When about twenty of them had assembled, Bone said to the Bloods, "These are the people I been tellin' y'all about. They've just got some things to say."

So we started talking just like we do at the Nabe, and they listened just like the guys and girls do at the Nabe, except more quietly. The only Blood who openly challenged what we said was one who came in late and drank from a bottle. It crossed my mind

—and I'm sure it crossed Doc's and Corey's—that there were killers in that room, but on the whole they were very hospitable. When
we were finished and walked back to the park, one of the brothers
said something to Ms. Norris about his eyes hurting when he
looked at her because she was so pretty. She laughed and later
commented that she felt safer with the Bloods than she often has
in the company of upwardly mobile businessmen.

We called Kershaun when we arrived back at the Embassy
Suite and invited his group to meet us in one of the rooms there.
Around seven that night, he strolled in with his homies C-Rag and
Youngster and about half a dozen other Crips. Shaun still hadn't
gotten past his skepticism about us—about all strangers, actually—
and joined the discussion very reluctantly. I attempted slowly to
gain his trust and the others', hoping the conversation would be
two sided. In addition to offering the gangsters ideas about peace-
making and about giving up their arms, my purpose there was to
acquire information concerning the dynamics of the Los Angeles
game and how it compared to the turf structure that we knew in
the Bay Area. Shaun continued to hold back, but Youngster and the
others engaged us in a rap session that made it clear that the
principal difference between southern California gangbanging and
northern California turf resulted from the depth of the Crip-and-
Blood wars, their history and tradition. Gang life was the legacy the
South Central brothers had inherited, and while they could see it
wasn't working, it was nonetheless all they knew; it was what they
had been raised on, much the same way an Iowa farmboy might be
raised on hard work. We were extremely encouraged, and in fact
blown away, by the introspection and open-mindedness of the OGs
in our midst. I could see that even Kershaun's interest was piqued.
We didn't want to leave.

Once a month for the next three months, Margaret and I
returned to Los Angeles to exchange ideas with the Crips and
Bloods, each time earning a little more of their confidence. I
helped two of them try to find jobs, and another of the erstwhile
gangsters agreed to go back to school. We were making headway.
My breakthrough with Kershaun, though, didn't occur until the

evening his documentary (*Eight-Tray Gangster: The Making of a Crip*) was shown at the Los Angeles Film Festival. Afterward, we stood out by Sunset Boulevard talking late into the night.

I had known quite a bit about Li'l Monster before we ever met. According to his brother's book, Kershaun was the one who had orchestrated the payback after Monster had been bush-whacked by rival gang members. Kody Scott (Sanyika Shakur) de-scribed Kershaun Scott as a serious, extremely dependable street warrior, one apparently destined to follow in the family tradition established during his big brother's legendary career as an Eight Tray Gangsta. Even as a young teenager, Monster had been a noto-riously fearless street guerrilla, dressing in black at night, mounting his bicycle, and setting out alone on murder missions deep in enemy territory. It was evident by Kershaun's intimidating de-meanor that he was every bit as hard and down (that is, dedicated to the set; ready to do whatever he had to do) as his brother. What I didn't know about Li'l Monster was the extent to which he, like Sanyika, had begun to grow out of his gangster persona.

My hope with Kershaun had been that I could persuade him to use his obvious influence to stop the madness in the streets and help save the generation. But as I found out that night on Sunset Boulevard, he was actually several steps ahead of me. From that point forward, I kept up a steady communication with him, and his devoted sense of citizenship—his deep desire to do right and ele-vate the race—emboldened me to take the next step: to bring the Crips and Bloods together. We had been flirting with the L.A. brothers for nearly two years, and it was high time to put our efforts to the test.

We decided to do it on Omega turf. The plan was for three Crips and three Bloods to fly to San Francisco, where they would be together for an entire week doing the things we do at the club. Bone couldn't make the trip because he had learned to be a film cameraman through Jim Brown's *Amer-I-Can* program and was busy shooting the movie *I Love Trouble*, but he helped round up three of his potnas—Wack, Ratman, and D-Dog. My only request to him and Kershaun was that they send us gang members who were willing to change. I didn't care what they had done or been capable of doing in the past; only that they were receptive to the prospect of a different lifestyle. Given that directive, Li'l Monster selected Youngster, who had been a regular at our Los Angeles sessions, and Stagalee, a hard-core OG who had been a sidekick of Monster Kody Scott and with whom I had become familiar through Monster's book.

I was fully aware that we were doing a dangerous thing, bringing such confirmed, hard-line enemies to the same place—we had even arranged for the motel rooms to be shared by a Crip and a Blood—but I figured that if the plane landed in San Francisco unscathed, it would be clear sailing after that. It was with considerable relief, consequently, that I welcomed six young men at the airport, each wearing his gang colors but still in one piece.

It was November 1993, and they arrived early in the afternoon of some heavyweight fight that I don't even remember; I never saw it. As the fellows pulled up desks and chairs in the large, open classroom next to the Omega office—by that time we had moved our office to an old frame school building on Tennessee Street, in the warehouse district between Potrero Hill and Hunters Point—they made it clear that they expected to talk a little bit, go out for a bite to eat, then settle in somewhere to watch the fight. Well, we sent out for food at five o'clock, and the fight came and went without another mention. It was about eleven that night when we finally broke up.

In one marathon session, Doc, Coach, and I showed clips from *Roots* and *Eyes on the Prize* and stormed through what amounted to Omega 101, with a few hours of Advanced Omega tacked onto the end. It was a crash course in essentially our entire antiviolence package, including the nine risk factors, the handling of anger, fear, and pain, and the four rules for living. In enumerating the risk factors—guns, drugs, destructive language, material values, and the rest—we were able to point out and even personalize the specific behaviors that essentially defined the gangsters' lifestyle. The discussion of anger, fear, and pain awakened them to the necessity of coming to terms with their emotions in a positive context. And the rules for living gave them new standards to use as their guides for rehabilitation.

Beyond the motive of education, we wanted to see if our formulas held up under the Crip-and-Blood test. "Does this stuff make any sense?" we would ask periodically. The answer, more often than not, was yes and no; that is, the guys bought into some of our rap but not all of it. Li'l Monster, for instance, despite our lecture on risk factors, remained adamant about his right to bear arms. He and I went back and forth on that issue, Kershaun asserting his constitutional privilege and I emphasizing the mortal recklessness that carrying a gun represented. "This is what is getting you guys killed," I argued.

Late into the night, as we plunged into the four rules for living, Doc went to the blackboard and wrote, "Life; Friendship; Change; Respect." Then we undertook to examine each of those things. We talked about the precious nature of life and the fact that, in the 'hood, the enemy is never killed; about friendship and the fact that a friend will never lead a friend to danger; about the courage to change and the fact that a real man or woman stands alone; and finally about respect. We talked longest and hardest about respect, especially how to get it. As always, this was a fundamental point of contention with the homies, who traditionally operated on the premise that respect is a function of reputation, and reputation, in turn, is earned through things like money and cars and jewelry and guns and women and being hard and down. Stagalee was one in particular who very evidently subscribed to all of this, a classic sort of gangsta. He had the reputation, he had the history, and he definitely had the look, with tattoos from top to bottom. He was also the most consistently skeptical brother in the room. So we ran down the whole subject of respect with him, and he acknowledged that he had spent most of his life trying to earn it.

"Stag," I inquired, "did you ever get respect from all the stuff you did—the killing, the robbing, the moving on each other?"

"Naw," he said. "I don't think so. I got it in prison."

"How did you get it in prison?" I asked. "When did you get it? What did you do to get it?"

"I gave it to myself," he answered slowly. "I never found it when I was out there lookin' for it, so I figured out I had to learn to respect myself."

It was a golden moment. Doc and Coach and I looked at each other with looks that said, "Damn! How about that?!" Here was one of our very own rules for living rolling straight off the tongue of one of the hardest, stubbornest, most notorious gangstas in South Central. After ten hours of talking things over and thinking things through, these guys were reaching the very same conclusions we had reached and preached over the course of countless long nights. We hadn't put those words in Stag's mouth. We hadn't written them on the board. They came from his experience. It was wonderful.

When they pulled into their motel just before midnight, the Crips and Bloods crammed into one room, popped the *Roots* tape into the VCR, and watched until dawn. The schedule didn't slow down for them the next day, however. The week was packed. They spoke to Bay Area gang members at Juvenile Hall, to Omegas at the Nabe, to students at a couple of area high schools, and to *The CBS Evening News*. During the *Street Soldiers* radio program on Monday night, Kershaun rapped with an angry teenager from Oakland bent on avenging the murder of his brother, who had been gunned down in a drug dispute. When he sensed that he needed to counsel the kid privately, Li'l Monster transferred him to another line, where he was able to draw from his own experiences without the radio audience listening in. Before hanging up, the boy promised Kershaun he would go to bed and hold his revenge for the time being. "Man," Kershaun said afterward, awed by the power of right reasoning, "I saved someone's life tonight."

As the week wore on, Li'l Monster became increasingly affected by the experience of saving lives. Ultimately, we got him to think hard about his own. Of all the gangsters who made the trip to San Francisco, Kershaun clearly was the one who most wanted to change his life. But weaning him from his weapon was no easier than getting a junkie off cocaine. Our challenge was to break down his dependence—to persuade him that if he didn't carry a gat, he wouldn't put himself in situations where he might need one. As much as he wanted to change, because of his habits he was still a dangerous character. There's a criterion I generally apply to the people I work with: Could I have my eight-year-old daughter around him, or does his lifestyle place her in danger? When I met Kershaun, I could not have left Cassie in his company. He understood that, and more importantly he also understood that as tough as he was and as fiercely as he protected his family, his own children were not safe with him, either. In a world of guns, nobody's safe.

Doc and I talked a lot about this, and she decided to make Kershaun a personal project. One Sunday afternoon, not long after our week together in San Francisco, Ms. Norris telephoned him to tell him that there was something pressing on her mind, and she couldn't let another day pass without talking to him about it. "Is this a good time, Shaun?" she asked.

"Oh sure, yeah. What's goin' on?"

"Shaun, you see, it's like this," Doc said. "I have a difficult time sugar-coating things. I believe in shooting straight from the hip, calling it as I see it; plain and simple, Shaun, just being honest. That's all. And I require that of myself at all times just as I trust you to always be honest with me."

"Uh-huh, okay," he mumbled, not quite certain where she was leading.

"Shaun, I really think the public does gangsters a disservice when they refer to them as gangbangers. You see, when someone is addicted to alcohol, we call them alcoholics. Those who are addicted to drugs are called drug addicts. Yet young men who are out on the streets killing others are referred to as gangbangers. The term becomes *en vogue*. And so does the behavior. People forget to attach faces to the bodies as they drop, and the perpetrators and prospective victims all become numb to what is actually happening. *Gangbanging* is too gentle a term for what you all are doing, Shaun. Let's face it, you are *killers*. Does this make any sense to you? What do you think?"

Kershaun's silence indicated that he was not ready to answer, so Doc continued to shoot bullets of information. "Shaun, when I tell you that you are a killer," she said, "I want you to understand that you are someone who has become addicted to killing. You have killed in the past, and you might kill in the future unless you realize that you are addicted to killing and your drug is the gun. It's necessary for you to see this in order for us to move to the next level. Now, work with me. If you were a recovering alcoholic, the last thing you would need around you is alcohol. Right?"

"Agreed," replied Kershaun.

"Likewise, if you were a recovering drug addict, it would make no sense for you to hang around a crack house, right?"

"Right."

"Well, Shaun, let's look at it. A *killer*. You're a recovering killer. What sense would it make for you to have your drug—guns —around your being if you seriously want to recover from this addiction? You see, we are all in recovery from bad habits. Your fatal habit is that of killing. And in the words of Malcolm X, 'To have been a criminal is no disgrace, but to remain a criminal is a disgrace.' Shaun, you are a good person recovering from a heinous addiction. If you are really serious about helping the people, it must begin with you freeing yourself from your drug of choice—the gun. And by the way, once you do that, I'll have no reservations about leaving my sons, my hearts—Marcus, Brandon, and Jonathan—in your presence. And even more immediate to you, your son's safety won't be at risk due to your own behavior."

More than a pregnant pause followed. When Kershaun finally spoke, it was clear that a new standard of behavior had given rise within him.

"Miss Norris," he said, "no one ever put it to me like that before. You really made me think, and what you're saying makes sense. I can see that you're right—I'm addicted to killing. All of us in this lifestyle are. And I can see that I gotta come clean if I want to do some good; there's no doubt about that. How can I talk to the homies and other gang members about saving the people if what I do contradicts what I say? I never thought of the gun as my drug, but from what you said I can see that it is. I can see that as long as

I keep my guns, I'm a part of the problem. I want to be part of the solution. You and Mr. Marshall know that.

"Thanks, Miss Norris."

"Thank you, Shaun. We love you and we're with you."

When Shaun finally made up his mind to quit packing, the environment around him changed immediately. The moment he put down his gun, I felt he had become the kind of man with whom I'd be pleased to leave my daughter. In the ensuing months, his life has not surprisingly taken on a new shape. He has become a full-time college student, and realizing he could function without firepower in his pocket, he has taken the additional step of changing his major from criminal justice to education—which means, among other things, that he is content with the prospect of life without material wealth. His freedom from materialism will permit Kershaun to be a leader in the movement to rehabilitate L.A.'s black community.

That effort in general is an urgent one that, I'm convinced, was jumpstarted by the week the Crips and Bloods spent in San Francisco. Once word got out that we had taken on the so-called untouchables, the alleged worst of the worst, Los Angeles was on its way to becoming an Omega town. The Crips and Bloods themselves aided this cause, letting it be known that the knowledge we gave them rang true. It was apparent that what worked for San Francisco worked for Los Angeles. The issues were the same, and so were the answers.

Having turned some heads, our next task was to escalate the process by somehow capitalizing on the momentum. We had no immediate plans to set up a branch office in Los Angeles, and I wasn't certain that was necessary as a starting point. Obviously, we could reach more people through the radio show if we could somehow get it into southern California. If that happened, *Street Soldiers* would be the centerpiece around which we could customize a violence-prevention program for the Crips and Bloods.

The general plan was to carry Omega to Los Angeles in fragments, an ambition that became possible when the James Irvine Foundation came through with a $100,000 grant targeted specifically for that purpose. The Irvine Foundation had previously earmarked $300,000 to sustain our ongoing violence-prevention activities in northern California (which came on top of $400,000 donated for scholarships by San Francisco's Bernard Osher Foundation), and the additional $100,000 enabled the L.A. program to take wing. Not only could we fly Crips and Bloods to San Francisco, but Margaret and Coach and I could travel regularly to Los Angeles to conduct workshops and make feasible the notion of periodically hosting *Street Soldiers* from there.

What made the latter possibility even more workable was the fortuitous fact that the company that owned KMEL in San Francisco, Evergreen Media, also operated one of the top music stations in Los Angeles—KKBT, known as "The Beat." What's more, Keith Naftaly, the program director with whom we had worked at KMEL, had by that time assumed a similar position with KKBT. Keith became our in-house crusader at The Beat, and if the management there wondered about his personal bias, he could simply point to the ratings for *Street Soldiers* in San Francisco and the remarkable media coverage the program had received. With all of that going for us, there was no salesmanship required on our part. It was simply a matter of working out the logistics and establishing a starting date.

In practically no time at all, it was determined that KMEL and KKBT would simulcast *Street Soldiers* two Mondays every month, one of the shows emanating from San Francisco and the other from Los Angeles. Given a schedule from which to make additional plans, we then arranged for Doc, Coach, and I to conduct antiviolence classes on the Mondays we had to be in L.A. for the radio program; we would start kickin' it at six in the evening and go straight from there to the KKBT studio. Maxine Waters, the activist congresswoman from Los Angeles, intervened to reserve us a meeting room in a youth building on South Vermont, deep in Eight Tray Gangsta territory and not more than twenty blocks from where I grew up. With all of that in place, it was officially on in L.A., and we couldn't wait for our first simulcast, scheduled for Monday, January 17, 1994.

It was an event that apparently made the earth shake—for real. Around four o'clock Monday morning, Doc and I were awakened in our hotel rooms by an ominous rumbling that felt like The Big One, and practically was. It was a hell of an earthquake. When the rocking and rolling stopped, power was out in much of the city. Suddenly the simulcast didn't seem nearly as feasible as it had the past couple of months.

I got through to Keith Naftaly later in the afternoon, and with power restored, the decision was made to go on with the show. A Los Angeles media personality named Dominique Diprima, who had been one of the early guest hosts for *Street Soldiers* in San Francisco and had since moved along to KKBT, sat behind the microphones with us to give the program a local identity. Other than that, it was *Street Soldiers* as we knew it.

"I'd like to dedicate this historic evening to my grandmother, who lives right here in Los Angeles," I said for openers, proud that Gue Gue—and my parents as well—would finally be able to listen to the show. "And to all grandmothers, for whom we have made the streets of the city unsafe."

The KKBT signal can be heard all over southern California, including San Diego, and northward it overlaps the KMEL coverage area. This meant that our simulcasts blanketed virtually the entire state, bringing in an audience estimated at two hundred thousand. Given such a broad audience, it was interesting that from the beginning, most of the calls on the simulcast shows came from greater Los Angeles. It was immediately apparent that *Street Soldiers* was hitting Los Angeles every bit as hard as it had hit the Bay Area, if not harder. As soon as we opened up the airwaves that night, the calls flooded in. They haven't stopped since.

One of our first calls on that memorable Monday came from a nineteen-year-old former gangster from South Central who had been incarcerated at age fifteen for robbery. His time in juvenile prison wasn't the thing disturbing him, however. "I had a homie I went to school with," the guy explained, "and he wasn't even gangbangin'. He was just followin' me wherever I went, looking up to me, and he ended up takin' the bullet I was supposed to take.

275

How can I face his parents, you know?" The brother didn't try to conceal the fact that he was crying as he spoke.

"I shed a tear every time I think about it," he said. "The way it is here, the Bloods and Crips, you know what I'm sayin', we gotta come together. We all black, you know what I'm sayin'? Red and blue is white man's colors. Put the white in there, and you got the flag. There's no white men livin' in South Central. We gotta come together, people."

For the purposes of *Street Soldiers*, the lessons of Los Angeles derive from the fact that the street life there is so thoroughly deep seated. One of our early L.A. callers, a fifteen-year-old mother from Inglewood named Lashona, had been raped and was an alcoholic by the age of eleven. Her best friend was shot in the head the day after the previous Christmas just for hanging around the wrong people, who happened to be his cousins. Lashona was trying to change her life for the benefit of her baby son, but the examples around her were not helpful. One of the mothers in the 'hood allowed her six-year-old to smoke weed and drink forty-ounce Hennessees. The boy, whose rough language and manner got him suspended several times from first grade, wore a blue rag on his head and claimed whatever set his mother's latest boyfriend belonged to.

Many of our L.A. callers are second-generation gangsters who have had the benefit of watching OGs mellow into middle age or die, and those not directly involved in the game have acquired a distanced perspective of it. One way or another, they can all talk the talk. It was evident from the very first simulcast that by coming to Los Angeles in search of meaningful urban dialogue, we had climbed the mountain and met the wise old man.

He took many forms, however, and used many unusual names. There was a brother named Entrepreneur who had recently graduated from college and told us he planned to be a drug dealer so that he could start at the top; there was a woman who appealed to us on behalf of her twenty-seven-year-old cousin, Wacky, a motel supervisor and mother of two who couldn't separate herself from the gang; and then there was this young man from Compton:

"Yo, my name is Duryea," he said, "and I'm nineteen years old. I joined the gang because my brother was in one. They called him Night. He died in my arms when I was thirteen. We went to the gas station, and we were in the wrong territory. So we went back to the car, he hopped in the car, and they shot him in the head. The blood splattered all over me, and he landed in my lap.

"That night, some of the older homies came to me and said, 'That's your brother. You got to be his little one. You got to follow in his footsteps. You got to be Little Night.' I knew who did it, so I went and got me a .380. They took me over there, cut off the lights, and told me to get out of the car. I got out of the car and shot somebody. A week later, somebody shot me in front of my mama's house. I kept on gangbangin' until I went to jail, spent a year in YA. I got caught holdin' dope for one of my homies. When I got out of jail, my homeboy turned his back on me. I had to sell dope to get by. One of my homies had me get out of the car and give the dope to somebody and turned out it was the police. I went to jail for that, too—two more years.

"Now I'm out of jail, and when my old homies see me, they always want to fight me. They want to run up on me 'cause I don't come to the 'hood no more. They think I'm showin' disrespect to the 'hood, not givin' the 'hood the time they supposed to have. I'm supposed to kick it with them, like that should be my first priority. But I feel they got me in too much trouble already. I done sold dope, I done shot people, and I did time for somebody else. I shot people because older people talked me into it. They came to my house and got me and told me I had to be like my brother. And that's what I did. I went and followed behind them and did what they told me. When my brother died in my arms, that should have told me right then not to follow in his footsteps."

This was one of those rare calls that put the whole problem in a nutshell. "You said it all right there," I told the brother. "A lot of people do not understand gangbangin'. They don't understand the mentality behind it. But you just explained it right there."

"My brother was my idol," Duryea said. "When he was thirteen, he had a car. My brother was my father. When he died in my arms, I didn't know what I was. So then the older homies come and say, 'They shot your brother—whoop-dee-whoop—you gonna let them shoot your brother?' Later, I come to find out they shot my brother for a reason. I come to find out my brother did all kinds of things. He killed people, took people's lives. I took on my brother's name, so I took on everything that he had. When I went to jail, people were chasing me and beating me up because my brother owed them money."

"Do you know what you want to do now?" I asked.

"I'm trying to get out of Compton," he said. "But it's not easy to get out. To get out of the gang, you got to get put off [ceremonially severed from the gang]. And when you get put off, you might die."

"We can help you with that. We can help you with the transition from the life you've been in to the life you want to be in."

"I want to go to college."

"I was hoping you'd say that," I replied. "You're getting into our territory now. If you are serious about helping yourself, we can help you get to college. There's nothing you can do about your past, but we can give you a number to call us to help you with your future."

Duryea did call, but he didn't follow through on the information we gave him. Whether or not he ultimately helped himself, though, he no doubt helped any number of homies out there who were listening to him. One of the things that made Duryea's such a valuable call was the fact that it gave us and our new audience a poignant model for all that we liked to teach and preach about friendship. True to our postulate concerning risk factors, he had placed his own life in jeopardy by mistaking fearship for friendship. He had also learned, the hard way, our rule for living that says a friend will never lead a friend to danger. As his and subsequent calls suggested, peer pressure is perhaps an even stronger force in Los Angeles than it is in the Bay Area—a situation due, no doubt, to the traditions and legacies involved, and also to the matter of proximity. In South Central, the nearest gang is literally next door, and the second nearest might be across the street. In any and most

every case, the life hits close to home. A caller named Neno demonstrated that to me during our first simulcast, and in the same
conversation I demonstrated it to him.

"I'm from Los Angeles but I originate from Inglewood," he
said. "My name is Credit, but everybody calls me Neno, Brother
Salaam. I'm Muslim now. I'm a former gang member.

"My boy Pluto died back on July Fourth, right? And the
dude who killed him lives right across the street from me. It's going
against my religion to do something to hurt him because God said
do unto others as you would have them do unto you. But this has
been eating me up, and it's hurting me so bad that I'm thinking
about going to take care of it myself. My homeboy Pluto, he just
made sixteen. It's horrible, man. So many of my other homeboys
died. All my homeboys died. It's so bad, it's like the Lord is sayin'
this is a test, what are you goin' to do?"

"It's always the ones closest to you that make the test," I told
Neno. "Man, don't do it, man."

"I be just shakin' thinkin' about it," he said. "I coulda took
him out when the blackout came, man [after the earthquake that
morning]. I been thinkin' negative, and I been sayin', I'm gonna
think positive. I need to get on the show here, man. I need to get
my feelings out."

"Think about your partner Pluto," Margaret suggested.
"Think about all the good things he was. Think of all your friends
who have been lost to this senselessness. Take the goodness of
their spirit and make it alive in you, just like we keep Malcolm X
alive and Martin Luther King alive and Harriet Tubman alive.
That's the way you avenge his death. You make his death an instru-
ment of peace. Believe me, what goes around comes around. He
thinks he's getting away with it, but don't worry about that."

"Yo," Neno replied, "at fourteen I was slingin' guns out of
junior high. I went to the penitentiary. But I changed my ways.
Right now I'm shakin' because I'm thinkin' if this brother's listenin',
what does he think when I come back to my neighborhood, and
how I'm gonna deal with the situation?"

"We've had instances just like that, where the brother was listening," Doc said. "You know what he ended up doing? He turned himself in because he couldn't stand it anymore."

Something about Neno's torment—about his pain and his conflict and his vulnerability—made me share something at that moment that I hadn't thought I could share with two hundred thousand strangers, or even two. It had seemed too personal, too hideous to contemplate publicly, but on the other hand, I had consistently encouraged other brothers and sisters to start the healing process by venting their anger and pain. That was the exercise. That was why we were there.

Finally, it just came out. "I'm not gonna say what happened, but you can think of the most heinous crime," I told Neno and everybody. "I only say this because I know my grandmother would let me do this. As I said when we started the show, my grandmother lives down here. She's eighty-six years old. And this nineteen-year-old brother did about the most despicable thing you can do to a woman. Let's put it that way." I can say it now that I've dealt with the anger and pain: The dude attacked and raped my grandmother at knifepoint. She used to call me in the middle of the night hysterical because of the flashbacks she was having.

"You know how I feel about this woman, man?" I said. "Since I was that little. I even cry when I think about it. I tell you, I was gonna get the dude. I was gonna fly down from the Bay Area and get the dude, but I didn't have to. The dude got it. He's in jail now. He got it. By not doing anything to him, I saved myself and I allowed myself to think about her. My concern is for her. We sat and talked about it. It wouldn't have done her no good for me to do something stupid. One of the reasons I help brothers is because of her. How am I gonna help brothers like you if I go out and do the kind of thing I'm telling you not to do? We got to get back to the point where life is the most precious thing. Right now it's death. Everything's death. We have to think about life. Brother's gonna get his, man. We're concerned about you. We don't want you going back."

* * *

A couple of weeks after I discussed Gue Gue's ordeal on the radio, I received a prison letter from a notorious South Central OG. It expressed sympathy for what had happened and then asked whether the offender was incarcerated in a California state prison, and if so, where. No specific plans or threats were mentioned, but the intimation was clear. "Certain things cannot be tolerated, irregardless of the perpetrator's illness," the author wrote. "I believe as the elders teach there at the Boys Club, that the treatment of women and children represents the degree of civilization reached by any people. Not the amount of wealth accumulated, or the numerical count of structures, but rather the ways in which social relations are conducted. I am a firm believer in this." Naturally, I declined to provide information concerning the rapist, but I was impressed by the writer's ideology and fascinated by the network we had apparently tapped into. Through radio, we were obviously dealing with a very powerful medium.

The responses to our shows, written and phoned in, increased sharply the moment *Street Soldiers* was carried into southern California. On Tuesday mornings after our simulcasts, it was common to find thirty phone messages waiting for us at the club from Los Angeles listeners. L.A. so embraced our work—not only the radio show, but also the meetings, conferences, and academic classes—that exactly one year after we placed the program on KKBT, we saw fit to start broadcasting all of our simulcasts from there. At that, we realized we hadn't begun to satisfy southern California's appetite for *Street Soldiers*; at two o'clock every Tuesday morning, when we were ready to sign off, all eight of our phone lines would still be lit.

It was a heady period for all of us involved with the Omega Boys Club. Jack was getting tangible results for his labor at Juvenile Hall, staying at it around the clock to salvage kids he knew well or barely, while Margaret, Coach, and I (actually, Coach was sort of a swingman, working both sides of our equation) pumped up the cause through outreach of unimagined, audacious proportion. We were thrilled by the concept of making Omega's lessons available to literally hundreds of thousands of brothers and sisters.

Because my co-founder preferred eyeballs in his audience and consequently chose to operate in more intimate circles, Omega's heightened public profile accrued largely to me. Various honors started coming my way at an embarrassing clip, culminating in 1994 with the Essence awards, sponsored annually by *Essence* magazine and presented on national television, and a very generous MacArthur Foundation fellowship. While the Essence award was a real trip—sharing the podium with famous people whom I had admired for years—the MacArthur grant, which came to me with a phone call out of the blue (when I realized what the lady was telling me, I had to find a chair and sit down), carries with it more prestige than I ever thought I'd be associated with as a street soldier (known as the "genius" award, it's usually given to the likes of poets and physicists), not to mention enough money to carry me over for several years. The real value of both awards, however, was that they called attention to the work Omega was doing and the lives we were saving.

After that little flurry of public recognition, I found it interesting that most of my friends in the black community congratulated me on the Essence award while my white friends and the media were much more impressed by the MacArthur fellowship. Most of the responses were of course gratuitous, but some—especially those I hadn't expected—were memorable. There was a very encouraging bundle of mail, for instance, from inmates at a correctional facility in Jackson, Michigan, who had formed a group called Prisoners Doing the Right Thing. And most satisfying of all was a letter I received from Sanyika Shakur, which arrived from Pelican Bay Prison. Captivated by his book and increasingly proud of his brother, I had written Monster to familiarize him with Omega's work, at the same time harboring the notion that he could become a very influential figure in the urban antiviolence campaign. His return letter reinforced my belief:

Rev. Greetings Bro. Joe,

I hope to find you, Ms. Norris & Mr. Jacqua doing well & in strong spirits. Yours has been received intact. It found me well here. You know, it's sort of an irony to have received a letter from you, being that I saw you on the Essence Award (Congratulations!); on the local Bay Area News & most recently on the World News with Tom Brokaw. I've been so changed by seeing you & hearing you speak that it just blew me away to receive some direct words from you.

I see that our dreams, Brotha Joe, are very much alike. U.N.I.T.Y. And much like you, I am optimistic about our ability to create this situation. I remember reading in Two Thousand Seasons, by Ayi Kwei Armah, who was explaining about the destruction from within:

"The way is not the rule of men. The way is never women ruling men. The way is reciprocity. The way is not barrenness. Nor is the way this heedless fecundity. The way is not blind productivity. The way is creation knowing its purpose, wise in the withholding of itself from snares, from destroyers." That is so profound to me. And altho Two Thousand Seasons is a novel, it's perhaps the most worthy book I've ever read. Well, my point is that the unity of our community begins, I feel, with the coming together of our family structures. We'll need to concentrate on certain segments of various 'hoods. From house to house, block to block, community to community. Admittedly, I am an idealist & feel that all things are possible. Equally, however, I overstand the thickness of the colonial mentality among us. People, nevertheless, are instinctively followers & participatory & as such, will move along a groove already created. Hence, we must be the trench diggers—groove makers—& not contributing grave diggers. I have grand theories for our unification. You have tapped into a strong groove & it is obvious by the grassroots response that you are reaching people.

Yes, I am quite proud of Ashanti's (Kershaun's) development. For he has done alot of what I have merely theorized about. He's a very practical cat who is genuinely concerned with our peaceful development. Dig this, when I was a prisoner in Quentin, on my first jolt, I would write to him & try, as best as I could then, to articulate some of the ills *affecting us as a people & he'd write back & confer his overstanding of the position, but also add that what could we do. Of course, that is where my knowledge fell short. Cause while I could "tell it like it is" & even articulate "how it should be," I could not put together a pragmatic blueprint to get us there. I went thru the usual flights of fancy that was the norm then in Quentin, i.e., Mao's countryside revolution; Castro's guerilla foco; Mark Essex's roof top solution and the Panthers' quixotic fix—none, however, seemed too practical in 1986. Lil Bro recognized this & urged me to continue my studies. By the time of my release in Nov. of '88, Bro had organized a study & struggle group of young street soldiers. He had ten to twelve cats daily in his room watching "Eyes on the Prize" tapes! The cat was organizing when I got there. He's been able to do out there what it has taken a cage to teach me. He will be/is a valuable asset to our struggle.*

Bro. Joe, my daughter just graduated junior high school Wednesday. Earlier this year, she was being pressured to clique with the local street org. And you know, the issue is never really as urgent until it hits home, dig? She has managed to steer clear of it thus far. Two of her friends have been gunned down in ride-bys. Tamu, my wife, is stumped on what to do. I, myself, am quite agitated. I need to be out, need to be there.

Free the Land!
Sanyika

While enlisting as a partner in our struggle, Sanyika also confirmed what I had observed about Li'l Monster. Although I had known him a relatively short time compared with many of the Bay Area Omegas, I considered Kershaun's transformation to be one of the greatest, most gratifying personal triumphs I had witnessed. By the middle of 1994, he had not only withdrawn from gang life but had stepped forward as a leading community activist, a true street soldier. Perhaps the most significant testimony ever delivered on a *Street Soldiers* program was the one in which Li'l Monster announced to all of California that he was no longer carrying a gun. That required an awesome degree of courage.

Additionally and especially pleasing to me was the fact that Kershaun had proven to be as sensible as he was courageous; he had become, in fact, a purveyor of knowledge on whom we could depend. When Kershaun was sitting in on *Street Soldiers* one night and a South Central gangsta phoned in to talk about the pressures of running with the set, my man said, "There's nothing wrong with standing by yourself. When push comes to shove, you are going to be all that you have. When you go to the pen or YA, you go yourself. So you got to stand on your own two feet. A man will stand alone and handle his business. I'm twenty-nine and I been in gangs since 1979. I did five and a half years for gang-related murder. And I roll by myself." It's one thing to hear those words coming from me or Doc; it's another thing entirely to hear them out of Li'l Monster's mouth.

In my years hosting *Street Soldiers*, I've found that there is only one type of individual who can speak to an audience as powerfully as a big-time gangsta, and that is a big-time gangsta's mother. I don't care how bad and hard he is, or how much of a fuck he doesn't give, there's not a homie out there who isn't touched by the words of a mother, any mother. And in Los Angeles—in California, in fact, and in all of America—the mother of all gangsta mothers is Monster's and Li'l Monster's. It was an unforgettable moment when that wonderful lady, Birtie, called in spontaneously just before two o'clock one Monday night.

Hers was a slow, deep radio voice, and it was punctuated by the starts and stops of a woman trying in vain not to cry. "This is Monster's mother," she said, then had to wait while all of us on the other end of the line made a considerable fuss.

"You guys are so marvelous," she continued. "You certainly have cooled me down. Listening to the brothers, I hurt so badly for them. I went through it not just for my sons but for all the parents and their children. The problem they had was the 77th Street police station. The big white brothers that wore the cowboy clothes. They were angry with each other, not just the big white country brother in the cowboy clothes. . . . Forgive me [for crying]. . . . These young brothers warring against each other, it didn't start out that way. When Tookie [Stanley "Tookie" Williams, the founder of the Crips] started the situation, it was supposed to be calm. Then they decided to war against each other with chains and pipes and things. And they went from there to the guns.

"Forgive me. . . . I hurt for all the brothers, and their mothers hurt for them. We suffer for them. We have been through hell for them. Bail bondsmen have taken our money. Monster would just like for the brothers to stop warring against each other. My son has been associated with Malcolm X, with Martin Luther King. I wish my son could have dealt with these two people, but they killed them, too. So I'm preparing myself. It's coming to that end, and I know it. Because there's one thing for sure—they don't want no black brother out there with a thought, an idea, and a mind of his own. And my little guy certainly does have it."

"Bertie, you ain't got to worry about them," I promised her. "You ain't got to worry about them, okay? Shaun is mine. Sanyika is mine. All the brothers is ours. I want you to rest. I'm on their case, day in and day out, and they know it."

If only it were that simple. I was confident that I could keep Shaun and Sanyika from *self*-destructing. I was certain that I could help them to significantly reduce their risks. But even as I was assuring Bertie about their protection—as much as I *wanted* to believe that her sons and any mother's sons were safe under Omega's wing—I also overstood, as Sanyika would put it, that it was never quite that simple.

13

The More You Know,
the More You Owe

In the summer of 1994 I was invited to join seventeen others
from the Bay Area on a ten-day tour of Israel, sponsored for
local community leaders by the Jewish Community Relations
Council. I wasn't sure why I had been chosen for the trip, but I had
never been out of the country before and was awed by the prospect
of flying halfway around the world into the heart of religious history.

We arrived in Tel Aviv late on a Friday evening and went
straight to the old city, Jerusalem, before our bags were unpacked.
(Actually, I had no bags to unpack; mine had been waylaid in
Paris.) Shabbat was beginning, and the Jews were streaming down
to the wailing wall by the thousands, men on one side and women
on the other; we were told that if a woman were to be caught on
the men's side, she would be beaten on the spot. I was transfixed
by the entire spectacle and wandered around for about an hour
taking it all in and wondering, all over again, what in the hell I was
doing there.

The question clung to me for the next several days as we
received a crash course in Holy Land history, from which I learned,

among other things, that Jerusalem has been conquered thirty-eight times and completely destroyed on sixteen occasions. It was plain to see that the religious significance of the city was inseparable from its bloody heritage, a biblical irony that left me pondering the essential nature of conflict. I tried to do this from the perspective of the Omega Boys Club. From my vantage point, Israel testified to the fact that religion, like ethnicity and in some cases a mere street address, is fundamental to identity. The protection and preservation of identity, in turn, can be found at the center of virtually every dispute involving homeland. All around the globe—in the Middle East, in Ireland, in Bosnia—the most severe regional strife has resulted when the sovereignty of one people's identity has been challenged. In San Francisco, we call that turf. In Los Angeles, where the tradition runs deeper, generations of hard combat have crystallized the two sides into Crips and Bloods.

Against the highlighted background of more than two thousand years of war, it was the growing prospect of peace that dominated the days we spent in Israel. Yasser Arafat visited Jericho and the West Bank, which prompted a demonstration of a hundred thousand Israelis who thought their government had taken leave of its senses by receiving the PLO leader. Meanwhile, our little group from the Bay Area met with Ariel Sharon and Yael Dayan (Moshe Dayan's daughter), both members of the Knesset, and Faisal Husseini, Arafat's point man in Jerusalem.

Our involvement in the peace process, however trivial, brought home to me the point that practically the entire world had become involved in the Arab-Israeli negotiations. Being in the Holy Lands further impressed upon me the relative smallness of the region; Israel is about the size of Delaware, one-fifteenth the size of California. Its borders are squeezed even tighter by being closed in on two sides by enemies—Lebanon to the north, Syria and Jordan on the west—not unlike the landscape of South Central, where the Eight Trays, for instance, border their archrivals, the Rolling Sixties.

The comparisons between the Middle East and urban America thickened the more I stirred them in my head. And so did the differences. The discrepancy that hit me the hardest was the fact that whereas the world has intervened for the purpose of bringing order to the Middle East, the Crips and Bloods continue to fight their deadly fight in virtual isolation. So do the homies of Sunnydale, Fillmore, Hunters Point, Chicago, Detroit, Newark, and East St. Louis.

Having moderated cease-fire talks between the Crips and Bloods, having observed players from Sunnydale and Hunters Point sitting side by side at the Neighborhood House, and having watched in amazement as a hundred thousand Jews protested the peace settlement with the PLO, I can say for a fact that the brothers in the 'hoods are more receptive to the concept of peaceful coexistence than are the Israelis and Palestinians. They have also taken more initiative toward that end. In the same way that political events—the breakup of the Soviet Union and the Persian Gulf War—facilitated the Israeli-Arab negotiations, the evolving Crip-and-Blood talks were precipitated by the Rodney King incident and the ensuing insurrection. The Crips and Bloods, however, have not been visited by presidents and constantly attended to by secretaries of state. They have not received hundreds of millions of dollars of aid from the United States government. They have not been near the top of political agendas around the world. Nobody helps the homies.

This is an extremely hard thing to justify or even comprehend. It's not as if the problems in the cities are a big secret. By dropping out of school, by having babies they can't take care of, by terrorizing their neighborhoods, by killing each other, the homies have been trying for years to get our attention. They've been all over the news. Some of them have even written to the president, like the nine-year-old from New Orleans named James Darby, who in April 1994 sent a letter to President Clinton pleading with him to stop the violence in the city or "somebody might kill me." Ten days later, James was murdered in a drive-by shooting as he and his mother walked home from a Mother's Day picnic.

A few months later, there was the much-publicized Chicago incident in which an eleven-year-old boy named Robert Sandifer fired a semiautomatic pistol into a group of neighborhood kids playing football and killed a fourteen-year-old girl. Robert had been arrested twenty-eight times between the ages of nine and eleven. A few days after he shot the girl, he was found dead in a pool of blood beneath a graffiti-covered underpass, and two teenagers from the same gang were arrested for his murder. The case was essentially solved, but bigger, more pressing questions remained: After being arrested twenty-eight times in two years, what in the hell was this kid doing out on the streets in the first place? What did he learn while he was in juvenile detention? Who was looking after him? Who gave a damn about him? Where was the system?

For all the attention that Robert's case attracted, and James Darby's before him, there was no mainstream national movement that took up the cause afterward. There was no special legislative session or presidential press conference. There were no new priorities declared. It was simply business as usual around America.

Our country's deafening indifference concerning its urban children has become a time-honored, practically sacred political tradition, and that was the thing that kept ringing in my ears the whole time I was in Israel. The obvious disparities that spoke to me there—the breakdowns in logic, priority, and responsibility—were not only disturbing but disorienting: If Americans are so willing to devote their effort and their money toward peace in the Middle East, why in the hell aren't they willing to do the same to achieve it in the cities of our homeland? Where is the commitment? In American terms, where is the money? The real question here is one that shouldn't even be asked but must be: Do we really want peace in our cities? The issue has been out there for a long time now, and America's silence on the subject speaks volumes.

Toward the end of our Israel trip, we visited the holocaust memorial, a spellbinding series of displays that includes a separate tribute to the million and a half Jewish children who were exterminated by Hitler. The children's memorial is stunning for its simplicity—a huge glass cylinder, completely darkened but for the refracted light of six candles. The only sound is the recorded roll call of young people more than fifty years gone. I was doubly moved

—for the Jewish children remembered with such powerful dignity, and for the African-American children for whom no candles are lit, no wreaths are laid, no silence is observed. As we bowed our heads and listened to the traditional Hebrew prayer, I was thinking, What about the African holocaust? What public memorials are there to the hundreds of thousands who died on slave ships, and to the survivors and the sons and grandsons of the survivors, who were burned, bludgeoned, shot, tortured, and lynched? What about the casualties of the wars that rage on the streets of cities like Los Angeles? What about the children? Does anybody really care about *our* children?

On the morning of our last day in the kibbutz, I woke up at five o'clock to write in my journal. When the sun rose about an hour later, I found myself walking alone in the glorious Israeli dawn toward the shore of the Sea of Galilee, where I stopped and sat down, pushed a Stevie Wonder tape into my Walkman, and listened to my boy singing "Ribbon In the Sky." I'm not sure why the tears started dripping off my cheeks. It was just one of those moments.

At that moment, though, I knew why I was there. I knew that it had to do with the peace process, and with the concept of help. I knew that, in some shape or form, I had to take a little bit of Israel back to California. The Israelis and the Palestinians couldn't find peace without help from the outside, and neither could the Crips and the Bloods or the homies ducking bullets in 'hoods from California to New York. I understood, that morning at the Sea of Galilee, that I was being prepared for the big task back home— stopping the violence in the streets. My job was to bring together all the resources I could marshal to help make peace in the urban centers of America.

While it was a blessed moment in Israel that galvanized my resolve on this score, the urgency of the mission had already been defined by the unprecedented moment in history that we occupy. Urban violence, however compelling on its own account, is only the most visible symptom of a contemporary disorder that plunges deep into the American anatomy. This disorder is fostered by conditions that aren't getting any damn better. And to the degree that crack cocaine, guns, and the lack of employment opportunity have conspired to drastically alter the fundamental dynamics of the black community over the last generation—to the degree that they have made this a time like no other in the urban neighborhoods of our nation—it will require an equally potent coalition to return the community to its native values. That's the only way to truly save the children.

While I hold firmly the position that the children must be saved by individuals, those three items—crack, guns, and employment—represent specific areas in which government can and must get involved. Government must spare no effort or expense in cutting off the flow of crack cocaine and punishing its purveyors; it must unequivocally rid the nation of guns; it must promote job training, public works programs, and any and all methods of putting city people to work. It must put its money where its political rhetoric is and take the kids into account.

In this country, government responses aimed at urban teenagers who are criminally connected—the element Omega so often works with—tend to be more concerned with the crime rate itself than with the kid; more concerned, that is, with making society safer than with nurturing the young man or woman. I honestly believe that there are people in high places—certainly in low places—who would rather lock up young black men, or even let them kill each other, than put forth the effort to save them. Reflecting this mentality, government programs, to a great extent, weigh in on the criminal-justice end of the continuum, reacting to the problem with more policemen and prisons. Government places its premium on *fighting* crime, not preventing it, and has created an industry to ostensibly do that. Symbolically, its response to a drive-by shooting is to tag the body, incarcerate the shooter, and recycle the bullet. In that tradition, the state's answer to crime in California has been three-strikes-and-you're-out, in which a third felony conviction automatically carries a life sentence. The young criminal's reply has been to go down shooting on the third strike, swearing, like Jimmy Cagney in *White Heat,* "You'll never take me alive."

For now, I've resigned myself to the fact that government's punitive, back-end involvement is a constant, and that the front-end work—the counseling and the nurturing—is left to the rest of us. The champions of the underprivileged—the true Americans, judging by the ideals on which the country was purportedly founded—have always been those who, like Frederick Douglass and Martin Luther King and Malcolm X, have taken the constitution at its word and made government live up to it. Now is the time for the rest of us to take up where they left off. We have to be the heroes now. Government is not going to take the lead in this struggle; it will only follow. The best we can hope for is that it will follow the heroes.

All I demand of government is what I demand of teachers and parents and counselors and citizens at large: Care. Do for the children of America's cities what you would do for the children of Israel and Palestine. Do for them what you would do for your *own* children. Move the agenda. Get involved. Do something. There is no higher priority. The measure of any society ought not to be its foreign policy or its gross national product but the way it raises its children. In that context, the prevailing commentary on our society —our government—is that we have no national youth policy. The indictment I would serve on America is that it simply hasn't put forth any meaningful effort on behalf of its young people.

While it is certainly not government's job to raise our children, what government *can* do is reconfigure the circumstances in which children are raised. For those raised in the inner cities, drugs, guns, and unemployment are circumstances. By addressing those issues, America can clean up its urban environment; it can recast the setting. That's a task I'm happy to leave for the likes of Maxine Waters and Jesse Jackson. Meanwhile, Omega's job my job and Jack's and yours—is to work within the circumstances, whatever they are, to nurture, counsel, love, teach, and be there for the children. We have to do the job that a family can do and even a village can do but that government can't.

At Omega, our slogan is the old African proverb, "It takes a whole village to raise a child," and as I see it, everyone is a citizen of the village. The African village is quintessentially an extended family, and that's precisely how our boys club thinks of itself. There's nothing revolutionary about our message or what we do. There's nothing novel or innovative about it. On the contrary, we're merely championing a cultural system that throughout history has always worked—in Africa and also in America.

At our level, what it boils down to is that if one of us—the elders or the Omega boys and girls themselves—sees a brother selling dope or carrying a gun or dissing a sister, it is that Omega's responsibility to set the brother straight. Tell him he's wrong and why he's wrong. That's what I would expect someone to do for my kids, and whatever one wants for his own kids, he should want for all kids. That's the principle on which the extended family operates. When someone joins Omega, he or she makes a commitment to be a family member. In the very same manner, I hope that when someone listens to *Street Soldiers*, he or she makes the commitment right then and there to be a family member—to help the village raise the child.

The operative question is: Are you willing to do it? Are you willing to be a street soldier? I don't ask for everybody out there to go to college or to put somebody through college, or to start a club or even join a club. The grandiose plan is not very grandiose at all when it comes down to the individual; it's simply a matter of being a family member. It's a matter of stepping up to the task, citizen by citizen. It's a matter of caring substantially. I don't expect everybody to be Harriet Tubman, but I do expect those who follow Harriet to take someone's hand and help them across the creeks.

The village spirit has never been as vital to the general welfare of our country, and our race, as it is now. In slavery times, the black man's freedom was denied and his basic human rights were trampled upon, but he had the village. Unless it was separated by a bill of sale, he had his family. Slavery did its best to tear apart the black family, and to a monumental degree it succeeded, but it was not as effective in that respect as crack cocaine has been in the past ten years. Slavery did not undermine the individual's worth like crack cocaine does. It did not disfigure his value system like crack cocaine does. It did not attack the mother in the mother like crack cocaine does. It could never defeat love like crack cocaine has.

I honestly don't know what it is about crack that makes it so formidable an enemy. I don't know if the power behind crack lies in its cheapness—anybody with five bucks in his pocket can get off —or in the high that it delivers, or in the addictiveness inherent to it, or as some speculate, in some mysterious, dastardly chemical agent specially formulated to bring down the black man. It doesn't matter. What matters is that this shit has driven much of the love out of the black village. Incredibly, it has driven much of the love out of the black mother. When Jack and I were working together in the junior high school, the horror stories we heard were all about kids; now we hear them about their mothers, too.

We all know that, for more than a generation, the black mother has been saddled with the burden of saving the race. Maybe the responsibility became too overwhelming and crack seemed like her only escape. Maybe crack is the black mother's equivalent of the banker jumping out the twelfth-floor window during the Depression. Maybe crack is her response to what she feels is the black man's disrespect. Whatever the reason, the bottom line is that a whole lot of children have been left on their own, with nobody giving a damn. The socialization process has broken down in the black community.

There's no getting around the fact that children have to have families—if not immediate, then at least extended. If the mother and father are not going to be there for them, then the rest of us have to step into the breach. We have to be the mom where there is no mom. We have to be the dad where there is no dad. That's what Omega does and what Omega wants everybody to do. This is the first time in our history that the bad guys—those black and white, far and near, who would destroy our neighborhoods—have outnumbered the good guys, which means that the good guys have to band together. We all have to extend ourselves beyond our immediate families and raise the children.

It's a colossal job that, in one capacity or another, is sure to require every able person in the village.

I returned from Israel energized by the conviction that Omega's next major challenge was to escalate the antiviolence campaign in Los Angeles and basically do there what we had done in San Francisco. The work was and is by no means finished in San Francisco —I don't suppose it ever will be completely—but there are unmistakable signs that we are succeeding. Former inmates are bringing home college diplomas. Kids can circulate between the 'hoods again without being shot at. The turf wars aren't as deadly as they once were. Where the ideology of violence was once systematically drilled into the heads of young homies, knowledge is now being passed down.

This was never more evident to me than it was during a Father's Day picnic at the Fillmore projects in 1994. All of the turfs were represented that day, and there was not a hint of drama. Given the recent history of the San Francisco 'hoods, this was nothing short of remarkable. It told me that, despite the skeptics who insist otherwise, things could change a lot in a few years, and they obviously had. I'm convinced that the same could happen anywhere, even Los Angeles.

By virtue of basic logistics alone, however, it would necessarily happen differently in Los Angeles than it had in San Francisco. To wit, there was this dilemma: In order to fully replicate our San Francisco model in L.A., we would have to break up the model. There are only four of us, after all. Jack can be in only one Juvenile Hall at a time. This promised to be an ongoing riddle, because we had no intentions of abandoning the Bay Area—or the six hundred Omegas there—and our long-range agenda put us in places much farther away than Los Angeles.

For starters, there was Chicago, where once a month for five months in 1994, Coach took one of our leading members—the list was made up of Corey Monroe, Nate Pique, Andre Aikins, Otis Mims, and Kershaun Scott—to meet in a westside housing project

with Vice Lords and Gangster Disciples. Our Chicago work originated when I ran into an energetic middle-aged woman named
Gloria Lewis while I was in Cincinnati to receive an award from
Marian Wright Edelman and the Children's Defense Fund. Gloria,
who worked for a community agency but whose main credential
was that she cared a lot about city kids, kept after me to come to
Chicago until I broke down and bought an airline ticket. Coach
came, too, and when we got there Gloria showed us around, then
set up a little rap session with about half a dozen tough guys. I
figured that would be the end of it, but she was determined.
Within a matter of months, she had established the Chicago Society for Youth. I advised Gloria not to call the group Omega, but to
do her own thing. That's what Coach and the Omegas have been
helping her do.

We've tinkered around also in Detroit, where Ms. Norris
took a group of Omega brothers for three days in May 1995. We'll
take Omega's message to any city, actually, that has a Gloria Lewis
(who has since accepted a position as director of violence prevention programs for the Chicago Department of Public Heath). Jack
and Coach and Ms. Norris and I can't be on hand in all of those
places, however, which means that we have to train other people
who can be there for the kids and who, like Gloria, sincerely want
to be there. That's the essential part of the formula. We can supply
the method by which someone else can save city kids, but the heart
has to beat in that person's chest.

To cope with the logistics involved—to make it feasible, that
is, for the four of us and some of our members to meet with people
from around the country who are interested in what we do and how
we do it—we've responded to the national demand by establishing
The Omega Institute (funded by a grant from the Kellogg Foundation), which, when up and running, will offer quarterly workshops
wherein our methods can be systematically taught. Through the
Institute, people like Gloria Lewis will be able to visit San Francisco for three- or five-day training sessions.

We will also operate our Institute program for school counselors, concentrating on what works and what doesn't work in the

way of violence prevention. For the most part, the schools don't have a clue when it comes to dealing with the violence in their halls. If educators were to educate themselves on the dynamics of the city kid—if they could at least learn to identify his anger, fear, and pain and help him handle it—they would substantially increase not only the safety of their buildings but also their graduation rates. As sort of a prototype for our school curriculum, Ms. Norris and I have been getting together regularly with students and staff members at Berkeley Continuation High School, a last-chance type of school for kids who have been kicked out everywhere else.

Another, more obvious way to spread Omega's message across the nation would be through syndication of *Street Soldiers*, which I consider to be virtually synonymous with the boys club. We've been working up to syndication incrementally, first by simulcasting into Los Angeles and then by hosting shows from remote locations; our initial location show was broadcast early in 1995 from the Mentoring Center in Oakland. The grand ambition for the radio show is that it inform the urban community at large, including those who specifically need Omega's lessons and those who don't—that is, both the student and the mentor. Magnified to a national scale, this would have an incalculable effect on the health and welfare of a generation. The way we figure it, for each individual that we reach, there is the real possibility of saving lives in the plural. A good mentor can do it by passing along life-saving knowledge, while every kid who saves himself probably saves others as well. My operating principle is that if I save one, I save four: There's the brother himself, the brother or brothers he was going to shoot, the girl he was going to impregnate, and the baby he was going to bring into the world. That's not taking into account the loved ones and children of whomever he might have maimed or murdered.

Because of the differences between Omega's curriculum and those of more traditional boys clubs or youth programs, radio—actually, the media in general—is sort of a custom vehicle for us. Our emphasis is on information, on knowledge, on the mindset of the young brothers and sisters. Our objective is to give them a different way of thinking about things. We're raising children not by giving them basketball and Friday night dances but by giving them Du Bois and Malcolm X and rules for living and risk factors and adults to talk to. We give them a family, and if the FM dial seems like a poor substitute for the dinner table, it beats the hell out of the crack house or the street corner.

Even with the power of the airwaves on our side, though, Jack and Coach and Doc and I obviously can't do it all by ourselves. We can't be the extended family for a whole nation of city kids. Through the radio, we can perhaps be there on Monday nights for a young brother in, say, Philadelphia, but somebody in Philadelphia has to be there for him the rest of the time. A family, among other things and perhaps foremost, is there for the long haul. That basic point was the common ground on which Jack and I established the Omega Boys Club. In many ways, Jack and I are dramatically different people with completely different philosophies, but both of us are in this thing until we die. One way or another, we're committed to saving everybody. We're going down with the ship. Coach is the same way. Ms. Norris is the same way. That's why Omega works. And that's also why there are only four of us—because the commitment required to make it work is extraordinary. It isn't casual. It isn't extracurricular. It's long-term, full-time, and chin-deep. In the final analysis, it's a matter of what you're willing to do. Are you willing to let the kids die, or are you willing to save them? I've made my choice. Jack, Ms. Norris, and Coach have made theirs. You've got to make yours.

Please don't misunderstand: The Omega Boys Club has no monopoly on commitment, and we certainly haven't cornered the market on saving kids. We like to think of Omega as a model for what can and must be done, but the fact is, there are programs all around the country that work miracles for young people at risk, although most of them are not really programs per se. At Omega, we think of ourselves fundamentally as a family rather than a program. A program—especially a state or federal program—inherently operates under predetermined parameters. It implies salaries and schedules and guidelines and a very temporal existence that concludes when the government budget cycle turns over. Necessarily, it also involves politics, a consideration that inevitably compromises its mission (and takes Jack out of the picture right off the bat).

Jack and I made a conscious effort from Omega's inception to avoid any ties with government, keeping the club independent of federal or state funding. Without a nickel of government aid, we've been able to build up a sizable scholarship program. When the scholarship fund was going strong, we broadened our options to include employment training and an entrepreneurship program. None of those things would have been possible, of course, without the financing provided by trusts, foundations, civic groups, and selfless private citizens. It's truly remarkable what can be done when people care in a substantial way.

I'd venture to say that every successful urban youth program in America is the direct result of people who care extraordinarily, from the benefactors to the staff to the volunteers. In the 1994 book *Nurturing Young Black Males,* edited by Ronald Mincy, a teenager named Shawn Satterfield illustrated this point while talking about a highly acclaimed organization in Baltimore called Project Roadmap. "People ask me what's so special about this program," he said. "It's the people. They care and they deliver. Whereas, the other programs, they never put their personal feelings in it; it was just like a nine-to-five type thing. Here, it's the counselors, the mentors, everybody involved in the program. They want to help you. It's real. . . . These people are in it with their heart." I swear he could have been talking about Omega.

Another program (for lack of a better term) that has shown very favorable results and received attending publicity is one called Quop (for Quantum Opportunities Program), which is being sponsored in four cities (Philadelphia, Saginaw, San Antonio, and Oklahoma City) by the Ford Foundation as a million-dollar experiment. By random selection from a computer, Ford identified twenty-five single-parent ninth graders in each city and matched them up with a full-time tutor/counselor/father-figure whose job was to monitor their schoolwork, spend time with them every day, and generally be a surrogate parent for the student's full four years of high school. The kids receive a little over a dollar for each hour they spend working on a computer or going to cultural events or playing checkers with senior citizens—for virtually anything, really, that constitutes constructive extracurricular behavior. For every dollar earned, another is placed in a fund for the participant's college or trade school fees. The supervisor's salary also increases in relation to the amount of money the teenagers earn. Not surprisingly, the early results show that Quop students graduate from high school and enroll in college at a rate more than double that of their statistically identical counterparts.

In California, meanwhile, Maxine Waters has introduced a program called Seventeen to Thirty that also uses the principle of bestowing financial incentives for young people involved in job training or higher education. We've capitalized on that concept, as well. Johnny Releford, the first Omega to attend the Glen Mills reform school in Pennsylvania, earns fifty dollars a week (the money was provided to us by the Cahill Foundation) for taking a course in electronics repair. For kids who once were awash in drug money, fifty bucks isn't much, but it's more than enough to get them bus rides to class and a few lunches along the way. We call it grubstake money. Omega offers the same for guys enrolled in GED class.

An additional function of grubstake money is that it shows the homies they don't need big bankrolls to get by. That's a hard lesson for most of them. When club members or even drug dealers argue that they aren't surviving on what they have, I often ask them, "How much do you need?" Invariably they say something like, "I don't know. I just need money. I feel like I got nothin' if I ain't got no money." I challenge them to articulate their needs more specifically than that. "Would fifty dollars a week do it? Twenty? A hundred? What is it that you *want*?" Once they identify what they really want and need, I say, "All right. Now let's see how we can get it." It might be a pair of shoes that they need; it might be a job; it might be a college education. Whatever it is, the drill is to make the homies realistic in their desires and expectations; to make them realize that big money—money for money's sake—isn't as essential as they thought it was. When they understand that, they begin to change.

For young people who are independently sincere about gainful employment—particularly those, for instance, who might be just out of jail, ready to start fresh, and need a little something to weigh against the temptations of the old life and the pressures of the old gang—cash rewards, however modest, can provide invaluable short-term relief. Money can help a kid who is spoiling for help, and money alone can help those who are otherwise poised to help themselves. But all of that notwithstanding, the dollars usually aren't what the brothers and sisters most need. What they most need is an extended family. For the majority of kids at risk, it's not enough to give them bus fare or to open the gym doors for midnight basketball, roll out the balls, and walk away. From where I stand, the key element of Quop, like Project Roadmap and the Omega Boys Club, is that the administrator—or more to the point, the father figure—is on duty full time and he's there for the long term. No matter how a program is structured and what it consists of, that's what it takes. It takes people who are going to be there day after night, year after year.

Which is what brings us to you. There's something I said to the joint congressional committee on children and families that I would like to say also to you: There are no more excuses. There is no excuse to plead ignorance, no excuse to pussyfoot, no excuse to remain on the sidelines anymore, because there's now a model that has been proven to work. There are answers written right on these pages. There are ways to save the children.

Two excuses I've grown particularly weary of hearing over the years are these: (1) there's no guarantee that your efforts will result in saving a kid, and (2) you can't save everybody. As general statements, both of those are undeniably true; as excuses, both of them are shamefully lame. Of course there are no guarantees. But we can guarantee what will happen if we *don't* get involved. Kids will keep selling crack to mothers. They will keep screwing up their own lives and those of their friends and relatives. They will keep terrorizing the neighborhoods. They will keep killing each other. Guaran-damn-teed. And of course you can't save everybody. But why should that prevent you from saving *somebody*?

Anybody can save somebody. In the business of saving kids, the Omega Boys Club admittedly has advantages that other people and programs don't and wouldn't have: We have a radio show that enables us to reach hundreds of thousands of young people every Monday night. We also had very fortuitous publicity early on, which enabled us to attract public support, which enabled us to send kids to college. The college scholarships, in turn, have given us something tangible and extremely valuable to offer the brothers and sisters who come to us for help; they have given us the luxury of handing out hope in heavy packages. But even so, it should be understood that the advantages from which we benefit—the scholarships and radio shows—are advantages only to the extent that they are co-sponsored by commitment.

And while we're quick to acknowledge our advantages at Omega, we're just as quick to point out that we didn't start with them. We started with Jack, me, and unconditional commitment. You can plug in different names for Jack and me, but you can't plug anything in for the commitment, not if you truly want to save the children. If Omega has proven anything, it is that effort saves lives. Effort is something that anybody and everybody has to give. That means you. At the risk of repeating myself—and I *intend* to repeat myself on this point and keep repeating myself until the nation responds—the question is: Do you want the kids of the inner cities to be productive citizens, or are you satisfied to have them shoot each other and go to jail? Do you want them to have access to the American Dream, like everybody else? Do you want them to live, or do you want them to die?

There are no more excuses if you genuinely want the homies to live, because now you know. You might not know about budgets and buildings and meeting agendas, but you know that you have to be there for the kids; that you have to help them deal with their anger, fear, and pain; that you have to provide them with the knowledge they need to recognize and steer clear of risky behavior; that you have to give them positive rules for living. Having read this far, you *have* to know these things now, and there's no getting around it: The more you know, the more you owe.

What you do with this knowledge is entirely up to you. My purpose in these pages has not been to tell you what to do but to show you what can be done. If you're able to establish something like Omega in your community, great. Obviously, though, everybody can't start a boys club, and I'm asking everybody to do *something*. You have to figure out for yourself what you're capable of contributing. I'm not going to let you off the hook by telling you to write a check or to write your congressman or to be a Big Brother or to invite a kid to dinner or take a kid to a ball game. There is no easy cookie-cutter solution. There is only you and me and whatever we can do.

Whatever you decide to do, it will be a profound privilege. What greater satisfaction could there be than helping a young person like Li'l Monster put down his gun? Than watching Joe Thomas graduate from college? Than hearing Jermaine King talk a teenager out of the gang? Than seeing Andre Aikins smile again?

That last one, by the way, that's the indicator I use—the smile coming back. A statistic I find very revealing is that until the 1970s, black people had the lowest suicide rate among any ethnic group in America. Now young blacks have the highest suicide rate. In the interim, the last quarter of a century, something has obviously happened in our society to make the young brother a tragically tortured, nihilistic individual. I blame crack. I blame guns. I blame the lack of employment opportunity. I blame the black father who has abandoned his family responsibilities. And like it or not, I blame anybody and everybody who is unwilling to step forward and take up the slack. I blame anybody and everybody who does not care enough to be a responsible citizen of the village and raise the child.

If you do that—if you embrace your citizenship and help us save the children—I can promise that you will see the smiles coming back like I do every Tuesday night at the Nabe. And believe me, it's a hell of a thing to behold, that smile—a ringing announcement not only that the homie has finally found something to smile about but that, at long last, we've wrecking-balled the facade he has been hiding behind for so damn long. The smile breaks through only when the mean-mug breaks down, and the mean-mug breaks down only when the brother understands that not everyone is going to judge him by his hardness; that not everyone is his enemy. The smile is a sign of a young man maturing into innocence. More than that, it's a sign of feeling returning to dude's face; of a street kid becoming human again, once lost and now found. All in all, the smile is a wonderfully enlightening indicator—one of two, actually, that tell me a brother has changed. The other is that his pants start coming up.

There's hardly a Tuesday night that I don't see some smiles I've never seen before, and some pants coming up. It makes my day, my week, my life. It's why I do what I do, and it's why, every Thursday and Saturday and Monday, I think, God, I can't wait until Tuesday night.